Early praise for *iOS Unit Testing by Example*

When it comes to testing strategies and patterns, Jon Reid is an absolute wizard! Few things have influenced me professionally as much as Jon's writings on TDD. I'm using many of his techniques from this book every single day in the development of our iOS applications.

➤ **Fred A. Brown**
   Enterprise Software Architect, Oracle

After reading this book, iOS developers will no longer wonder how to unit test or why to unit test. They'll be equipped to get all the benefits unit testing offers.

➤ **Josh Justice**
   Web and Mobile Developer, Big Nerd Ranch

Jon Reid is the designated expert on unit testing in the iOS space. This helpful and informative book will help you avoid common pitfalls. The wrong test is as bad as no tests at all.

➤ **Janie Larson**
   Red Queen Coder, LLC

Jon has given us the definitive guide on unit testing with XCTest. Techniques, tips, tricks, and tons of Jon's wisdom.

➤ **Jeff Langr**
   Langr Software Solutions, Inc.

Jon is one of the most experienced TDD devs in the Cocoa world; for years he shared interesting techniques one could apply in their codebases. This book is a massive compendium of knowledge and should be read by anyone that wants to get up to speed with proper iOS testing techniques.

➤ **Krzysztof Zablocki**
   CEO and Cofounder, Pixie

Becoming a disciplined test-driven iOS developer takes patience, knowledge, discipline, and practice. *iOS Unit Testing by Example* will provide a major head start on this journey and supply the toolbox of skills you need to start writing better, more maintainable code. I know of no one better placed and better qualified to help than Jon Reid.

➤ **Andrew Ebling**
   Founder and Developer, Tenero Mobile Limited

iOS Unit Testing by Example

XCTest Tips and Techniques Using Swift

Jon Reid

The Pragmatic Bookshelf

Raleigh, North Carolina

Many of the designations used by manufacturers and sellers to distinguish their products are claimed as trademarks. Where those designations appear in this book, and The Pragmatic Programmers, LLC was aware of a trademark claim, the designations have been printed in initial capital letters or in all capitals. The Pragmatic Starter Kit, The Pragmatic Programmer, Pragmatic Programming, Pragmatic Bookshelf, PragProg and the linking *g* device are trademarks of The Pragmatic Programmers, LLC.

Every precaution was taken in the preparation of this book. However, the publisher assumes no responsibility for errors or omissions, or for damages that may result from the use of information (including program listings) contained herein.

Our Pragmatic books, screencasts, and audio books can help you and your team create better software and have more fun. Visit us at *https://pragprog.com.*

The team that produced this book includes:

Publisher: Andy Hunt
VP of Operations: Janet Furlow
Executive Editor: Dave Rankin
Development Editor: Michael Swaine
Copy Editor: Adaobi Obi Tulton
Indexing: Potomac Indexing, LLC
Layout: Gilson Graphics

For sales, volume licensing, and support, please contact *support@pragprog.com.*

For international rights, please contact *rights@pragprog.com.*

ISBN-13: 978-1-68050-681-5
Book version: P1.0—June 2020

For Kay, who believed in me

Contents

Part II — iOS Testing Tips and Techniques

Part III — Using Your New Power

Foreword

In these days of social media, direct marketing, and sponsored "influence," there seems to be an arms race to devalue words as rapidly as possible. A mere two thousand years ago, a "passion" was a commitment to a cause or belief so powerful that it led to suffering, abandonment, and rejection from your closest personal friends, even to the greatest of personal sacrifices. Today, on my LinkedIn screen as I write this, I can see people who tell me that they are "passionate" about "digital talent," "advertising and marketing," and "blockchain and broader financial technology." The message that each is conveying appears to be that they're open to recruiters talking to them about paid work in those fields. Similarly, "evangelism" has shrunk in scope from announcing the good news from on high to working in marketing for a technology company.

Nonetheless, I have no hesitation in describing Jon Reid as a passionate evangelist for test-infected—test-driven is not strong enough—development, and improving the quality of iOS apps. I worked with Jon at Facebook back in 2014, where he brought his trademark combination of enthusiasm, commitment, kindness, patience, and humility to bear on some particularly challenging problems. We had already met and collaborated both online and at conferences, and I knew this about Jon: everything he says about testing with iOS is not because *he* is the expert, but because he wants *you* to become the expert too. Not necessarily straight away, but he wants you to share in the beauty and power he sees and to develop the same care and appreciation about the topic.

This book will support you in that journey. Whether you picked it up because you're wondering why Xcode always asks you to "include unit tests" when you start a project, or because you're looking for specific tips to solve tricky problems and increase your test coverage, you'll find help in here. I did. On the day that Jon sent me the manuscript, I was struggling with writing a test to show that one view controller presented another modally. I searched this book, and there was the answer. That makes it easy to write a conclusion for this foreword: read this book, because we've tested it, and it works.

Graham Lee

Head Labrarian at https://labrary.online

Warwick, United Kingdom, November 2019

Preface

One of the principles of agile software development is to "respond to change."[1] Agility sounds appealing, but these days it is often approached as a project-management tool. Yet we are developers, working in code. The more the code itself resists change, the harder it will be to adopt agility in any meaningful way.

But we can change this—because we are developers, working in code. There are disciplines that fall under the term "technical agile practices." Among these are unit testing, refactoring, and test-driven development. These are some of the tools we can use to make code pliable so we can safely bend that code into new shapes.

I've been learning to apply these disciplines in the workplace since 2001. Lately I've been teaching "Test-Driven Development for iOS" workshops.[2] So it seemed a safe bet that if I ever wrote a book, it would be about TDD.

But I realized that folks can learn theoretical TDD, but still be stuck on iOS particulars. Because if you don't know how to write unit tests for iOS code, how can you ever TDD it? So my book plans pivoted, and here we are. My goal is to give you solid handholds so you can unit test your iOS code.

Apple's framework for the user interface, UIKit, lies at the center of iOS code. And the center of UIKit is view controllers. That's why I focus on unit testing view controllers.

It may seem counterintuitive to test UI-centric code using unit tests. As soon as one sees "UI" or "view," it's easy to assume that "UI tests" are the best fit. But UI tests don't provide the level of control and fast feedback that unit tests give. UI tests are more about automating tests for quality assurance. Unit tests, when they are very fast, serve a different purpose. They become a development tool, helping you bend the code so you can "respond to change."

---

1. https://agilemanifesto.org
2. https://qualitycoding.org/services/

So let's learn how to write unit tests for iOS apps. But keep in mind that the unit tests themselves aren't the goal. They're not the end, they're the means.

How This Book Is Organized

This book explores its ideas using coding examples. Each chapter has a section describing how to make "a place to play." One can learn things by reading, but learning by doing is more effective. If you take the trouble to set up each project, trying the changes and experiments, your learning will go deeper.

I've organized the book into three parts: Foundations, iOS Testing Tips and Techniques, and Using Your New Power. Here's a quick summary of each part.

Part I: Foundations

The first part covers the foundations of using XCTest with iOS apps. The first three chapters cover XCTest. We start with test assertions, move on to managing test suites, and then how to use code coverage to reveal holes.

The next two chapters get into iOS apps. We explore how the app launch sequence may interfere with test isolation. Then we'll see how to load view controllers from test code. This varies, depending on whether a view controller is storyboard-based, XIB-based, or code-based.

The last chapter of Part I examines dependencies that make testing difficult. Managing dependencies and replacing them is a foundational skill for unit testing. We'll see what options are available to us in the Swift programming language.

Part II: iOS Testing Tips and Techniques

The second part is a grab bag of techniques for testing iOS specifics. You can jump around these chapters more freely. You can follow the cross-references that appear where the chapters build on each other.

We start with the basics of making sure outlets are connected, and how to tap buttons. This alone opens up a world of testing possibilities.

Then we'll see how to test presented views. This includes alerts and navigation from one view controller to the next.

Things become more challenging as we get into persistent data and networking. These topics lead us into test doubles. We'll see how to use fakes, spies, and mocks.

For examples of more complicated UI elements, we'll examine text fields and table views. They'll take us into the topic of how to test delegate methods. Finally, we'll see how to test view appearance using snapshot tests.

Part III: Using Your New Power

The last part demonstrates what a solid set of unit tests empowers you to do.

Chapters 17, 18, and 19 focus on refactoring. Contrary to common usage, the word "refactoring" doesn't mean rewriting. Instead, it's a structured discipline of moving in small, verified steps to change the design of code.

Unlike most of the book, the examples in these chapters build on each other, so do them in order. In Chapter 17, we create a working view controller, bring it under test, and begin refactoring. We do this with the most common refactoring moves. These moves belong in your tool belt.

To illustrate how much we can change code design by applying small steps, the UI pattern starts from model-view-controller (MVC). In Chapter 18, we refactor our way from MVC to model-view-view-model (MVVM). Then in Chapter 19, we transform the view controller to use model-view-presenter (MVP). The point isn't to promote any particular UI pattern but rather to show how refactoring makes it possible to do large transformations.

Finally in the last chapter, we'll do test-driven development. This code example is unrelated to the earlier chapters. TDD combines unit testing and refactoring with emergent design. Having covered unit testing and refactoring, you'll be most of the way there by the time you start this chapter.

Disclaimer: No SwiftUI Support

SwiftUI is Apple's new declarative UI paradigm. They unveiled their first version of it at WWDC 2019. Since there's a lot of excitement around this paradigm, you may wonder why it's not covered in this book.

The main difficulty is that as I write this, SwiftUI is still quite new. This makes it a moving target, which Apple will iterate on over the next few years. Not only that, but I simply haven't used it yet.

And Apple has initially focused on making SwiftUI work and not on making it testable. In the first round, there don't seem to be any clean ways of testing the behavior or data flow of SwiftUI code. Some folks in the iOS developer community are coming up with their own patterns and helpers as workarounds. Will we come to agree on any standards for unit testing SwiftUI? My guess is that this will happen when Apple decides to put their weight into the problem.

So this book uses the well-established declarative paradigm of UIKit. As you create new projects for the worked examples, be sure to select "Storyboard" as the user interface, not "SwiftUI."

Online Resources

The source code shown in this book can be found under the "Source code" link on the Pragmatic Bookshelf website.[3] You can also help improve this book by submitting errata, from typos to content suggestions.

Acknowledgments

First, I must thank my wife, Kay Reid. She's been my constant "go for it" voice, encouraging me to grow my initial teaching into a book and a consultancy.

Daniel Steinberg was the first person who advised me to write a book. Daniel, I owe you a drink.

I also want to thank Graham Lee. He was the first "voice in the wilderness" with his book *Test-Driven iOS Development [Lee12]*. Thank you for that book, for being an encouraging friend, and for writing the foreword to this book. Who else but Graham would turn a technical foreword into a reflection spanning thousands of years?

I rely on feedback loops for software development, but had no idea that writing a book worked in the same way. I'm deeply grateful to the technical reviewers whose feedback made this book so much better. The reviewers were Andrew Ebling, Fred Brown, Janie Larson, Josh Justice, Liz Marley, and Mark Dalrymple.

Besides the "official" reviewers who worked with my editor, many of you emailed me directly. Thank you for your corrections and suggestions. I especially want to thank Simon Rofe, who struggled with me to find a way to unit test storyboard segues. Cheers, mate.

Finally, I want to thank all the students at my workshops on test-driven development for iOS. Several innovations came from those discussions, and some were discovered by the students. Every time I teach, I learn something new.

Jon Reid
jon@qualitycoding.org
San Jose, California, USA, April 2020

---

3.   https://pragprog.com/book/jrlegios

Part I

Foundations

What are the basic tools and skills you need to write unit tests for iOS code?

There are subtleties around how unit tests work in XCTest. They're not difficult but are often overlooked. Let's get this right to avoid problems down the road.

As we get into iOS specifics, it's helpful to know how your normal application launch affects testing. And you'll need to know how to load your view controllers so you can test them.

But typical iOS code contains dependencies that interfere with testing. Let's learn how to identify which dependencies are problematic and how to box them off. Previously untestable code will become testable.

CHAPTER 1

Assert Yourself

Every company wants to reduce their costs. In software, making changes is inexpensive: we wiggle our fingers on keyboards. So where do the costs lie? Aside from development time, they lie in errors, and how much time it takes to detect these errors. (They also lie in building the wrong thing, which is beyond the scope of this book.)

To detect problems, mobile developers use all kinds of feedback loops. For example, we keep an eye on crash reports and customer complaints. But that's the longest loop. After making an incorrect change, it takes a long time to get that feedback.

To try to prevent errors from making it all the way to customers, companies use manual testing. The best quality experts apply talent and creativity to do exploratory testing. Let's not waste their time asking them to follow steps in mind-numbing repetition. Besides, the time between making an error and getting feedback from testers is still long.

What if we could do a large amount of testing using computers? In fact, what if the developer's own computer could provide feedback? And what if this feedback were so quick, you could get it on every change you made? This kind of rapid feedback is a game changer. It not only catches problems quickly, it can change the way you code.

This is what unit tests are for. Maybe you haven't done any unit testing in your iOS apps yet. Or maybe you've been able to test some logic, but your tests don't cover the iOS-specific parts. (And those are important parts.) Wherever you are in your unit testing journey, the goal for this book is the same: to reduce your costs.

What Are Unit Tests Anyway?

There's some confusion about what makes a test a *unit test*. Many people try to focus on the "unit" part of the name, thinking it describes testing a unit of production code. I'll continue to use the term because it's widespread, but let's forget about asking "What's a unit?" Instead, here's my definition:

Unit tests are a subset of automated tests where the feedback is quick, consistent, and unambiguous.

Quick: A single unit test should complete in milliseconds. We want thousands of such tests.

Consistent: Given the same code, a unit test should report the same results. The order of test execution shouldn't matter. Global state shouldn't matter.

Unambiguous: A failing unit test should clearly report the problem it detected.

In our first chapter, we'll explore the fundamental tool of unit testing: assertions. You'll learn the most common assertions in the Swift XCTest framework in a hands-on way.

If you're a seasoned unit test writer, you may want to skip ahead to the Key Takeaways, on page 16. But even if you've written some tests, it can be good to go over the fundamentals. What are assertions for? What do they report? Do you know how to choose the right assertion for the right job? This chapter will help you get familiar with these tools, which we're going to be using all the time.

Create a Place to Play with Tests

Assertions give unit tests a way to state their expectations. The tests fail if these expectations aren't met. Let's make a place outside of your actual projects where we can experiment with how they work. Throughout this book, you'll learn new concepts by playing in these safe spaces. Then in the exercises at the end of each chapter, you'll begin applying these concepts to your own code.

When it comes to learning, reading doesn't come close to *doing*. If you take the code from the examples and type them into your computer, your learning will go deeper. So I encourage you to open your IDE of choice and give it a go. (The examples will use Xcode.)

Let's start by making a place where we can play with tests. Xcode playgrounds are tricky to use with XCTest, so we won't do that. Instead, we'll make a new project. In the Xcode menu, select *File* ▶ *New* ▶ *Project…* or press Shift-⌘-N.

It doesn't matter what type of project we make as long as it comes with unit test support. But since we're going to focus on testing iOS apps, we may as well get used to what that feels like. First, create an iOS Single View App.

Next, choose any options you like for your new project. In the examples that follow, we'll use the project name AssertYourself. But make sure to do the following:

- Choose "Swift" as the language.
- Choose "Storyboard" as the user interface. (Don't select "SwiftUI.")
- Select the check box for "Include Unit Tests."

You now have a project set up to run unit tests on an iOS app, which we'll use for our learning experiments.

Select the initial test file that the new project created. Its name will be the project name followed by Tests. So for this project, find AssertYourselfTests.swift.

Delete every method in the AssertYourSelfTests class, leaving only an empty shell:

```
class AssertYourselfTests: XCTestCase {
}
```

Make sure your destination is set to an iOS simulator. Any simulator will do.

Now in the Xcode menu, select *Product ▶ Test* or press ⌘-U. You might want to learn this keyboard shortcut—you'll be doing this often. Think U for "unit test" to remember it.

This will perform several steps and then run the tests. You won't see any test failures because there are no tests. You may see this image show briefly on your screen:

Test Succeeded

If you didn't see that image, go to Xcode Preferences and select the Behaviors tab. There you can customize what happens when testing succeeds. To display the image, select the check box "Notify using bezel or system notification," as shown in the image on page 6.

Now we're ready to play. In the following sections, we'll experiment with assertions to learn more about them.

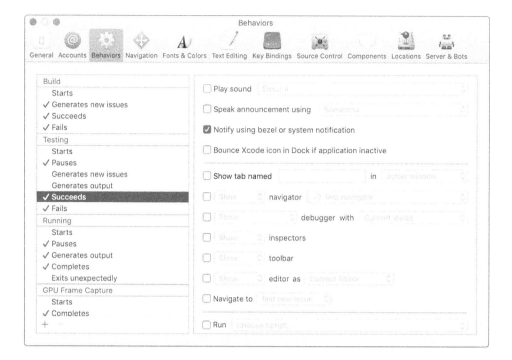

Write Your First Assertion

Now that we have a home for tests, let's go over how to use the testing mechanism. How does a test communicate success or failure? What does Xcode show you when a test fails? What does it show when a test succeeds?

The way a test reports a failure to XCTest is through assertions. Let's start with the simplest assertion. Add the following method to the AssertYourselfTests class:

AssertYourself/AssertYourselfTests/AssertYourselfTests.swift
```
func test_fail() {
    XCTFail()
}
```

First, what makes this function a test?

- It lives within a subclass of XCTestCase.
- It isn't declared private.
- Its name starts with test.
- It takes no parameters.
- It has no return value.

Why the underscore in the test name? This goes against Swift's normal "camel case" naming conventions. But good test names often contain three parts. I like to use underscores to separate these parts and camel case within each part. I'll explain this further when we have a test name describing its inputs and expected output. For now, know that the underscores separate the test name into parts, which we'll look at in Add Tests for Existing Code, on page 40.

This test does nothing but fail. Run it by pressing ⌘-U and observe what happens. First, you may see this image show briefly on your screen:

Test Failed

(If you didn't see that image, go back to the Behaviors tab in Xcode preferences. Only this time, customize what happens when testing fails.)

Looking at the earlier source file within Xcode, you'll see the *Test Status Icon* in the left-hand gutter, like the image to the right.

X marks the spot in two places: the method and the class containing the method. The method is a *test*, also known as a *test case*. The class represents a *test suite*, which is a collection of tests. The X icon shows a failure at both the test level and the suite level. You'll also see that Xcode highlighted the XCTFail() line and added an annotation to its right.

XCTFail()   ◇ failed

So Xcode has marked the following:

- The class containing a failing test
- The method defining a failing test
- The line with the failed assertion

Now add // before XCTFail() to comment out the assertion. Press ⌘-U to run the tests. You'll see the following:

- The annotation disappears from the assertion line
- The test status icons change from red Xs to green check marks, like the image to the right.

This may look trivial, but it's significant. It means we have a way to fail a test, with Xcode showing us where the test reported the failure. You can also see that when a test finishes without triggering any assertions, the test passes.

> As you progress in your testing ability, you'll even be able to write assertions defining what you *want* the code to do. Then you can change the production code until it passes the tests. We'll return to this topic in Chapter 20, Test-Driven Development Beckons to You, on page 297 at the very end of the book.

Add a Descriptive Message

Seeing the location of a test failure is a good start. But when a test fails, we have to diagnose what went wrong. We can save time for ourselves in the future by having the assertion explain anything we know at the point of failure.

XCTFail() can take a String parameter as an *assertion message*. Let's see how it works. Add the following method to the class:

AssertYourself/AssertYourselfTests/AssertYourselfTests.swift
```
func test_fail_withSimpleMessage() {
    XCTFail("We have a problem")
}
```

Run the tests. Note how Xcode puts the message in the annotation:

```
XCTFail("We have a problem")                    ◇  failed – We have a problem
```

Since the annotation is on the same line as the failure, you may ask, "Couldn't we have put a message to ourselves in a code comment?" But this isn't the only place the message appears.

In the Xcode menu, select *View ▶ Navigators ▶ Show Issue Navigator* (or press ⌘-5). The Navigator column on the left will show any issues, including test failures. You may need to click the Buildtime selector, shown here:

As you can see, the descriptive failure message appears in the Issue Navigator. It also appears in the test logs, which other tools may process—especially on *continuous integration* servers.

Thanks to Swift's string interpolation, XCTFail() can do more than spit out a string literal. Add this to the suite:

```
AssertYourself/AssertYourselfTests/AssertYourselfTests.swift
func test_fail_withInterpolatedMessage() {
    let theAnswer = 42
    XCTFail("The Answer to the Great Question is \(theAnswer)")
}
```

(Strings are italicized in code samples. That's a backslash \ for string interpolation, not a pipe |.)

Run the tests, and you'll see the following:

```
failed - The Answer to the Great Question is 42
```

Avoid Conditionals in Tests

We can report failures and include descriptive messages. Now that you've tasted the power of XCTFail, it's tempting to use it everywhere. All it takes is a little more code in the test, right? That may be true, but "more code" is code that can go wrong. Let's learn how to simplify our test code by introducing more assertions.

For example, it might be tempting to test a Boolean result like this:

```
AssertYourself/AssertYourselfTests/AssertYourselfTests.swift
func test_avoidConditionalCode() {
    let success = false
    if !success {
        XCTFail()
    }
}
```

That would be fine if we didn't have other assertions. But we do. Try adding and running this next test. It achieves the same result but in a more declarative way.

```
AssertYourself/AssertYourselfTests/AssertYourselfTests.swift
func test_assertTrue() {
    let success = false
    XCTAssertTrue(success)
}
```

By using the Boolean assertions XCTAssertTrue() and XCTAssertFalse(), we can avoid many conditionals in our test code.

Eliminating branches from test code makes it easier to understand. I want test code to be extremely simple. In fact, *xUnit Test Patterns [Mes07]* lists *conditional test logic* as a *test smell*.

Let's look at the three types of control flow constructs we use daily:

- Statements in a sequence
- Conditionals
- Loops

These control flows fall into a paradigm called *structured programming*. They've become the building blocks of programming.

If our test code can avoid conditionals and loops, then we're left with one thing: statements executed in sequence. The best test code is dead simple to read. Of course, there are still conditionals inside there somewhere. But by using assertions that have more power, our test code becomes simpler.

Describe Objects upon Failure

Wouldn't it be nice if we had assertions that came with descriptive messages? The assertions we've seen so far can only say that they failed, but they can't tell us why. But there are some assertions that describe objects. We'll also look at how to customize the way objects describe themselves in these messages.

Here's an assertion to confirm that an optional value is nil. Add this test and give it a run:

AssertYourself/AssertYourselfTests/AssertYourselfTests.swift
```
func test_assertNil() {
    let optionalValue: Int? = 123
    XCTAssertNil(optionalValue)
}
```

This is the first assertion that gives us more information upon failure:

```
XCTAssertNil failed: "123" -
```

Instead of nil, we got "123". But why is it in quotes when the type is an optional integer with value 123? That's the way XCTest reports strings, and assertions ask objects to describe themselves as strings. We can see this better with a struct instead of an Int:

AssertYourself/AssertYourselfTests/AssertYourselfTests.swift
```
struct SimpleStruct {
    let x: Int
    let y: Int
}
```

```swift
func test_assertNil_withSimpleStruct() {
    let optionalValue: SimpleStruct? = SimpleStruct(x: 1, y: 2)
    XCTAssertNil(optionalValue)
}
```

Running this test gives us this message:

```
XCTAssertNil failed: "SimpleStruct(x: 1, y: 2)" -
```

That's pretty readable for a simple struct. But some types have complicated descriptions. This can make failure messages hard to read. We can control how a type describes itself by making it conform to CustomStringConvertible.

Here's a structure that is identical to the previous one, but it adds the protocol to give itself a custom description:

```swift
AssertYourself/AssertYourselfTests/AssertYourselfTests.swift
struct StructWithDescription: CustomStringConvertible {
    let x: Int
    let y: Int

    var description: String { "(\(x), \(y))" }
}
func test_assertNil_withSelfDescribingType() {
    let optionalValue: StructWithDescription? =
            StructWithDescription(x: 1, y: 2)
    XCTAssertNil(optionalValue)
}
```

Running this test gives us the following simplified failure message:

```
XCTAssertNil failed: "(1, 2)" -
```

XCTAssertNil() is one assertion that gives more information. That's because it takes an object instead of a Boolean value. The assertions for equality also give more information, and we'll look at them next.

Even in the cases where we provide our own descriptive messages, it's good to have an option to simplify the output. Keep CustomStringConvertible in your tool belt.

Test for Equality

We've tried a few different assertions so far, including one that gives more output. And we have a way to customize its output. But now we're coming up to the workhorse of assertions, the one you'll use most often.

The most common assertion takes a result and checks if it's equal to an expected value. Try entering and running this test:

AssertYourself/AssertYourselfTests/AssertYourselfTests.swift
```swift
func test_assertEqual() {
    let actual = "actual"
    XCTAssertEqual(actual, "expected")
}
```

Here's the resulting failure message:

```
XCTAssertEqual failed: ("actual") is not equal to ("expected") -
```

It's worth noting that other unit testing frameworks usually use (expected, actual) for their equality arguments. The order matters because the failure message states which is which in the following format:

```
expected: <"expected"> but was: <"actual">
```

But with XCTAssertEqual(), the argument order doesn't matter. It simply reports ("A") is not equal to ("B"). Since we can put them in any order, there's no need to place the expectation first, as in

```swift
XCTAssertEqual("expected", actual)
```

But it does change the failure message. I prefer to flip the order, placing the expectation last. Whichever style you prefer, it doesn't matter to XCTest. But to make assertions easier to read, try to be consistent across your project.

Test Equality with Optionals

Let's explore equality further. One of Swift's core features is optional values. When one of the arguments to XCTAssertEqual() is optional, what happens? Enter and run the following test:

AssertYourself/AssertYourselfTests/AssertYourselfTests.swift
```swift
func test_assertEqual_withOptional() {
    let result: String? = "foo"
    XCTAssertEqual(result, "bar")
}
```

The failure message is

```
XCTAssertEqual failed:
    ("Optional("foo")") is not equal to ("Optional("bar")") -
```

Yet we typed a plain string literal "bar" as the second argument. How did it become optional?

Well, XCTAssertEqual() requires both arguments to be the same type. Swift knows that if a value of type T is being assigned to a variable of type T?, it can wrap it. This promotes the value from non-optional to optional.

All this makes it easier to write equality assertions when optionals are involved. There's no need to balance out both sides of the equation ourselves. This helps make test code more readable.

> Why do I emphasize readability for test code? Isn't it good enough to have things pass or fail?
>
> Change happens. The production code will evolve, so test code will need to change with it. To change test code, we need to understand it. And every time we need to understand code, we read it. Making test code readable is an act of kindness to your coworkers, and to yourself.
>
> As *Clean Code: A Handbook of Agile Software Craftsmanship* *[Mar08]* says, "Test code is just as important as production code."

Fudge Equality with Doubles and Floats

We've looked at the equality assertion. We've seen how it continues to work fine with optional values. Now let's see how it works with floating-point numbers. If you're not already aware of what can go wrong, buckle your seat belt.

Enter this next test. But don't run it yet:

AssertYourself/AssertYourselfTests/AssertYourselfTests.swift
```
func test_floatingPointDanger() {
    let result = 0.1 + 0.2
    XCTAssertEqual(result, 0.3)
}
```

Before running the test, try predicting the outcome. Do you have an expected result in your head?

Okay, now run the test. You'll see the following failure message:

```
XCTAssertEqual failed: ("0.30000000000000004") is not equal to ("0.3") -
```

What in the world is going on?

We're used to using ten digits to represent numbers. Can you write $\frac{1}{3}$ in decimal notation? No. The sequence 0.3333... goes on forever, so anything you write down is an approximation.

That's just the way math works. Computers face the same problem, but everything boils down to 1s and 0s, so the tricky numbers are different. We can't write $\frac{1}{10}$ in binary notation. You can learn more about this at "What Every Programmer Should Know About Floating-Point Arithmetic."[1]

Let's get back to assertions. Since floating-point numbers are approximations, we need a hand-wavy way to assert equality—something that says, "These two numbers should be equal, more or less." Enter the following test:

AssertYourself/AssertYourselfTests/AssertYourselfTests.swift
```
func test_floatingPointFixed() {
    let result = 0.1 + 0.2
    XCTAssertEqual(result, 0.3, accuracy: 0.0001)
}
```

The accuracy parameter gives us a way to express the "more or less" fudge factor. Run this test and you'll see that it passes.

It's hard to predict in advance which floating-point numbers will cause problems. So just use the accuracy parameter whenever you want to use XCTAssertEqual() with Double or Float types.

Avoid Redundant Messages

Let's finish up our examination of the equality assertion by looking at its descriptive message.

As you may have guessed from Add a Descriptive Message, on page 8, each assertion can have an optional message. When you first learn this power, it's easy to get overly excited. But consider the following test:

AssertYourself/AssertYourselfTests/AssertYourselfTests.swift
```
func test_messageOverkill() {
    let actual = "actual"
    XCTAssertEqual(actual, "expected",
                   "Expected \"expected\" but got \"\(actual)\"")
}
```

The resulting failure message is:

```
XCTAssertEqual failed: ("actual") is not equal to ("expected") -
    Expected "expected" but got "actual"
```

The added message may be a little more precise. But if you're consistent with the order you use for actual value versus expected value, it doesn't add much. Getting all that formatting right took extra work for little benefit.

Remember, when XCTAssertEqual() or XCTAssertNil() fail, they provide a fair bit of information. It's usually enough. XCTAssertTrue() and XCTAssertFalse() only say they

---

1. https://floating-point-gui.de

failed, but that too is often enough. We're going to aim for tests that are so short, we won't need to add any messages of our own.

So for now, resist the temptation: unless you're using XCTFail(), leave the message out. We'll find a use for assertion messages later.

> ### Testing Without Assertions, Back in the Stone Age
>
> Before the invention of unit testing frameworks, it wasn't like programmers didn't run any tests. We wrote little main() functions in our source files, conditionally compiled out. By building a single file with its main() function enabled, we'd make a little program to exercise that one file. It would print() to the console, and we'd read the output to see if it matched what we wanted.
>
> Life is much easier now. Instead of having a human read the output, assertions give us *self-checking tests*. And we have test suites, which let you run a set of tests in one shot.

Choose the Right Assertion

That wraps up our tour of the most common XCTest assertions. With these choices and more, how do you choose which one to use for a particular test? Since all automated tests come down to a true/false decision, it may be tempting to forget the choices and simply use XCTAssertTrue() for all your tests. For example, you may think about writing assertions like these:

```
XCTAssertTrue(a == b)
XCTAssertTrue(optionalValue == nil)
```

These assertions will fail correctly when a is not equal to b, or when optionalValue is not nil. But the failure messages would only say

```
XCTAssertTrue failed -
```

Then we'd have to diagnose what went wrong.

Assertions like these throw away valuable information. As *xUnit Test Patterns [Mes07]* explains, test assertions have two goals:

- Fail the test when something other than the expected outcome occurs.
- Document how the system under test is *supposed* to behave (i.e., *tests as documentation*).

In other words, it's not enough to report that a test failed. What was the actual result? How did it differ from the expected result? These are the questions we should be able to answer from failure messages.

So pick the assertion function that's closest to what you want to say. While XCTest provides sixteen assertion functions,[2] these are the ones you'll use the most:

Assertion	Purpose
XCTAssertEqual(_:_:)	Asserts that two values are equal
XCTAssertEqual(_:_:accuracy:)	Asserts that two floating-point values are equal within a certain accuracy
XCTAssertNil(_:)	Asserts that an optional value is nil
XCTAssertNotNil(_:)	Asserts that an optional value is not nil
XCTAssertTrue(_:)	Asserts that an expression is true
XCTAssertFalse(_:)	Asserts that an expression is false
XCTFail()	Fails the current test. You should always provide a descriptive message.

Key Takeaways

What are the key points from this chapter that you should apply to your coding?

- A test case is a function in a subclass of XCTestCase where the function has the following traits:
    - Its name starts with test
    - It has no parameters, and no return value
    - It isn't private

- Press ⌘-U (think U for "unit test") to run tests.

- An assertion failure marks the test as failing. Otherwise, the test case passes.

- Avoid conditional branches in test code to keep test code simple. You can do this by choosing an assertion that expresses the condition you need.

- When comparing floating-point numbers, use XCTAssertEqual() with an accuracy: argument.

- If your test needs a condition that the built-in assertions don't provide, then put an XCTFail() (with a description message) inside a conditional clause.

---

2. https://developer.apple.com/documentation/xctest

- Check the failure reporting of your tests. If the description of an object is hard to read, provide a custom description by conforming to the Custom-StringConvertible protocol.

Activities

Now it's time for you to put this chapter into action. Read through this list, pick one of the activities, and do it. It's only in doing that we actually learn.

1. Read Apple's documentation of test assertions so you know what your other options are.

2. Is there any production code you can begin testing today? Look for low-hanging fruit—functions that use only their input arguments to calculate a return value. This includes failable initializers: write one test checking for a nil return value and another for non-nil. (Pro tip: Any time you add a new test, make sure you see it fail by temporarily breaking the production code.)

3. If your code already has some unit tests, then do the following:

   a. Read through the tests you have.

   b. Select a simulator, and press ⌘-U to run your own tests. Make sure they all pass. If there are any test failures, delete those tests.

   c. Is each test using the best assertion for the job? Improve any you can.

   d. Check calls to XCTAssertEqual() to see if the argument order is consistent. Try to stick to a consistent order for actual/expected.

   e. Look for any XCTAssertEqual() assertions that compare floating-point numbers. Do they use the accuracy parameter? Add any that are missing.

   f. Consider whether there are any optional assertion messages you can delete because they're redundant.

   g. Add descriptive messages to any XCTFail() assertions that are missing them.

   h. If you've changed any assertions or messages, make sure their failure output is helpful. You can check this by introducing temporary errors in either the test code or the production code. Afterward, don't forget to remove these errors, then run the tests to make sure they pass.

What's Next?

We'll talk more about assertions as we put them to use, especially when we make our own test helpers.

You still have plenty of tricks to learn. But you now carry assertions in your tool belt, and you can begin writing simple tests of your own code.

Now that you've written some unit tests, how are these tests run? In the next chapter, we'll clarify common misunderstandings of the life cycle of test cases. You need a mental model that matches what's actually going on. In particular, we'll see how to avoid the most common mistakes that Swift programmers make.

CHAPTER 2

Manage Your Test Life Cycles

There's more to tests than the assertions. When does XCTest create and run the tests? Swift programmers are particularly prone to making wrong assumptions about test life cycles. These assumptions lead to mistakes in test design.

Picture a test case that passes when it's run by itself but fails when it's run as part of a test suite. Perhaps you've had this happen to you. The noisy results keep us from trusting our tests. Flaky tests are worse than having no tests. To build the safety net under our legacy code, we need reliable tests.

To avoid flaky tests, we want to run each test in a virtual *clean room*. There should be no debris left over from previous tests or from manual runs.

Setting up a good clean start for a test can be tricky. As Swift programmers, we've become used to the way Swift creates objects. It's easy to assume these ideas apply to test cases as well. But XCTest manages the life cycle of tests: it decides how tests are made, run, and terminated. So let's go over what it's doing and get our mental model right.

In this chapter, we'll explore the life cycle of tests, the different phases within a test, and how to manage the objects they need. In particular, we'll look at setUp() and tearDown(). Read on and you'll see how to give each test its own clean room. Along the way, you'll also learn useful tricks for creating new test suites and for looking at test results.

Make a New Place to Play

Let's create a new project for this chapter. Follow the steps for Create a Place to Play with Tests, on page 4, but use the project name LifeCycle. Go ahead and create the project now.

Now let's make a new file in the production code. In the Project Navigator, select the LifeCycle group in the LifeCycle project. Create a new file, choosing the Swift file type. Give it the name MyClass. Then double-check the targets. This is production code, so it belongs in the app target, not the test target. In the new file, create the following class:

LifeCycle/LifeCycle/MyClass.swift
```
class MyClass {
    func methodOne() {
        print(">> methodOne")
    }

    func methodTwo() {
        print(">> methodTwo")
    }
}
```

As you can see, this class has two methods. All they do is print to the console. We won't be testing them with assertions. Instead, we're going to examine the console output to see what gets logged when we run them.

Let's make a test suite to exercise MyClass. By convention, the name of the test suite starts with the name of the type we're testing, and it ends with Tests. So we'll call this suite MyClassTests.

 Name your test suites to match the thing they test. If you want to test a Foo type, name your suite FooTests. This makes it easier to find the tests for any component.

In the Project Navigator, select the LifeCycleTests group in the LifeCycle project. Make a new file, choosing the unit test case class type. Give it the nameMyClassTests.

The important thing to double-check is that the test file goes into the test target, not the app target. Your Save dialog options should look like this:

You should now see MyClassTests.swift. Delete every method in the MyClassTests class, leaving only an empty shell:

LifeCycle/LifeCycleTests/MyClassTests.swift

```swift
import XCTest

class MyClassTests: XCTestCase {
}
```

Whenever we make a new project that includes unit tests, Xcode creates an initial test file. We won't be using this file, so let's delete it. Select LifeCycleTests.swift in the Project Navigator and press ⌫. In the confirmation alert, select Move to Trash, and wave bye-bye. Cleaning up test code is at least as important as cleaning up production code, if not more so.

Before we start experimenting with the life cycle of test objects, let's look at a few techniques. First, we'll see how helpful it is to have a stepping-stone test that precedes the first real test. Then we'll see how to hook up your tests so they can access your production code. And finally, we'll look at how to examine the console output for specific tests.

Start from Test Zero

Now we have a home for our next set of tests. Before we get into our experiments around life cycles, I'd like to show you a trick. First, whenever I create a new test suite, I start with a special test I call *Test Zero*. Add the following test to MyClassTests:

LifeCycle/LifeCycleTests/MyClassTests.swift

```swift
func test_zero() {
    XCTFail("Tests not yet implemented in MyClassTests")
}
```

I call it *Test Zero* because it precedes the first real test we want to write. Go ahead and run tests to make sure it fails. Why? This is a check of our infrastructure. It confirms that our basic test plumbing is correct.

Test Zero helps separate our problems so we can tackle them one at a time. When we create a new test suite, we're usually thinking about that first test. But before we get lost writing that test, let's make sure the suite runs. Otherwise, basic infrastructure problems will interrupt our thinking flow.

This is an example of a larger principle: *take a small step, get feedback*. If you learn nothing else from this book, take that principle home with you.

 Start a new test suite with a test that does nothing but fail. Run your tests to make sure you get the expected failure.

I never write Test Zero by hand. Instead, I use custom XCTest templates to make new test files. You can download the templates I use from my website.[1]

Hook Up Tests to Production Code

While we've confirmed some plumbing, we haven't checked that the test code can reach the production code. We'll confirm that as we write our first test. Essentially, we're transforming Test Zero into our first real test that accesses MyClass.

First, once we've confirmed the expected failure, Test Zero has served its purpose. Let's delete it and add a test that uses MyClass. Add the following test:

LifeCycle/LifeCycleTests/MyClassTests.swift
```
func test_methodOne() {
    let sut = MyClass()

    sut.methodOne()

    // Normally, assert something
}
```

The name sut stands for *system under test*, which is usually abbreviated as SUT. It's a common term for "the thing we're testing." Unlike this simple example, tests often have many objects in play. Using a consistent name like sut makes it clear which object the test is going to act on. It also makes it easier to reuse snippets of test code.

As it stands, the test won't compile. It doesn't know what MyClass is. We need to add this line at the top of the file:

LifeCycle/LifeCycleTests/MyClassTests.swift
```
@testable import LifeCycle
```

Why do we need the @testable attribute on the import statement? That's because we didn't specify access control for MyClass, so it defaulted to internal access. @testable makes internal declarations visible.

Note that anything declared private remains off-limits, even to tests. This is different from Objective-C, where nothing is truly private.

The test should now build and run. Unlike an actual unit test, there is no assertion. Instead, we'll use tests together with console output as *learning tests* to probe the behavior of code we don't own.

---

1.   https://qualitycoding.org/files/XCTest-Templates.zip

Examine Console Output

To experiment with test life cycles, we need a way to go beyond test results. We'll need to examine detailed test logs, the information the tests write to the console output. Let's go over how to see these logs.

Add a second test, test_methodTwo(), that invokes methodTwo():

```
LifeCycle/LifeCycleTests/MyClassTests.swift
func test_methodTwo() {
    let sut = MyClass()

    sut.methodTwo()

    // Normally, assert something
}
```

With two tests in our suite, press ⌘-U to run tests. Then let's go find the log so we can read the nitty-gritty details of this test run.

You can see the console output of the latest run by going to the Xcode menu and selecting *View* ▶ *Debug Area* ▶ *Activate Console*. But we can do one better.

In the Xcode menu, select *View* ▶ *Navigators* ▶ *Show Report Navigator* (or press ⌘-9). The Navigator column on the left will show a history of recent activity. Find the latest test run and click on its log. It will look something like this:

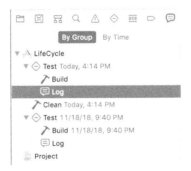

This allows us to see not only the latest output, but also any recent test run (and other activities).

In the central panel, select the "All Messages" filters at the top. Then select the line that says, "Run test suite All tests." A log icon will appear on the right side, as shown in the image on page 24.

Click this icon to reveal the transcript. It will look something like this:

```
Test Suite 'All tests' started at 2019-06-22 19:08:40.422
Test Suite 'LifeCycleTests.xctest' started at 2019-06-22 19:08:40.422
Test Suite 'MyClassTests' started at 2019-06-22 19:08:40.423
Test Case '-[LifeCycleTests.MyClassTests test_methodOne]' started.
>> methodOne
Test Case '-[LifeCycleTests.MyClassTests test_methodOne]' passed
    (0.002 seconds).
Test Case '-[LifeCycleTests.MyClassTests test_methodTwo]' started.
>> methodTwo
Test Case '-[LifeCycleTests.MyClassTests test_methodTwo]' passed
    (0.000 seconds).
Test Suite 'MyClassTests' passed at 2019-06-22 19:08:40.426.
   Executed 2 tests, with 0 failures (0 unexpected) in 0.002 (0.003)
   seconds
Test Suite 'LifeCycleTests.xctest' passed at 2019-06-22 19:08:40.426.
   Executed 2 tests, with 0 failures (0 unexpected) in 0.002 (0.004)
   seconds
Test Suite 'All tests' passed at 2019-06-22 19:08:40.426.
   Executed 2 tests, with 0 failures (0 unexpected) in 0.002 (0.005)
   seconds
```

What does this show? First, that we have several test suites. Like Russian dolls, each suite contains another one, until we reach MyClassTests.

Within MyClassTests, we have our two test cases. Don't be afraid of the funny notation:

```
-[LifeCycleTests.MyClassTests test_methodOne]
```

That's in the style of Objective-C logging. The minus sign indicates a message to an instance. The square brackets show the message, with the recipient on the left and the content on the right.

So first we see that test_methodOne() started. The transcript shows any output, especially messages from failed assertions. In our case, it shows the output from the print(_:) statement, showing that the test successfully ran methodOne(). Then it reports whether the test passed or failed, along with the time it took.

We get a similar report for test_methodTwo(). Then counts of how many tests passed or failed bubble up to each test suite level.

We can also look at the output for individual tests only. Click the up arrow on the right side to collapse the "All tests" transcript. Then option-click the disclosure triangle to the left of "Run test suite All tests." A regular click will expand one level, while an option-click expands all levels. Click on a test case to reveal the log icon, or hover your mouse along the right until it appears. Then click the log icon at this level to see the transcript for a single test case, like this:

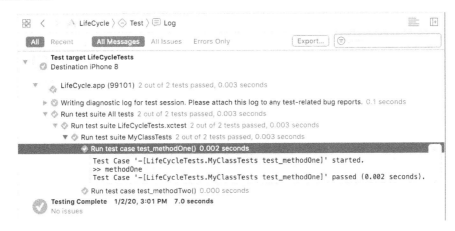

Let's review this method of examining reports. In the Navigator column, we can select which report we want to examine. For that report, we can filter by the following options:

- All Messages
- All Issues (which includes any warnings, for build logs)
- Errors Only

Then, by using the disclosure triangles, we can select how much of the transcript we want to see—even down to individual test cases. So while you can view the full console output of the latest run, the Report Navigator offers history and granularity. Choose whichever works best for your needs.

Now we're ready to run experiments to learn about object management. First, we'll see how tests have separate phases and how this relates to objects being created and destroyed. Then, we'll try a common Swift approach to properties in XCTestCase and observe how it breaks the object management rules. We'll learn how XCTest actually manages test cases in memory. Finally, we'll fix the problem by using the setUp() and tearDown() methods.

Observe Object Life Cycles to Learn the Phases of a Test

Now that we can examine the transcripts of test runs, we can log more information and see the results. This is what we'll use to run our experiments on test life cycles. Let's record information to learn when objects are created and destroyed.

(This experiment may feel a little tedious. But memory management is important in test code, as well as in production code. And the test life cycle is different than what most folks expect. Let's lay proper foundations to avoid making common mistakes.)

Add the following properties and methods to MyClass:

```swift
LifeCycle/LifeCycle/MyClass.swift
class MyClass {
    private static var allInstances = 0
    private let instance: Int

    init() {
        MyClass.allInstances += 1
        instance = MyClass.allInstances
        print(">> MyClass.init() #\(instance)")
    }

    deinit {
        print(">> MyClass.deinit #\(instance)")
    }

    func methodOne() {
        print(">> methodOne")
    }

    func methodTwo() {
        print(">> methodTwo")
    }
}
```

This keeps a running count of MyClass instances, printing messages when init() and deinit are called.

Then for the completeness of this example, add an XCTFail() assertion to the end of test_methodOne(). Something like this will do:

```swift
XCTFail("Failed, yo")
```

Now run the tests. Then find the latest log in the Report Navigator and drill down to the transcript of test_methodOne(). You'll see something like this:

```
Test Case '-[LifeCycleTests.MyClassTests test_methodOne]' started.
>> MyClass.init() #1
>> methodOne
LifeCycle/LifeCycleTests/MyClassTests.swift:10: error:
    -[LifeCycleTests.MyClassTests test_methodOne] : failed - Failed, yo
>> MyClass.deinit #1
Test Case '-[LifeCycleTests.MyClassTests test_methodOne]' failed
    (0.005 seconds).
```

This shows that for test_methodOne(), the following occurs:

1. The test creates an instance of MyClass.
2. It invokes a method on the instance.
3. It asserts an outcome.
4. It destroys the instance.

This is what *xUnit Test Patterns [Mes07]* calls the *four-phase test*. You can think of these four phases as set up the thing, call the thing, check the thing, destroy the thing.

This helps create a virtual clean room for each test. Every test needs to start from nothing, setting up what it needs. With no changes to the code, tests should reach the same outcomes regardless of the following:

- Whether a single test is run by itself
- Whether all tests are run together
- Whether the test order changes

FIRST is a helpful acronym for unit test principles: unit tests are fast, isolated, repeatable, self-verifying, and timely.[2] Here, we're focusing on "I" for isolated. Tests should not have different outcomes due to external changes. They should be isolated from each other and from the world.

The four-phase test also creates a predictable structure. For local variables, the final cleanup phase is handled by the compiler. So the four phases are usually shortened to three phases and abbreviated as AAA:

- Arrange
- Act
- Assert

Following *The Art of Unit Testing: with examples in C#, Second Edition [Osh13]*, I recommend separating these phases by blank lines.

---

2. https://pragprog.com/magazines/2012-01/unit-tests-are-first

Separate the Arrange, Act, Assert sections of your tests with blank lines. Then each line of test code identifies its purpose. This helps clarify what we're testing. When their intent is clear, tests become documentation of how the code is supposed to work.

The Wrong Way to Reduce Duplicate Test Code

Now we're reaching the critical goal of this chapter: avoiding the testing mistake most Swift programmers make. Let's apply a common Swift programmer approach to duplication. We'll see how it creates problems for test code. Delete the XCTFail() assertion in test_methodOne(). This brings the MyClassTests suite back to this:

LifeCycle/LifeCycleTests/MyClassTests.swift
```swift
class MyClassTests: XCTestCase {

    func test_methodOne() {
        let sut = MyClass()

        sut.methodOne()

        // Normally, assert something
    }

    func test_methodTwo() {
        let sut = MyClass()

        sut.methodTwo()

        // Normally, assert something
    }

}
```

See how each test starts with the same line, creating an instance of MyClass? A typical Swift programmer would think, "Why not promote sut from local variables to a property?" It would look like this:

LifeCycle/LifeCycleTests/MyClassTests.swift
```swift
class MyClassTests: XCTestCase {
    private let sut = MyClass()

    func test_methodOne() {
        sut.methodOne()

        // Normally, assert something
    }

    func test_methodTwo() {
        sut.methodTwo()

        // Normally, assert something
    }
}
```

Everything looks cleaner, and more "Swifty." So what's the problem? Run the tests and look at the test transcript. If you drill down to the "All tests" level, you'll see something like this:

```
>> MyClass.init() #1
>> MyClass.init() #2
Test Suite 'All tests' started at 2019-06-22 20:12:15.128
Test Suite 'LifeCycleTests.xctest' started at 2019-06-22 20:12:15.128
Test Suite 'MyClassTests' started at 2019-06-22 20:12:15.129
Test Case '-[LifeCycleTests.MyClassTests test_methodOne]' started.
>> methodOne
Test Case '-[LifeCycleTests.MyClassTests test_methodOne]' passed
    (0.001 seconds).
Test Case '-[LifeCycleTests.MyClassTests test_methodTwo]' started.
>> methodTwo
Test Case '-[LifeCycleTests.MyClassTests test_methodTwo]' passed
    (0.000 seconds).
Test Suite 'MyClassTests' passed at 2019-06-22 20:12:15.131.
   Executed 2 tests, with 0 failures (0 unexpected) in 0.001 (0.002)
   seconds
Test Suite 'LifeCycleTests.xctest' passed at 2019-06-22 20:12:15.131.
   Executed 2 tests, with 0 failures (0 unexpected) in 0.001 (0.003)
   seconds
Test Suite 'All tests' passed at 2019-06-22 20:12:15.131.
   Executed 2 tests, with 0 failures (0 unexpected) in 0.001 (0.004)
   seconds
```

Look for the logging of the init and deinit calls.

Two instances of MyClass are created before tests are even run. And they're never destroyed.

This is no longer the clean room we want for our tests. Problems can potentially multiply:

- If there's a problem creating MyClass, it will happen before any tests run.

- If there's a problem destroying it, we'll never know because the instances aren't destroyed.

- If instantiating MyClass has any global side effects, such as swizzling methods or touching the file system, all bets are off.

What is going on? Keep reading.

The problems that come with "legacy" code don't apply to only production code. You can have "legacy" test code as well. Like any code, test code requires ongoing care to keep it in shape. Any tests that fail to preserve the clean room create potential problems. These problems can go unnoticed for a long time. So make sure to review the quality of test code, old and new, with the same rigor you apply to production code.

Learn How XCTest Manages Test Cases

By applying the wrong way to reduce duplication, we've stumbled onto a mystery. Why are objects piling up before we run a single test? To solve this mystery, we're going to dig into how XCTest creates and runs test cases.

It's easy to assume that when XCTest runs a test case, three things happen:

1. It creates an instance of the XCTestCase subclass.
2. It runs the specific test method.
3. It destroys the XCTestCase instance.

Or, you may have assumed that XCTest creates one instance to run all the tests in a suite.

But both are incorrect. Here's what really happens:

1. XCTest searches for all classes that inherit from XCTestCase.

2. For each such class, it finds every test method. These are methods whose names start with test, take no arguments, and have no return value.

3. For each such test method, it creates an instance of the class. Using Objective-C runtime magic, it remembers which test method that instance will run.

4. XCTest collects the instances of the subclass into a test suite.

5. When it's finished creating all test cases, only then does XCTest begin running them.

What this means for our example is that XCTest finds MyClassTests. It searches for method names starting with "test," and it finds two. So it creates two instances of MyClassTests: one instance to run test_methodOne(), another to run test_methodTwo().

And it assembles these instances into a test suite before running any tests. Since each instance has a MyClass property, we've accidentally created two instances of MyClass.

When Is XCTestCase a Test Case?

Why does XCTestCase look like a test suite, when it has a name that says it's a test case? The difference is between when we're writing test code and when XCTest is running them.

We can put several test methods inside an XCTestCase subclass. From our point of view of writing or reading test code, MyClassTests is a test suite. But it's more accurate to say it will *become* a test suite.

When XCTest runs, it creates a separate instance for each test method. So each instance of MyClassTests is a single test case, from XCTest's point of view.

Use setUp() and tearDown()

Having looked at the wrong way to tackle test code duplication, what's the right way? XCTestCase provides special methods for us to use.

First, let's set a term for "stuff the test needs in order to run." The term we're looking for is *test fixture*. Since our two tests use the same test fixture, we want to move it outside the tests. But simply promoting sut to a property didn't work. So what do we do? XCTestCase defines two methods, setUp() and tearDown(). They're designed to be overridden in subclasses. Combined with careful use of optionals, we get this:

LifeCycle/LifeCycleTests/MyClassTests.swift
```swift
class MyClassTests: XCTestCase {
    private var sut: MyClass!

    override func setUp() {
        super.setUp()
        sut = MyClass()
    }

    override func tearDown() {
        sut = nil
        super.tearDown()
    }

    func test_methodOne() {
        sut.methodOne()

        // Normally, assert something
    }

    func test_methodTwo() {
        sut.methodTwo()

        // Normally, assert something
    }
}
```

Run the tests and examine the log. You'll see that XCTest created and destroyed the MyClass instances within each test run. Hurray!

For Swift in particular, the trick is to declare the objects in our shared test fixture using var instead of let. We also add the ! to make these variables implicitly unwrapped optionals:

LifeCycle/LifeCycleTests/MyClassTests.swift
```
private var sut: MyClass!
```

This may cause you some initial discomfort. Experienced Swift programmers call ! the "crash operator," and do their best to avoid it. But the implicitly unwrapped optional is a necessity here, just as it is for an IBOutlet.

XCTest is a framework, meaning it calls back to our code. setUp() and tearDown() are *template methods* as defined by *Design Patterns: Elements of Reusable Object-Oriented Software [GHJV95]*. The test runner in XCTest *guarantees* the following sequence for each test case:

1. Call setUp().
2. Call the test method.
3. Call tearDown().

So rest easy. As long as you create what you need inside setUp(), the implicitly unwrapped optionals won't crash. And without them, we're creating a context of unpredictable chaos for our tests. Type the exclamation point. It's the right thing for XCTestCase properties.

Note that setUp() alone isn't enough. XCTest creates test instances, but it never destroys them. Their properties will live on, so we need tearDown() to clean up any remains of our shared test fixtures.

 Every property you create in setUp() should be destroyed in tearDown().

Don't Abuse setUp()

Whenever we programmers learn a new trick, we have a tendency to overuse it. Be careful not to overuse setUp(). It can become a dumping ground for things used by only some of the test cases. This in turn makes it hard to reason about the tests when we read them. Try to limit setUp() to things that matter to most tests in a suite.

Key Takeaways

Here are the main points from this chapter you should take with you:

- Name your test suites to match the thing they test.

- When you create a new test suite, start with Test Zero, a test that does nothing but fail. This will help you confirm that your test plumbing is correct.

- Use @testable import to import the code you want to test.

- Inside each test case, there are the Arrange, Act, and Assert phases. Adding blank lines between the phases helps clarify the function of each line of code in your tests.

- Remember that each test method runs in a separate instance of its XCTestCase subclass. These instances live inside a collection of all tests, which the test runner is iterating over. So they all exist before test execution and are never deallocated (at least, not until the test runner terminates). And so...

- Inside XCTestCase subclasses, stored properties should always be implicitly unwrapped optionals—that is, var with an exclamation point. Set their values in setUp(). Set them back to nil in tearDown(). Otherwise you won't be able to predict or control what objects exist during any test case.

Activities

Solidify your reading by turning it into action. Pick one of the following activities, and try it.

1. Use Test Zero the next time you create a new test suite.

2. If your code already has some unit tests, do the following:

    a. Run your own unit tests. Look at the test logs using the console area. Look at the test logs in the Report Navigator, drilling down to specific tests. It's good to know both approaches.

    b. Do any test files import the module under test without the @testable attribute? Add the attribute—at the very least, it helps identify what you're testing. Then see if you can remove public from production code types or functions those tests touch.

    c. Add blank lines to your test code to separate tests into the AAA sections: Arrange, Act, Assert.

    d.   Assuming you have an automated build system that runs your tests, look at the output. Introduce a temporary test failure. Does your system make it easy to identify the failure?

3.   Fix any test code that doesn't handle shared test fixtures correctly:

    a.   Look for test suites that initialize stored properties. Change these properties from let to var. Make them implicitly unwrapped optionals with ! on the end. Move their creation into setUp().

    b.   Look for missing or incomplete tearDown(). Make sure they set properties back to nil so the test fixture is destroyed.

    c.   If you're bold enough to try an alternative to Xcode, look into App-Code.[3] Among its many features, it supports plugins. There's a third-party plugin that automatically generates tearDown() code.[4] It can even do so across the whole project.

What's Next?

XCTest has other facets that we'll introduce as we need them. But now you've seen the different phases of a single test case. We make these phases clear by organizing code within a test method into three sections: Arrange, Act, Assert. Just remember AAA.

Particularly, you know the biggest mistake Swift programmers make: they don't take into account that properties in XCTestCase can interfere with the life cycle of test fixtures. And you know how to use setUp() and tearDown() to avoid this mistake.

But as we write unit tests, how will we measure our progress? That's where code coverage comes in. In the next chapter, we'll see how to measure coverage in Xcode. In particular, we'll see how coverage can mislead us and how to use it well. We'll also look at a useful technique for adding tests to existing code.

---

3.   https://www.jetbrains.com/objc/
4.   https://qualitycoding.org/swift-teardown-appcode-plugin/

CHAPTER 3

Measure Code Coverage and Add Tests

Chipping away at legacy code can be a long process. A good way to add positive feedback to the process is by measuring code coverage. That way, you'll be able to have a sense of progress.

Code coverage is a way of measuring how much production code the test code exercises. But it's often misunderstood, and the results can be misleading.

In this chapter, you'll see what a coverage report tells you about your unit tests—and what it doesn't tell you. You'll learn how to use code coverage to find holes in your test suites. We'll look at rules of thumb for covering different types of control flows. And you'll get positive feedback as you bring your legacy code under test.

And how should we go about writing tests for existing code? We'll look at whether you should even write such tests. We'll also go over a cool trick for testing well-established code.

Make a New Place to Play

Let's make a new project. Follow Create a Place to Play with Tests, on page 4, but use the project name CodeCoverage.

Now let's make a new file in the production code. Name it CoveredClass. Import UIKit (we'll need it later in the examples), and let's give it a small static function:

CodeCoverage/CodeCoverage/CoveredClass.swift

```
import UIKit

class CoveredClass {

    static func max(_ x: Int, _ y: Int) -> Int {
        if x < y {
            return y
        } else {
            return x
        }
    }
}
```

In the test target, delete the initial test file for this project, CodeCoverageTests.swift. Create a new test suite CoveredClassTests, starting with Test Zero:

CodeCoverage/CodeCoverageTests/CoveredClassTests.swift

```
@testable import CodeCoverage
import XCTest

class CoveredClassTests: XCTestCase {

    func test_zero() {
        XCTFail("Tests not yet implemented in CoveredClassTests")
    }
}
```

Run your tests to make sure you get the expected failure.

We'll add more code as we go, but for now, we'll start with this to learn the basics of examining code coverage. First, we'll turn on coverage. Then we'll see how to drill into a partially covered line to see what is and isn't executed. Then we'll learn about characterization tests, a powerful technique for adding tests to existing code.

Enable Code Coverage

Now let's enable code coverage on this project. Follow these steps to get to the check box, as shown in the image on page 37.

1. In the Xcode menu, select *Product* ▶ *Scheme* ▶ *Edit Scheme...* or press ⌘-<.

2. In the scheme editor, select Test in the left column.

3. Then from the tabs, select Options.

4. Finally, enable the Code Coverage check box to "Gather coverage for all targets."

This will measure code coverage every time we run tests using this scheme.

Examine Code Coverage Results

We need to run the tests another time for our new code coverage settings to take effect. Do so, then let's see where the results are shown. In the Xcode menu, select *View ▶ Navigators ▶ Show Report Navigator* (or press ⌘-9). In the latest test run, you will see a new entry labeled Coverage. Select it, as shown here:

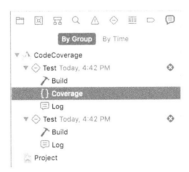

The main area to the right will show the app and a coverage percentage. Click the disclosure triangle. You'll see code coverage for each file, as shown in the image on page 38.

The coverage measurement for CoveredClass.swift is 0%, with an empty bar. You may be surprised to see the non-zero coverage for other files, though. We'll address that in Chapter 4, Take Control of Application Launch, on page 53.

Try clicking the column headers labeled Name and Coverage. You can sort the list by either column. Clicking the same header again reverses its order. This makes it easy to sort your project's files by ascending (or descending) coverage percentage.

Hover your mouse cursor over a row. An arrow will appear next to the file name. Clicking that arrow will take you to that file. Try doing that for Covered-Class.swift.

The source code editor now shows a coverage gutter along the right side, like this:

To the right of the max() function, the gutter is colored red. It shows a count of 0, which means this section of code was traversed by tests zero times.

If you don't see a right-hand gutter showing red, select *Editor ▶ Code Coverage* in the Xcode menu.

Drill into a Partially Covered Line

Let's start writing a test for the max() function, keeping an eye on the code coverage as we progress. Delete test_zero(), then add the beginnings of the new test:

CodeCoverage/CodeCoverageTests/CoveredClassTests.swift
```swift
func test_max_with1And2_shouldReturnSomething() {
    let result = CoveredClass.max(1, 2)
}
```

Note that there's no assertion yet. Run tests and go to CoveredClass.swift to see the line-by-line coverage. It should look something like this:

The code coverage gutter now shows a smaller red area and two numbers. The 0 marks the section that tests haven't touched. Above that is a 1, marking a section the test touched once. Between the two, the gutter shows a red-striped area. Hover the mouse cursor in that area, and you'll see things change, as shown here:

The green section shows the code we've touched. The line with the else clause is part green, part red. This gives us a way to see code coverage inside lines.

Whenever you see a red-striped area, place your mouse cursor there to examine which parts of the line remain untouched.

Of course, the problem with our test is that it has no assertion. This demonstrates the dangerous part of code coverage. Coverage says nothing about the quality of the tests.

> Lack of code coverage proves lack of testing. But positive code coverage doesn't prove anything.

Add Tests for Existing Code

Our incomplete test results in a warning:

```
warning: initialization of immutable value 'result' was never used;
consider replacing with assignment to '_' or removing it
```

This is a good clue that we should write an assertion for the result value. Let's bring this code under test.

We can write tests for existing code in two different ways. They depend on whether the code has proven itself with real use:

- If the code hasn't yet shipped, we should write tests that express the requirements for that section of code. This means we need to reason about how the code is supposed to behave. The tests may even catch some bugs.

- If the code has shipped, then real users are exercising it. As long as no one has found any bugs, that section of code does its job. This means we don't need to try to reason about the code's behavior. The tests just need to capture the existing behavior.

Does Old Code Need Tests?

Most code in a shipping app has been in use for some time. Do you even need to write tests for such code? No. That is, not as long as that code doesn't change.

But as soon as you need to change a section of code, write tests for that section before making any changes.

Our max() example is trivial, but let's imagine both cases. If the code hasn't shipped, we need to ask, "What are the requirements? That is, what is it supposed to do?" We know we wrote this function to return the greater of two integers, so we'd write tests that express this.

But if the code is in use, we don't need to work backward from the require-ments. Instead, we can write what *Working Effectively with Legacy Code [Fea04]* calls *characterization tests*. These are tests that capture the actual behavior of the code.

To write a characterization test, do the following:

1. Call the code from a test, yielding some kind of result.
2. Write an assertion comparing the result to a value you know won't match.
3. Run the test. The failure message will tell you the actual result.
4. Adjust the assertion so that it expects the actual result.
5. Rerun the test to see it pass.

This creates a test that guarantees a piece of the code's behavior. By building up coverage with characterization tests, we're making a safety net. It's an early warning system that will tell us if we changed any existing behavior. With such tests in place, you'll be able to move faster. Why? Because you won't need to spend as much time manually checking that you haven't broken anything.

For max(), we've done step 1. What we want for step 2 is an assertion that will tell us the actual value. We can get that by doing an XCTAssertEqual() against a value we know won't match:

CodeCoverage/CodeCoverageTests/CoveredClassTests.swift
```
func test_max_with1And2_shouldReturnSomething() {
    let result = CoveredClass.max(1, 2)

    XCTAssertEqual(result, -123)
}
```

Step 3, run the tests. This gives us a failure message that tells us the actual value:

```
XCTAssertEqual failed: ("2") is not equal to ("-123") -
```

For step 4, we copy the actual value 2 from the failure message and paste into the assertion:

CodeCoverage/CodeCoverageTests/CoveredClassTests.swift
```
func test_max_with1And2_shouldReturn2() {
    let result = CoveredClass.max(1, 2)

    XCTAssertEqual(result, 2)
}
```

Finally, step 5: run the test to confirm that it passes. You can also update the last part of the test name to shouldReturn2. This way, the test name itself expresses the behavior we've captured.

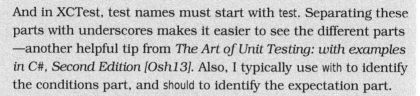

A good test name has three parts:

1. What the test is exercising. This is usually a function name.

2. The conditions of the test. What are the inputs that make a difference?

3. The expected result.

And in XCTest, test names must start with test. Separating these parts with underscores makes it easier to see the different parts —another helpful tip from *The Art of Unit Testing: with examples in C#, Second Edition [Osh13]*. Also, I typically use with to identify the conditions part, and should to identify the expectation part.

So in test_max_with1And2_shouldReturn2(), the name says we are exercising max. The conditions are that we're calling it with 1 and 2. The expected result is that it should return 2.

Those are the basics of code coverage. In the following sections, we'll explore techniques for effectively covering different types of code constructs, such as conditionals, loops, and statements in a sequence.

Cover a Conditional

How do you write tests that cover different types of control flows? Let's look at the three types of structured programming constructs we use daily:

- Statements in a sequence
- Conditionals
- Loops

Let's go over some rules of thumb for covering these control flows with tests. We are partway through covering max(), which has a conditional in the form of an if-else statement. We've written a test that covers the first half.

Now let's add a test to cover the second half. The conditional is if x < y, so let's choose values that will make this if-statement false. We'll apply the characterization test technique, giving the assertion a known mismatch. Running the test gives us the actual value. We plug that value into the assertion, giving us this test:

CodeCoverage/CodeCoverageTests/CoveredClassTests.swift
```
func test_max_with3And2_shouldReturn3() {
    let result = CoveredClass.max(3, 2)

    XCTAssertEqual(result, 3)
}
```

This should give us 100% coverage. Sadly, we're robbed of that satisfaction: The closing brace is marked as uncovered, as you can see here:

```
import UIKit

class CoveredClass {

    static func max(_ x: Int, _ y: Int) -> Int {
        if x < y {
            return y
        } else {
            return x
        }
    }
}
```

What's going on? This is a side effect of multiple early return statements: program execution never reaches the end of the function. There are ways to avoid this, of course. But why? Code the way you want without being a slave to coverage metrics.

 Don't fret trying to cover code you know to be unreachable.

It took two tests to cover this function: one for each side of the if-else. Even when there's no else clause, an if statement calls for at least two tests. Code coverage won't show it, but we need to test for what happens when a section of code behind a conditional isn't run.

For max(), we're satisfied with our two tests. But with the greater-than and less-than comparison operators, you'll often want a third test with an equal value. Equality is an interesting boundary condition for Comparable types.

Conditional expressions often use logical AND (&&) and logical OR (||) operators. For a && b, you'll want to test:

a	b
false	true
true	false
true	true

For a || b, you'll want to test:

a	b
false	false
true	false
false	true

Where's the fourth row of these truth tables? Adding tests for them doesn't add much value, so you can usually omit them. The three sets of inputs for each AND or OR as shown in the tables is enough to specify their behavior.

Stay aware that if statements aren't the only conditionals in town. Swift has the following:

- if statements
- Ternary conditional a : b ? c
- guard statements
- Nil-coalescing operator ??
- Optional chaining
- switch statements

Try to cover every side of a conditional. Remember that an if without an else still requires two tests, checking the behavior when the statements are *not* executed.

What If There Are Too Many Paths?

We should try to have one test for each independent path through a function. But in legacy code, the number of paths (and as a result, the number of tests) can explode.

One way to tame this explosion is to extract a nested conditional into its own method. So if you have an if inside another if, select the inner clause. Then in the Xcode menu, select *Editor ▶ Refactor ▶ Extract to Method*. Remove the fileprivate declaration from the new function so that tests can access it. Now you can write tests to cover the new function on its own.

Another way to tame the explosion is to look for combinations that shouldn't exist. We can often eliminate impossible states by using enumeration cases with associated values. To explore this further, see Mislav Javor's "Swift Enums Are 'Sum' Types. That Makes Them Very Interesting."[a]

Code analysis tools that measure *cyclomatic complexity* can help you identify functions that need too many tests.

---

a. https://mislavjavor.github.io/2017-04-19/Swift-enums-are-sum-types.-That-makes-them-very-interesting/

Cover a Loop

Let's move on to a new function that has a loop. Add the following static function to CoveredClass:

CodeCoverage/CodeCoverage/CoveredClass.swift

```swift
static func commaSeparated(from: Int, to: Int) -> String {
    var result = ""
    for i in from..<to {
        result += "\(i),"
    }
    result += "\(to)"
    return result
}
```

Again, let's write characterization tests instead of trying to reason through the code. We'll start with looping a few times—at least twice through. Since this function returns a string, start with an assertion you're confident will fail. Silly text is more likely to fail than an empty string.

CodeCoverage/CodeCoverageTests/CoveredClassTests.swift

```swift
func test_commaSeparated_from2to4_shouldReturnSomething() {
    let result = CoveredClass.commaSeparated(from: 2, to: 4)

    XCTAssertEqual(result, "FOO")
}
```

Run the tests. This gives us a failure message that tells us the actual value:

```
XCTAssertEqual failed: ("2,3,4") is not equal to ("FOO") -
```

Plug "2,3,4" into the assertion and rerun to confirm. Update the test name to express the actual result:

CodeCoverage/CodeCoverageTests/CoveredClassTests.swift

```swift
func test_commaSeparated_from2to4_shouldReturn234SeparatedByCommas() {
    let result = CoveredClass.commaSeparated(from: 2, to: 4)

    XCTAssertEqual(result, "2,3,4")
}
```

Now let's look at the resulting coverage that the Xcode shows in the image on page 46.

The numbers in the gutter show one execution of the part before the loop, two executions of the loop, and one execution of the part after the loop. It looks like we have 100 percent coverage. But that doesn't mean we're done.

```
CodeCoverage ⟩   CodeCoverage ⟩   CoveredClass.swift ⟩ No Selection

    static func commaSeparated(from: Int, to: Int) -> String {
        var result = ""
        for i in from...to {
            result += "\(i),"
        }
        result += "\(to)"
        return result
    }
}
```

It's tempting to cover a loop with a single test that loops several times. But this misses an important boundary condition. What if the loop is never entered? We want to see what happens if the statements inside are skipped.

Here's a characterization test that uses the same values for from and to. This will show the function's behavior when it loops zero times:

CodeCoverage/CodeCoverageTests/CoveredClassTests.swift
```
func test_commaSeparated_from2to2_shouldReturnSomething() {
    let result = CoveredClass.commaSeparated(from: 2, to: 2)

    XCTAssertEqual(result, "FOO")
}
```

Run the tests. This gives us a failure message that tells us the actual value:

```
XCTAssertEqual failed: ("2") is not equal to ("FOO") -
```

Plug "2" into the assertion and rerun to confirm. Update the test name to state the result:

CodeCoverage/CodeCoverageTests/CoveredClassTests.swift
```
func test_commaSeparated_from2to2_shouldReturn2WithNoComma() {
    let result = CoveredClass.commaSeparated(from: 2, to: 2)

    XCTAssertEqual(result, "2")
}
```

 To cover an arbitrary loop, use zero times through and a few times through—say, two or three times.

Cover Statements in a Sequence

Finally, let's look at the most common building block of structured programming: statements in a sequence. Add the following code to CoveredClass:

```
CodeCoverage/CodeCoverage/CoveredClass.swift
private(set) var area: Int

var width: Int {
    didSet {
        area = width * width
        let color: UIColor = redOrGreen(for: width)
        drawSquare(width: width, color: color)
    }
}
init() {
    area = 0
    width = 0
}
private func redOrGreen(for width: Int) -> UIColor {
    width % 2 == 0 ? .red : .green
}

private func drawSquare(width: Int, color: UIColor) {
    // ...
}
```

The statements in sequence we'll focus on are the didSet observer on the width property. Let's test the outcome of the first line, which calculates the area from a given width. We can do this with the following characterization test:

```
CodeCoverage/CodeCoverageTests/CoveredClassTests.swift
func test_area_withWidth7_shouldBeSomething() {
    let sut = CoveredClass()

    sut.width = 7

    XCTAssertEqual(sut.area, -1)
}
```

Running the tests gives us this failure message:

```
XCTAssertEqual failed: ("49") is not equal to ("-1") -
```

Plug 49 into the assertion and rerun. Don't forget to update the test name to match:

```
CodeCoverage/CodeCoverageTests/CoveredClassTests.swift
func test_area_withWidth7_shouldBe49() {
    let sut = CoveredClass()

    sut.width = 7

    XCTAssertEqual(sut.area, 49)
}
```

Now let's examine the coverage, which will look like this:

```
CodeCoverage ⟩ CodeCoverage ⟩ CoveredClass.swift ⟩ width

        private(set) var area: Int

        var width: Int {
            didSet {
26              area = width * width
                let color: UIColor = redOrGreen(for: width)
                drawSquare(width: width, color: color)
            }
        }

        init() {
            area = 0
            width = 0
        }

        private func redOrGreen(for width: Int) -> UIColor {
            return width % 2 == 0 ? .red : .green
        }

        private func drawSquare(width: Int, color: UIColor) {
            // ...
        }
    }
```

It looks like we have near-100 percent coverage. But we have only one test, which checks the calculation of the area property on line 26. We know there's nothing checking how redOrGreen() determines a color or checking how drawSquare() renders a view. If we were only using positive code coverage as our guide, we might falsely conclude that almost everything has test coverage.

This shows how misleading coverage can be. We can't count on positive code coverage alone—especially for statements in a sequence. We covered line 26. The other lines in the didSet observer are touched incidentally, not meaningfully. If you can delete lines of production code and the tests still pass, then those lines aren't covered.

 When you test a statement in a sequence of statements, the test touches the entire sequence. It's easy to have statements that look covered but lack tests.

As for drawSquare(), we'll look at how to write tests of rendered views in Chapter 16, Testing View Appearance (with Snapshots), on page 193.

Now we've seen how to cover different types of code constructs, and what to be careful with. Let's wrap up this chapter by taking a step back to think about the big picture. We want code coverage to be a helpful tool—not harmful, and not irrelevant.

Avoid Percentage Targets, Embrace Forward Movement

Adding tests to a legacy project is a long endeavor. Let's take a step back from code examples and look at practices to avoid—and practices to embrace.

Avoid setting percentage targets for code coverage. Goodhart's Law expresses the problem with such targets:[1]

> When a measure becomes a target, it ceases to be a good measure.

As you've seen, it's easy to raise the numbers without having meaningful tests. That's exactly what folks will do if the team uses coverage as a target instead of as a measurement of trends.

Another thing to avoid: don't write tests that set and get stored properties. Such tests don't say anything about the code—they only show that the compiler works. Those properties are there for a reason. Find the reason, and test the reason instead.

(But computed properties are just functions without arguments. Do test those.)

Rather than setting a percentage target, your team might try this goal: move the needle forward. Any forward progress is significant and worth celebrating.

Measure your total code coverage on a regular cadence—maybe every two weeks or every month. It's helpful to capture more than the percentage alone. Use a tool like cloc[2] to count lines of code. Then apply the percentage to calculate how many lines of code are covered and how many aren't. For example, if something with 5,000 lines has 20 percent line coverage, then 4,000 lines of code are definitely not covered. This will give you a clearer picture of totals, not just percentages.

Observe the code coverage gutter every time you add a test. It may be a long road, but the positive feedback of seeing the red blocks disappear will boost your motivation.

Key Takeaways

Here are the main things from this chapter to remember:

- To enable code coverage reporting, edit your scheme under Test/Options.

- Code coverage can be misleading, but lack of coverage is always true.

---

1. https://en.wikipedia.org/wiki/Goodhart%27s_law
2. https://github.com/AlDanial/cloc

- Covering a conditional takes two tests—one for when the condition is true, and one for when it's false. (That's not counting && and || operators.)

- When testing a loop, try to test what happens if the loop is executed zero times and also two times.

- If you can deliberately introduce a problem (such as deleting code) and your tests still pass, then that code isn't completely covered.

- Use the characterization test technique to capture the behavior of existing code: write assertions that capture the actual values. Then plug those values back into the assertions.

- Don't write tests that aren't meaningful just to juice your numbers. But do celebrate any genuine forward movement.

Activities

Ready to take action? Pick an activity below and give it a try. The first one is a prerequisite for the others, so do that if nothing else.

1. Enable code coverage on your project. Run your tests to get an initial percentage.

2. Combine your coverage percentage with cloc to calculate how many lines are covered and how many aren't. Record this in a spreadsheet you update periodically.

3. Look for any static func without tests. These will be easier to test than instance methods. Find a simple one. Use the characterization test technique to capture its actual behavior.

4. Look for tested code that has conditionals. See if there are at least two tests, one for true and one for false. Don't worry about "this should never happen, but Swift requires it" guard statements. (But do test guards that could fail in real use.)

5. Look for tested code that has loops. If any loop can be empty, make sure there's a test for that case.

6. After doing a few of these, check your overall coverage percentage again. If you moved the needle, celebrate!

What's Next?

You've learned how to enable code coverage in Xcode and how to read the results. You know how to cover the structured programming types:

1. Statements in a sequence will give false positives from a single test.

2. Conditionals should have at least two tests: one for true and one for false conditions.

3. Loops also need tests for zero times through, which coverage will never show.

You've also seen how positive coverage alone can be misleading. There's already a bit of a lie in your current coverage report. It shows that your application delegate has test coverage. That's not true. Let's fix that in the next chapter by giving the test target control of the application launch sequence.

CHAPTER 4

Take Control of Application Launch

We want to run tests in a clean environment. It's important that we control any surrounding state that may affect test outcomes. As we discussed in Chapter 2, Manage Your Test Life Cycles, on page 19, this is part of having isolated tests, which is one of the FIRST properties of unit tests.[1]

But unit tests for an iOS application won't have a clean environment—unless we take steps to create it. We saw a hint of this in Chapter 3, Measure Code Coverage and Add Tests, on page 35 when we saw the non-zero code coverage for the app delegate and view controller. Unless we're careful, the app will continue to use its normal launch sequence, even for test runs. This could create unwanted side effects that affect test runs. It can also slow down the test feedback loop. Tests don't start running until the app finishes launching.

In this chapter, we'll go over how to use a separate app delegate when running tests. By keeping your regular app delegate out of the way, you'll have greater control over your test environment. This will also make your code coverage results a little more accurate.

Make a New Place to Play

Okay, time for a new project. Follow the steps in Create a Place to Play with Tests, on page 4, but name the project name AppLaunch. Make sure to select Storyboard as the user interface, not SwiftUI.

This time, don't delete the initial test file AppLaunchTests.swift. But add one do-nothing test, deleting the other methods:

---

1. https://pragprog.com/magazines/2012-01/unit-tests-are-first

AppLaunch/AppLaunchTests/AppLaunchTests.swift
```
class AppLaunchTests: XCTestCase {
    func test_emptyJustSoWeHaveAPassingTest() {
    }
}
```

Then edit AppDelegate.swift to add a print(_:) statement to application(_:didFinishLaunch-ingWithOptions:):

AppLaunch/AppLaunch/AppDelegate.swift
```
@UIApplicationMain
class AppDelegate: UIResponder, UIApplicationDelegate {
    func application(
            _ application: UIApplication,
            didFinishLaunchingWithOptions launchOptions:
                    [UIApplication.LaunchOptionsKey: Any]?) -> Bool {
        print(">> Launching with real app delegate")
        return true
    }
}
```

Now let's use this project to run experiments about app launch. First, we'll see what happens with test execution if we don't take precautions. Then we will learn about the test launch sequence. After this, we'll see how to bypass the normal app delegate.

Observe the Default Behavior

With the print(_:) statement in the app delegate, let's see what happens. Make sure your destination is set to an iOS simulator. Build and run the app by clicking the play button (or press ⌘-R). Then press the stop button (or press ⌘-.).

Let's check the console output by going to the Xcode menu and selecting *View* ▶ *Debug Area* ▶ *Activate Console* (or press Shift-⌘-C). After a line about AppLaunch, you'll see this:

```
>> Launching with real app delegate
```

No surprises so far. But now press ⌘-U to run tests. Go to console output and scroll to the top. We still see the print(_:) statement output from the app delegate, even during testing—surprise!

Learn About the Test Launch Sequence

Let's see why the app delegate fires off during testing. Xcode runs tests within the context of a running app. The testing sequence goes like this:

1. Launch the simulator on macOS.
2. Dynamically inject the test bundle into the app.
3. Launch the app in the simulator.
4. Run the tests.
5. Terminate the app.

This gives tests the ecosystem they need to verify interactions with UIKit. As part of step 3, UIKit gives the app delegate a chance to set up anything the app needs to launch. This may include things like the following:

- Setting up core data
- Sending an app-specific key to an analytics service
- Sending a request to fetch data it needs before going to the first screen

These are things we don't want to have happen while running unit tests. Core data should be set up and populated by test code without using or changing any stored data. We don't want any network requests.

But we do want these things during normal launch. Since app delegate behavior depends on the needs of the app, Apple can't standardize it—or safely bypass it. But *you* can.

Bypass the Normal App Delegate

Here's how you can use a different app delegate for test runs only. In the test target, create a new file TestingAppDelegate.swift. Copy the contents of AppDelegate.swift from the main target, but make these changes:

1. Remove the @UIApplicationMain attribute from the class declaration.

2. Change the name of the class to TestingAppDelegate, and add a declaration @objc(TestingAppDelegate). By giving it an Objective-C name, we can refer to it without a namespace.

3. Remove all methods except application(_:didFinishLaunchingWithOptions:).

4. Customize the remaining method. For our example, let's change the print(_:) statement.

Putting this together, here's what TestingAppDelegate.swift looks like:

AppLaunch/AppLaunchTests/TestingAppDelegate.swift

```
import UIKit

@objc(TestingAppDelegate)
class TestingAppDelegate: UIResponder, UIApplicationDelegate {
    func application(
            _ application: UIApplication,
            didFinishLaunchingWithOptions launchOptions:
                    [UIApplication.LaunchOptionsKey: Any]?) -> Bool {
        print("<< Launching with testing app delegate")
        return true
    }
}
```

On the regular app delegate, the @UIApplicationMain attribute tells the Swift compiler to generate a "main" routine that starts the application with the designated app delegate. Since we're taking control, remove @UIApplicationMain from AppDelegate.swift as well as from TestingAppDelegate.swift. Then it's up to us to provide main.swift. Add the following file to the main target:

AppLaunch/AppLaunch/main.swift

```
import UIKit

let appDelegateClass: AnyClass =
        NSClassFromString("TestingAppDelegate") ?? AppDelegate.self
UIApplicationMain(
        CommandLine.argc,
        CommandLine.unsafeArgv,
        nil,
        NSStringFromClass(appDelegateClass))
```

This code tries to find a class named TestingAppDelegate outside of any namespace. If we're running tests, the test bundle will be present, so the class will be there. But on regular runs, the test bundle will be missing, so NSClassFromString() will return nil. Then the nil-coalescing operator ?? will fall back to using the regular AppDelegate.

It's time to give the new setup a try. First, run the app to verify the message from the normal app delegate in the console log. Then run the tests to verify the message from the testing app delegate. The console log will show

```
<< Launching with testing app delegate
```

We've managed to avoid the regular app delegate during testing. This is important because we want the tests to be in full control of what's going on during test execution.

Put Up with the Initial View Controller

The app delegate isn't the only code that UIKit runs at app launch. It also shows and activates the root view controller.

iOS 13 introduced scenes to support apps with multiple windows. Before this, there was one root view controller, in one window. And the app delegate owned that window. So with a separate app delegate for tests, it wasn't hard to supply an empty window with no root view controller.

But these days, the scene delegate owns the window. It would be nice if we had a simple way to use a separate scene delegate for tests. However, iOS caches the scene, which throws a wrench into our clean room goals.

Is there a way to suppress the initial view controller during tests? If you're lucky, your initial view controller doesn't do any work without the user taking some action. In this case, I'd shrug and ignore the fact that tests will start with the initial view controller present. Just be aware that your code coverage will be misleading for this view controller.

But you may have an initial view controller that immediately starts work, such as firing off a network request. In this case, try the approach described in the post "How to Switch Your iOS App and Scene Delegates for Improved Testing."[2]

For now, let's set aside the initial view controller, and finish this chapter by stepping back to think about what you might want your testing app delegate to do.

Tweak Your Testing App Delegate

You now have control over more of the app launch sequence during testing. Remember, the goal is to set up an environment that's suitable for tests. But your app may make assumptions about its environment, so your TestingAppDelegate may need more than the simple code in our example.

For testing, we want the environment to avoid doing any actual work. Depending on what your normal app delegate does, the testing app delegate may do things like the following:

---

2. https://medium.com/@hacknicity/how-to-switch-your-ios-app-and-scene-delegates-for-improved-testing-9746279378c3

- Setting up core data with an in-memory store. This will keep production data from interfering with test data and vice-versa. It will also help tests to run faster.

- Providing a testing-specific key for an analytics service. Unit tests shouldn't make any actual network calls, but they'll still happen until you change the legacy code. So at the very least, use a different key to avoid polluting the data you collect.

On the other hand, your app may not need anything in the testing app delegate. If all you're left with is an application(_:didFinishLaunchingWithOptions:) method that does nothing but return true, just delete the method.

Key Takeaways

The main thing to take away from this chapter is that due to app launch, running tests will execute other code. If left unchecked, we could have objects doing work outside the context of test execution. For unit tests, the tests need to be in full control of their environment. To give tests full control, use a separate app delegate during test runs.

This doesn't mean the regular app delegate is off-limits during testing. It means that if we call anything in the regular app delegate, it will be because we wrote a test to call it.

Activities

Ultimately, the goal is to change the way your app launches during testing. But that might be a big job, depending on your app delegate. Try doing the first activity to solidify your learning from this chapter. Then continue down this list in order, depending on how much you want to do.

1. Measure the code coverage of your current unit tests. If you don't have any, add a do-nothing test. See how much coverage is reported for your app delegate.

2. Does your app delegate contain anything that's not related to the application life cycle? Move such things out, even if that means placing them in their own singletons. Make sure your app continues to work.

3. Copy your app delegate to make a testing app delegate. Remove @UIApplicationMain. Set up main.swift. Gradually cut away anything you can from the testing app delegate. Make sure all tests continue to run.

4. After all this, see if the code coverage for your normal app delegate has gone to zero.

What's Next?

You've learned how to manage the app launch sequence. You can use a separate app delegate during testing.

This will give you a better clean room for testing. Except for the initial root view controller, your code coverage report will be more accurate. This gives you a clearer picture of where your app lacks unit tests.

Using the characterization test technique from Chapter 3, Measure Code Coverage and Add Tests, on page 35, you can write tests for any well-isolated business logic. But a lot of iOS code is in view controllers, so what do we do about that? In the next chapter, we'll pave the way for unit testing view controllers by learning how tests can access them.

CHAPTER 5

Load View Controllers

UIViewControllers play a central role in iOS code. They're the main way for UIKit to call most of our code. Does that mean your view controller code is out of reach of unit tests? Nope, not at all.

After all, UIKit manages to load and call your view controllers. So unit tests can do the same. To write tests for a view controller, the test first needs to load it. This will open the door to all sorts of tests.

In this chapter, we'll look at different ways tests can load view controllers. How you do this depends on how you like to write view controllers. You may use storyboards, XIB files, or straight code. After making a new project to hold this chapter's experiments, feel free to jump to the section you need:

- Set Up a Storyboard-Based View Controller for Experiments, on page 62
- Set Up a XIB-Based View Controller for Experiments, on page 66
- Set Up a Code-Based View Controller for Experiments, on page 68

Make a New Place to Play

It's time to make a new project. Follow Create a Place to Play with Tests, on page 4, but use the project name LoadViewControllers. Then delete the initial test file for this project, LoadViewControllersTests.swift.

There's no need to apply the techniques from Chapter 4, Take Control of Application Launch, on page 53 to bypass the app delegate. That's important to do in real code, but we're just experimenting here. (But if you want the practice, go for it.)

With this project skeleton in place, we can set up a particular style of view controller, then learn how to load it from unit tests. We'll do this for storyboards, XIB files, and code-based view controllers.

Set Up a Storyboard-Based View Controller for Experiments

Let's make a storyboard-based view controller we can play with. We'll want it to have some of the basics:

- The view controller itself
- An outlet to control some UI

The default storyboard already contains a view controller, but let's add a new one. Storyboards usually contain more than one view controller, so we need to be able to access any of them, not just the initial one.

Define the New View Controller

First, let's define a new view controller for the storyboard-based version. Select the LoadViewControllers group. Create a new file, selecting Cocoa Touch Class. Name it StoryboardBasedViewController and make it a subclass of UIViewController, like this:

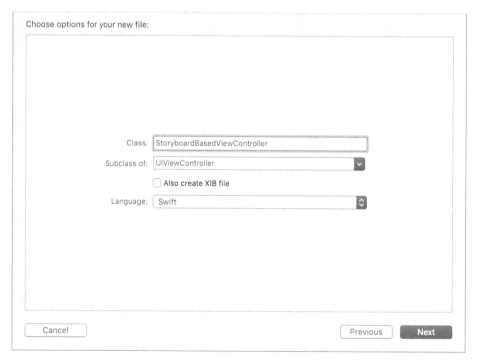

In the Save dialog, double-check that the app target is selected, not the test target.

Now let's define an outlet—a simple label will do. Change the code as follows:

LoadViewControllers/LoadViewControllers/StoryboardBasedViewController.swift

```
class StoryboardBasedViewController: UIViewController {
    @IBOutlet var label: UILabel!
}
```

Add the New View Controller to the Storyboard

Next, let's add this view controller to the storyboard. Open Main.storyboard and select *View* ▶ *Libraries* ▶ *Show Library* from the Xcode menu, or press Shift-⌘-L. This will bring up the Object Library. Find "View Controller" and double-click it to add a new view controller to the storyboard. (If you can't see the View Controller item, make sure you've selected Main.storyboard.)

This will create a generic view controller, which we need to change to our specific type. Select the second "View Controller Scene," which is the one we just added, as shown here:

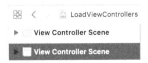

In the Xcode menu, select *View* ▶ *Inspectors* ▶ *Show Identity Inspector* or press ⌥-⌘-4. In the Identity Inspector on the right, the Custom Class section will show that the class of the selected view controller is UIViewController. (If it shows ViewController, that's the wrong one.) It will appear as follows:

Click the down arrow for Class to reveal the pull-down menu, and select StoryboardBasedViewController.

Let's add a label so we can connect it to the view controller's outlet. Open the Object Library again and drag a label onto the view controller in the main editor area. For this experiment, don't worry about positioning the label or setting any Auto Layout constraints.

Finally, connect the outlet to this new label. (One way to do this is to open StoryboardBasedViewController.swift in the Assistant Editor. Click in the open circle next to @IBOutlet and drag it to the label on the storyboard to establish the connection.)

Load a Storyboard-Based View Controller

We added a second view controller because storyboards usually have more than one of them. How can we access an arbitrary view controller within a storyboard? We'll do this by assigning a *Storyboard ID* to the view controller we want.

Create a new test suite named StoryboardBasedViewControllerTests. (Remember to start with Test Zero to confirm that the new suite is hooked up.) Add this import declaration at the top of the file:

LoadViewControllers/LoadViewControllersTests/StoryboardBasedViewControllerTests.swift
```
@testable import LoadViewControllers
```

Then add the following test case:

LoadViewControllers/LoadViewControllersTests/StoryboardBasedViewControllerTests.swift
```
func test_loading() {
    let sb = UIStoryboard(name: "Main", bundle: nil)
    let sut = sb.instantiateViewController(
        identifier: String(describing: StoryboardBasedViewController.self))
}
```

The first line loads the Main storyboard. Then the call to instantiateViewController(identifier:) takes an arbitrary identifier. It can be anything as long as it's unique within the storyboard. Using the class name as the identifier is an easy way to do this.

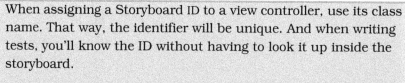

When assigning a Storyboard ID to a view controller, use its class name. That way, the identifier will be unique. And when writing tests, you'll know the ID without having to look it up inside the storyboard.

(There is an edge case: the class name won't be unique if your storyboard has multiple instances of the same view controller type. Don't worry—if you use the same Storyboard ID twice, Xcode will tell you.)

Run the tests. The results log will show "1 unexpected failure" with the following message:

```
failed: caught "NSInvalidArgumentException", "Storyboard
    (<UIStoryboard: 0x6000032d7bc0>) doesn't contain a view controller with
    identifier 'StoryboardBasedViewController'"
```

Let's assign this Storyboard ID to the view controller. Open Main.storyboard, select the "Storyboard Based View Controller," and look in the Identity Inspector on the right. (If the Identity Inspector isn't showing, press ⌥-⌘-4.) In the Identity Inspector, copy and paste the Class name field into the Storyboard ID field, like this:

Run the tests. This time this test will pass.

But the UIStoryboard method instantiateViewController(identifier:) returns a UIViewController that won't know about the outlet. We need to downcast this to the actual type of our system under test (or sut). Thankfully, the method returns a generic type. To get the type we want, we can explicitly specify the type of sut:

LoadViewControllers/LoadViewControllersTests/StoryboardBasedViewControllerTests.swift
```
let sut: StoryboardBasedViewController = sb.instantiateViewController(
    identifier: String(describing: StoryboardBasedViewController.self))
```

(Make sure you're using the new method which has the argument name identifier, not the old one named withIdentifier.)

If the type is wrong, this will crash the test run—we won't get any further test case reports. But it will give a useful message in the console log. And in my experience, programmers don't often introduce typos in the storyboard Class field. Since it's a rare occurrence, I don't mind if the tests crash. (But only for storyboards.)

We now have an sut of type StoryboardBasedViewController. Let's add an assertion to confirm that the outlet is set:

LoadViewControllers/LoadViewControllersTests/StoryboardBasedViewControllerTests.swift
```
XCTAssertNotNil(sut.label)
```

Run the tests. This will fail, but don't be disheartened. There's a trick to making this work: we'll ask the view controller to loadViewIfNeeded(). This will load the view controller's view from the storyboard, including outlet connections. Here's a complete test using the simpler force-cast approach:

LoadViewControllers/LoadViewControllersTests/StoryboardBasedViewControllerTests.swift
```
func test_loading() {
    let sb = UIStoryboard(name: "Main", bundle: nil)
    let sut: StoryboardBasedViewController = sb.instantiateViewController(
            identifier: String(describing: StoryboardBasedViewController.self))

    sut.loadViewIfNeeded()

    XCTAssertNotNil(sut.label)
}
```

Run the tests to watch this pass. This demonstrates that a unit test can load a specific view controller from a storyboard, with outlets connected.

Set Up a XIB-Based View Controller for Experiments

Now let's make a XIB-based view controller we can play with. As with the storyboard version, we'll want it to have two things:

- The view controller itself
- An outlet to control some UI

Define the New View Controller

Let's define a new view controller for the XIB-based version. Select the Load-ViewControllers group in the Project Navigator. Create a new file, selecting Cocoa Touch Class. Name it XIBBasedViewController and make it a subclass of UIViewController. This time, select the check box labeled "Also create XIB file." Your selections should look like this:

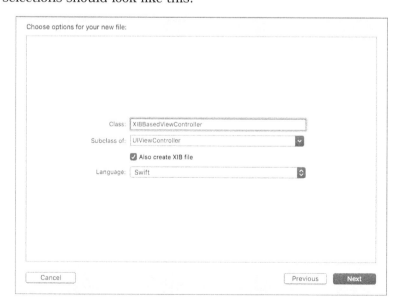

In the Save dialog, double-check that the app target is selected, not the test target, then press Create. This will add XIBBasedViewController.swift and XIBBasedViewController.xib to the project.

Now define an outlet—a label will do for our experiment. In the Swift file, use the following code:

```
LoadViewControllers/LoadViewControllers/XIBBasedViewController.swift
class XIBBasedViewController: UIViewController {
    @IBOutlet var label: UILabel!
}
```

Connect the View Controller Outlet to the XIB

Next, let's add a label so we can connect it to the view controller's outlet. Open XIBBasedViewController.xib and select *View* ▶ *Libraries* ▶ *Show Library* from the Xcode menu, or press Shift-⌘-L. Drag a label onto the view in the main editor area. For this experiment, don't worry about positioning the label or setting any Auto Layout constraints.

Then connect the outlet to this new label. (One way to do this is to show XIBBasedViewController.swift in the Assistant Editor. Click in the open circle next to @IBOutlet and drag it to the label on the view to establish the connection.)

Load a XIB-Based View Controller

Now let's experiment with a test that loads this view controller. Create a new test suite named XIBBasedViewControllerTests. (Remember to start with Test Zero to confirm that the new suite is hooked up.) Add the @testable import LoadViewControllers declaration to the top of the file. Then add the following test case:

```
LoadViewControllers/LoadViewControllersTests/XIBBasedViewControllerTests.swift
func test_loading() {
    let sut = XIBBasedViewController()

    XCTAssertNotNil(sut.label)
}
```

Run the tests. This will fail because there's a trick to making this work. We need to ask the view controller to perform loadViewIfNeeded(). This will load the view controller's view from the XIB, including outlet connections. Here's a complete test:

```
LoadViewControllers/LoadViewControllersTests/XIBBasedViewControllerTests.swift
func test_loading() {
    let sut = XIBBasedViewController()

    sut.loadViewIfNeeded()

    XCTAssertNotNil(sut.label)
}
```

Run the tests to watch this pass. This demonstrates that a unit test can load a view controller with an associated XIB.

> ### Where's the XIB Name?
>
> The designated initializer of UIViewController is init(nibName:bundle:). So why am I not calling this in the test? How is this even working?
>
> Initializing a UIViewController without arguments calls through to the designated initializer, passing nil arguments. Since our view controller class name XIBBasedView-Controller ends with Controller, UIKit will first look for a XIB file named XIBBasedView. (More accurately, it will look for a NIB file created from a XIB file with that name.) If that doesn't work, it will try to look for a XIB that matches the full name XIBBasedViewController.
>
> Apple describes these rules more fully in the documentation for the nibName property.[a]
>
> ———————
> a.   https://developer.apple.com/documentation/uikit/uiviewcontroller/1621487-nibname

Set Up a Code-Based View Controller for Experiments

Let's make a code-based view controller we can play with. Unlike the storyboard or XIB versions, a code-based view controller has no outlets. Instead, we create the views in code.

Since UIKit instantiates storyboard or XIB-based view controllers, their designated initializers can't change. But in a code-based view controller, we're free to define a new designated initializer. This lets us pass data as initializer arguments instead of setting them as properties afterward.

Let's define a new view controller for the code-based version. Select the LoadViewControllers group. Make a new file, selecting Cocoa Touch Class. Name it CodeBasedViewController and make it a subclass of UIViewController. In the Save dialog, double-check that the app target is selected, not the test target.

Now let's define an initializer that takes some data. For our example, we'll pass a string and store it in a property:

```
LoadViewControllers/LoadViewControllers/CodeBasedViewController.swift
class CodeBasedViewController: UIViewController {
    private let data: String

    init(data: String) {
        self.data = data
        super.init(nibName: nil, bundle: nil)
    }
}
```

Go ahead and try to build this. In the Xcode menu, select *Product ▶ Build* or press ⌘-B. Below the initializer, Xcode will show the following error:

> ⊘ 'required' initializer 'init(coder:)' must be provided by subclass of 'UIViewController'

This is a common error when writing code-based view controllers. We get this error because we're defining a designated initializer. But UIViewControllers conform to the NSCoding protocol so that UIKit can create them from storyboards and XIBs. Since we're using a code-based approach, we don't need to add actual NSCoding support. Still, we have to appease UIKit by providing the method it requires.

The icon on the left of the error shows that this is something Xcode can fix for us. This is an easy way to provide a do-nothing method. In the Xcode menu, select *Editor ▶ Fix All Issues*. Xcode will generate the following code:

LoadViewControllers/LoadViewControllers/CodeBasedViewController.swift

```
required init?(coder aDecoder: NSCoder) {
    fatalError("init(coder:) has not been implemented")
}
```

That's a fine implementation. For a code-based view controller, we don't expect anything to call this method, ever.

Load a Code-Based View Controller

A test can create a code-based view controller by calling its initializer. But there's one trick we need to borrow from its storyboard and XIB cousins. To explore this, let's create a learning experiment.

Create a new test suite named CodeBasedViewControllerTests. (Remember to start with Test Zero to confirm that the new suite is hooked up.) Add the usual @testable import LoadViewControllers to the top of the file. Then add the following test case:

LoadViewControllers/LoadViewControllersTests/CodeBasedViewControllerTests.swift

```
func test_loading() {
    let sut = CodeBasedViewController(data: "DUMMY")

    // Normally, assert something
}
```

We have to pass a string argument because the initializer requires it. But we won't be using the string's value in this experiment.

> Sometimes we need to pass an object just to satisfy Swift, but we don't care about its value. *xUnit Test Patterns [Mes07]* says,
>
> > We can use a *Dummy Argument* whenever methods of the SUT take objects as arguments and those objects are not relevant to the test.
>
> Clearly communicate to your readers which arguments are dummy arguments. For a string, this can be done by setting the value to "DUMMY" or "". For numbers, 0 is often clear enough. For other types, extract a variable and give it a name starting with dummy.

Code-based view controllers usually set up their views in viewDidLoad(). For this experiment, let's cheat by using a print(_:) statement instead of defining views. In the view controller, add the following:

LoadViewControllers/LoadViewControllers/CodeBasedViewController.swift
```
override func viewDidLoad() {
    super.viewDidLoad()
    print(">> create views here")
}
```

Run the tests. Applying the techniques from Examine Console Output, on page 23, drill down to the output of test suite CodeBasedViewControllerTests. You'll see something like:

```
Test Suite 'CodeBasedViewControllerTests' started at 2018-12-01 11:50:49.035
Test Case
    '-[LoadViewControllersTests.CodeBasedViewControllerTests test_loading]'
    started.
Test Case
    '-[LoadViewControllersTests.CodeBasedViewControllerTests test_loading]'
    passed (0.001 seconds).
Test Suite 'CodeBasedViewControllerTests' passed at 2018-12-01 11:50:49.037.
    Executed 1 test, with 0 failures (0 unexpected) in 0.001 (0.002) seconds
```

Notice that between "started" and "passed," we don't have any output from our print(_:) statement. So nothing calls viewDidLoad() automatically.

One way to address this is by having the test call viewDidLoad(). While this works, it deviates from the style we need for storyboards and XIBs. Rather than using one way here and another way there, it's simplest to use the same approach of calling loadViewIfNeeded().

Add the following line to the test:

LoadViewControllers/LoadViewControllersTests/CodeBasedViewControllerTests.swift
```
sut.loadViewIfNeeded()
```

Run the tests again, and drill down to the console output for CodeBasedViewController Tests. This time, the output for the test will include

```
>> create views here
```

This demonstrates that a unit test can load a code-based view controller, asking it to create its views.

Key Takeaways

What should you take from this chapter back to your code? That depends on which idioms you use for view controllers.

For storyboard-based view controllers you can do the following:

- Assign a Storyboard ID to the view controller.
- Instantiate a UIStoryboard. Then pass the Storyboard ID to instantiateViewController(identifier:).
- Assign the view controller to a variable with its explicit type, so that the test can access its properties and methods.
- Call loadViewIfNeeded() which connects the outlets and actions. It also calls viewDidLoad().

For XIB-based view controllers, you can do the following:

- Instantiate the view controller. As long as its XIB shares the same name as the view controller (or otherwise follows Where's the XIB Name?, on page 68), it will find the associated XIB file.
- Call loadViewIfNeeded() which connects the outlets and actions. It also calls viewDidLoad().

For code-based view controllers, you can do the following:

- Instantiate the view controller.
- If you want the test to execute viewDidLoad(), call loadViewIfNeeded().

Activities

This chapter has one activity, consisting of three steps:

1. Pick a view controller in your production code. Start with one of your simpler ones.
2. Make sure that its viewDidLoad() won't trigger any network calls or write anything to disk. If it does, pick a different view controller.

3. Write a unit test that loads this view controller. Don't forget to call load-
ViewIfNeeded().

This test isn't useful by itself because it has no assertions. But it's an
important stepping-stone that will enable further testing. Give it a try to
cement your learning from this chapter.

What's Next?

Whether you use storyboards, XIBs, or straight code, you can write tests that
reach your view controllers. We've covered the techniques you'll need for each
type. And regardless of the type, call loadViewIfNeeded(). That way, the view
controllers will load up everything they need.

But loading a view controller is just part of the battle. We want tests that call
various methods on view controllers. Unfortunately, view controller methods
often have hard-coded dependencies that get in the way of testing. In the next
chapter, we'll look at ways to isolate these dependencies. This will give tests
a way to control them so that we can test the methods.

CHAPTER 6

Manage Difficult Dependencies

When you realize you can write unit tests against view controllers, it's exciting. At first, you may think this will unlock your codebase to automated testing: "I can test anything!"

Unfortunately, as you try to make progress, you'll experience setbacks and frustrations. Sure, you can write a test that accesses a particular view controller. But as soon as you try to have a test call some method, you find the code inside the view controller is fighting you.

This is true of any types, not only view controllers. Code written without tests often has implicit hardwired dependencies. These dependencies can complicate testing. It so happens that view controllers are especially susceptible to such problems. It's easy to lump functionality (and the dependencies needed to perform it) into a view controller.

When testing is difficult, this reveals flaws in the architectural design of the code. By making changes to enable testing, you'll be shaping the code into cleaner design. Design decisions that were once hidden and implicit will become visible and explicit.

In this chapter, we'll learn how to identify difficult dependencies. Having identified them, we'll explore some techniques for isolating these dependencies. This will give you ways to write unit tests against previously untestable code.

Be Okay with Problem-Free Dependencies

Law enforcement agents learn how to detect counterfeit money by studying genuine money. Let's apply this idea to dependencies. Before looking at difficult dependencies, let's see what makes some dependencies problem-free.

Consider the following function:

```
func shoutHello(to name: String) -> String {
    return "HELLO, \(name.uppercased())!"
}
```

What dependencies does it have? This is a trick question because it's easy to reply, "It has no dependencies." But it *does* depend on the Swift String type. Our function calls the uppercased() method. Swift takes the result and does string interpolation. String interpolation prefers calling the description property of the CustomStringConvertible protocol.

There are word lawyers who insist that a test is not a unit test if it exercises more than one type. Yet no one would blink an eye at writing tests for shoutHello(to:) and calling them unit tests. So why is this dependency okay to test without isolating it?

To answer this, let's start with three of the FIRST unit test principles.[1] The first three apply to dependencies:

F for Fast Both functions—the uppercased() method and the description computed property—are fast. We're not in any danger of pushing up against the rule of thumb from *Working Effectively with Legacy Code [Fea04]*:

> A unit test that takes 1/10th of a second to run is a slow unit test.

I for Isolated Neither function has any side effects that would persist beyond the test run. Tests that exercise shoutHello(to:) won't get different results due to external factors. And the tests won't have any effect on each other.

R for Repeatable Calling these two functions with the same input will always yield the same output. There are no external services that might fail. There are no race conditions. The time of day (or phase of the moon) will make no difference.

(The last two of the FIRST principles don't apply to dependencies. So you're not left wondering what they are, S is for self-verifying. This means using assertions to pass or fail without human verification. And T is for timely. This means tests have more value when written before the production code.)

After fast, isolated, and repeatable, there's one more question that helps us classify dependencies.

Easy to Test? When something calls a dependency, how can we know if the call was correct? If there's a return value, it's easy. We can check the

---

1. https://pragprog.com/magazines/2012-01/unit-tests-are-first

return value, or any computation that uses the return value. For shoutHello(to:), the calls to String's uppercased() and description affect the function's return value. Tests can simply check the return value.

What if there is no return value? Chances are good the call causes some state to change. If we can check a property of the dependency for an expected value, that's also easy.

But if a call has an external effect we can't access, that dependency is harder to test.

If we take fast, isolated, and repeatable and combine it with easy to test, we get FIRE. If a dependency satisfies the FIRE rules, we can use it as is. Writing tests with it won't be difficult.

Identify Difficult Dependencies

Now that we have some rules to gauge if a dependency is problem-free, let's break each FIRE rule. This will help us learn which kinds of dependencies get in the way of simple tests.

F for Fast iOS programs often include code that will execute in response to some external trigger. In later chapters, we'll see how to unit test delegate methods. But if there's no way for tests to trigger the code execution immediately, that's a slow dependency. Examples include the following:

- Calls to web services
- Timers

I for Isolated Dependencies break the rule of isolation in two common ways: global variables and persistent storage.

Global variables come in different varieties:

- Variables defined outside of any type
- Singletons
- Static properties

Globals aren't a problem if they're read-only, such as string constants. It's when we can change the value of a global that we run into the challenges of *shared mutable state*. One test can set a value that affects a following test.

Persistent storage is similar, except that we store the state in something that outlasts the app's life cycle. This includes the following:

- The file system
- UserDefaults
- The keychain
- A local database
- A remote database

Recall from Chapter 2, Manage Your Test Life Cycles, on page 19 that we need each test to run in a clean room. Earlier test runs or manual testing should not change the outcome of automated tests. And automated tests should leave no trace that affect later manual testing.

R for Repeatable What dependencies are there that yield different results when called? We expect different results for the following:

- Current time or date
- Camera or microphone input
- Face ID or Touch ID
- Core Motion sensors
- Random numbers

We can anticipate those differences. But there are also unpredictable differences:

- External services—they can fail.
- Writing to a log file—we can run out of disk space.
- Time zone of the machine running tests—when writing tests, it's easy to assume they'll always run in your own time zone. Hidden problems will surface if your development team grows globally.

Easy to Test? It's not hard to test functions that return values or change properties. But there are also functions that cause side effects outside of the invoked type. Such dependencies take commands but offer no way to access the effects of those commands. Examples include the following:

- Analytics
- Playing audio or video

Analytics includes any system of logging events to a server. We can send events, but there's no way for the mobile API to ask for the last batch of events you sent.

This isn't a complete list of difficult dependencies. But they illustrate guidelines that will help you identify most of them. Next, we'll see how to isolate them.

Create Boundaries to Isolate Dependencies

Once we've identified dependencies that make testing difficult, what do we do with them? We need to find ways to isolate them behind boundaries. Having isolated them, we can replace them with substitutes during testing.

In well-structured code, we can summarize our code as boxes of functionality. An arrow line from one box to another represents a dependency. With careful design, these boxes and arrows form a *directed acyclic graph*. By avoiding cycles, we make it easier to replace functionality. This brings benefits to ongoing maintenance that extend beyond testability.

We can implement boundaries using Swift protocols. With protocols in place, we can substitute different concrete types. But to even begin using a protocol, we need a place where we make the current type explicit. Once we spell out the type, we'll be able to switch it to a protocol.

There are various techniques for making dependencies explicit. To illustrate them, let's make another project for our experiments.

Make a New Place to Play

Now we're ready to create a new project for this chapter. Follow the steps for Create a Place to Play with Tests, on page 4, but name the project HardDependencies. Also delete that initial test file, HardDependenciesTests.swift.

We don't need to apply Chapter 4, Take Control of Application Launch, on page 53 to bypass the app delegate, since this is an experiment. (This will be true for most of the book, so I won't continue to repeat this.)

To simulate a difficult dependency, let's pretend we're using an analytics API to track events. Make a new file in production code named Analytics.swift:

HardDependencies/HardDependencies/Analytics.swift
```
class Analytics {
    static let shared = Analytics()

    func track(event: String) {
        print(">> " + event)

        if self !== Analytics.shared {
            print(">> ...Not the Analytics singleton")
        }
    }
}
```

This API provides a shared instance to use as a singleton. As a "soft" singleton, it doesn't restrict us from creating separate instances.

Let's pretend the track(event:) instance method sends the event to a web service. We'll simulate it with a print(_:) statement, and observe the results in the console log. It also prints a message if the Analytics instance is not the singleton.

Besides an API we can't control, we'll also see an approach for singletons we own and can change. Make a second file in production code named MySingletonAnalytics.swift:

HardDependencies/HardDependencies/MySingletonAnalytics.swift
```
class MySingletonAnalytics {
    static let shared = MySingletonAnalytics()

    func track(event: String) {
        Analytics.shared.track(event: event)

        if self !== MySingletonAnalytics.shared {
            print(">> Not the MySingletonAnalytics singleton")
        }
    }
}
```

It's similar but wraps a call to the original Analytics class. We'll use this for Add Backdoors to Singletons You Own, on page 80.

Add Storyboard-Based View Controllers

To experiment with different techniques, let's make several view controllers. First let's add two view controllers to the storyboard. Select the HardDependencies group. Make a new file, selecting Cocoa Touch Class. Name it InstancePropertyViewController and make it a subclass of UIViewController. In the Save dialog, double-check that the app target is selected, not the test target.

Now let's add this view controller to the storyboard. Open Main.storyboard and select *View ▶ Libraries ▶ Show Library* from the Xcode menu, or press Shift-⌘-L. This will bring up the Object Library. Double-click "View Controller" to add a new view controller to the storyboard.

This will create a generic view controller, which we need to change to our specific type. Select the second "View Controller Scene" that we just added, like you see here:

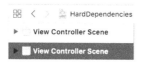

In the Xcode menu, select *View ▶ Inspectors ▶ Show Identity Inspector* or press ⌥-⌘-4. In the Identity Inspector on the right, the Custom Class section will show that the class of the selected view controller is UIViewController. (If it shows ViewController, that's the wrong one.) Click the down arrow for Class to reveal the pop-up menu, and select InstancePropertyViewController.

We're going to have a test load this view controller, so we need to apply the trick from Load a Storyboard-Based View Controller, on page 64. In the Identity Inspector, copy and paste the Class name into the Storyboard ID.

Now we have one storyboard-based view controller we can use in a test. Repeat these steps to create another view controller, naming it ClosurePropertyViewController. You should end up with three scenes in Main.storyboard—the first there by default, and the two you just added.

Add XIB-Based View Controllers

Now we'll add view controllers that use XIBs. Select the HardDependencies group in the Project Navigator. Make a new file, selecting Cocoa Touch Class. Name it OverrideViewController and make it a subclass of UIViewController. This time, select the check box labeled "Also create XIB file."

In the Save dialog, double-check that the app target is selected, not the test target. Pressing Create will add OverrideViewController.swift and OverrideViewController.xib to the project.

Now we have one XIB-based view controller we can use in a test. Repeat these steps to make the following additional view controllers:

- InstanceInitializerViewController
- ClosureInitializerViewController
- MySingletonViewController

Track Analytics on the New View Controllers

With two systems for tracking events (Analytics and MySingletonAnalytics), let's use them in the view controllers. In each view controller except MySingletonViewController, add the following method:

```
override func viewDidAppear(_ animated: Bool) {
    super.viewDidAppear(animated)
    Analytics.shared.track(event: "viewDidAppear - \(type(of: self))")
}
```

Copy the same method to MySingletonViewController, but change the singleton from Analytics.shared to MySingletonAnalytics.shared.

We now have a simulated setup of analytics, called from view controllers using differing styles. In the rest of this chapter, let's look at ways to replace these hard-coded dependencies. We'll start with two techniques that are easier to apply to legacy code but come at the cost of weak design. We'll move from there to techniques that take more work but yield more robust designs.

Add Backdoors to Singletons You Own

You can't change the behavior of singletons you don't own. But any singleton you do own provides an opportunity to add a *singleton backdoor*. We can use conditional compilation to ensure that the backdoors aren't available in release builds.

For this experiment, let's assume MySingletonAnalytics is code we own. It uses the *Adapter design pattern*[2] to wrap the actual analytics API:

HardDependencies/HardDependencies/MySingletonAnalytics.swift
```
class MySingletonAnalytics {
    static let shared = MySingletonAnalytics()

    func track(event: String) {
        Analytics.shared.track(event: event)

        if self !== MySingletonAnalytics.shared {
            print(">> Not the MySingletonAnalytics singleton")
        }
    }
}
```

 Any time you use a third-party framework, consider wrapping it in an Adapter. This will let you change or augment the underlying implementation without changing the call sites.

---

2. *Design Patterns: Elements of Reusable Object-Oriented Software [GHJV95]*

MySingletonViewController uses this singleton to track calls to viewDidAppear(_:).

HardDependencies/HardDependencies/MySingletonViewController.swift
```
override func viewDidAppear(_ animated: Bool) {
    super.viewDidAppear(animated)
    MySingletonAnalytics.shared.track(
            event: "viewDidAppear - \(type(of: self))"
    )
}
```

Using this singleton is fine. But during testing, we want to use something else. Later, we'll learn how to create mock objects that can record calls. For now, let's just get it to use a different instance.

We'll add a layer of indirection around the singleton. In the other cases where we don't own the singleton, we'll do this at the calling code. But if you own the singleton, you can add indirection inside the called code.

Add a new static instance of MySingletonAnalytics. Declare it private to restrict its visibility. Then change shared from a stored property to a computed property returning the new instance:

HardDependencies/HardDependencies/MySingletonAnalytics.swift
```
private static let instance = MySingletonAnalytics()

static var shared: MySingletonAnalytics {
    return instance
}
```

Also wrap the track(event:) method's print statement in a conditional, to compare against the new static instance. This way, it'll report when we're not using the regular singleton:

HardDependencies/HardDependencies/MySingletonAnalytics.swift
```
if self !== MySingletonAnalytics.instance {
    print(">> Not the MySingletonAnalytics singleton")
}
```

Build to confirm these changes, which are transparent to the call sites.

Now let's add the backdoor, wrapped in #if DEBUG conditional compilation. What we want is a way for test code to provide a different object in place of the singleton:

HardDependencies/HardDependencies/MySingletonAnalytics.swift
```
private static let instance = MySingletonAnalytics()

#if DEBUG
static var stubbedInstance: MySingletonAnalytics?
#endif
```

```swift
static var shared: MySingletonAnalytics {
    #if DEBUG
    if let stubbedInstance = stubbedInstance {
        return stubbedInstance
    }
    #endif

    return instance
}
```

Now if a test provides a stubbedInstance, the shared property will return it instead of the singleton. To ensure that we're doing this substitution consistently, inject the stub in setUp() and remove it in tearDown(). Add a new test suite MySingletonViewControllerTests:

HardDependencies/HardDependenciesTests/MySingletonViewControllerTests.swift

```swift
@testable import HardDependencies
import XCTest

class MySingletonViewControllerTests: XCTestCase {

    override func setUp() {
        super.setUp()
        MySingletonAnalytics.stubbedInstance = MySingletonAnalytics()
    }

    override func tearDown() {
        MySingletonAnalytics.stubbedInstance = nil
        super.tearDown()
    }

    func test_viewDidAppear() {
        let sut = MySingletonViewController()
        sut.loadViewIfNeeded()

        sut.viewDidAppear(false)

        // Normally, assert something
    }
}
```

Run tests. Since this is an experiment, the test case has no assertion. But our fake implementation of event tracking has print(_:) statements in Analytics.swift. By examining the console output (see Examine Console Output, on page 23) we can see the log for this test case:

```
Test Case '-[HardDependenciesTests.MySingletonViewControllerTests
    test_viewDidAppear]' started.
>> viewDidAppear - MySingletonViewController
>> Not the MySingletonAnalytics singleton
Test Case '-[HardDependenciesTests.MySingletonViewControllerTests
    test_viewDidAppear]' passed (0.001 seconds).
```

The log shows the event tracking works. The message "Not the MySingleton-Analytics singleton" also shows that we replaced the singleton with something else.

In general, you should avoid mixing test code into production code. Conditional compilation makes code hard to read, reason about, and maintain. *Dependency Injection Principles, Practices, and Patterns [vS19]* describes the singleton backdoor as an anti-pattern called *Ambient Context*. It's far preferable to use other means of injection, especially constructor injection. We'll look at this in Inject Instances Through Initializers or Properties, on page 85.

But if you already have a singleton you own, and it's already in wide use, adding a backdoor can provide a small *enabling point*[3] to switch behavior. It's like a hidden panel on a home theater system, concealing controls you don't need for daily use. It doesn't improve the singleton-centric design. But it allows you to test code that uses that singleton, without modifying the call sites. That's progress, and any progress is good.

Subclass and Override: A Legacy Code Technique

Let's move on to singletons we don't own. To add a layer of indirection around the singleton, we'll extend the calling code. An important dependency-breaking technique from *Working Effectively with Legacy Code [Fea04]* is *Subclass and Override Method*.

The idea is to create a subclass of production code that lives only in test code, or a *test-specific subclass*.[4] It gives us a way to override methods that are problematic for testing.

Let's apply this to OverrideViewController, which starts with this initial method:

HardDependencies/HardDependencies/OverrideViewController.swift
```
override func viewDidAppear(_ animated: Bool) {
    super.viewDidAppear(animated)
    Analytics.shared.track(event: "viewDidAppear - \(type(of: self))")
}
```

We want a way to replace Analytics.shared, so extract it to its own method. Select Analytics.shared, then select *Editor ▶ Refactor ▶ Extract to Method* from the Xcode menu. Name the new method analytics().

---

3. *Working Effectively with Legacy Code [Fea04]*
4. *xUnit Test Patterns [Mes07]*

HardDependencies/HardDependencies/OverrideViewController.swift
```
fileprivate func analytics() -> Analytics { Analytics.shared }

override func viewDidAppear(_ animated: Bool) {
    super.viewDidAppear(animated)
    analytics().track(event: "viewDidAppear - \(type(of: self))")
}
```

 When an IDE provides automated refactoring options, lean on them. Automated refactoring reduces human error, so it's especially important when there is no test coverage yet.

Remove the fileprivate modifier from the new method so that tests can override it.

Now create a new test suite OverrideViewControllerTests. (As usual, add @testable import HardDependencies.) Somewhere in the test file, define this test-specific subclass:

HardDependencies/HardDependenciesTests/OverrideViewControllerTests.swift
```
private class TestableOverrideViewController: OverrideViewController {

    override func analytics() -> Analytics { Analytics() }
}
```

The naming convention I use is to add the prefix Testable to the name of the original class. That's why this is named TestableOverrideViewController. It overrides the analytics() method to provide a different instance from the singleton.

Test code can then instantiate the testable subclass instead of the original. Add the following test case:

HardDependencies/HardDependenciesTests/OverrideViewControllerTests.swift
```
class OverrideViewControllerTests: XCTestCase {

    func test_viewDidAppear() {
        let sut = TestableOverrideViewController()
        sut.loadViewIfNeeded()

        sut.viewDidAppear(false)

        // Normally, assert something
    }
}
```

Run tests. The test case has no assertion, but we can check the console output (see Examine Console Output, on page 23) for the fake event tracking printed by Analytics.swift.

Subclass and Override Method can only be applied to a class that permits subclassing:

- Swift doesn't allow subclassing of structs.

- The final modifier prevents classes from having subclasses. Remove it to apply this technique.

- Storyboard-based view controllers can't be subclassed because the storyboard stores an instance of a predetermined type.

With these restrictions in mind, this technique is powerful. It provides a way to wrangle previously untestable classes. Subclass and Override Method is useful for short-circuiting any problematic methods. The changes to production code are minimal, which is important when you don't yet have test coverage.

 Once you learn Subclass and Override Method, be careful not to apply it excessively. I recommend using this technique only for preexisting code without tests. For new code, or old code with test coverage, try to use the techniques that follow in the rest of this chapter.

Inject Instances Through Initializers or Properties

Subclass and Override Method lets you replace entire methods, not only dependencies. It's great for legacy code but puts almost no design pressure on the code. It also keeps dependencies somewhat hidden. Using *dependency injection* means making more changes, but these changes bring greater clarity.

On the surface, dependency injection (DI) means we pass dependencies into an object. Instead of allowing the object to decide its dependencies, we tell the object what to use.

DI is more than passing in instances. It promotes loosely coupled code that depends on protocols instead of concrete types. But we don't have to go full-on with protocols to get benefits from DI. By providing a default, we give the object a way to specify its own dependency—unless it's told otherwise.

Use Initializers

Constructor injection is the preferred form of DI because it makes dependencies explicit. We can use it on any type that lets us add parameters to the initializer. This includes view controllers that are XIB based or code based.

InstanceInitializerViewController is a XIB-based view controller. We'll start by giving it a private property set by its initializer:

HardDependencies/HardDependencies/InstanceInitializerViewController.swift
```
private let analytics: Analytics

init(analytics: Analytics = Analytics.shared) {
    self.analytics = analytics
    super.init(nibName: nil, bundle: nil)
}
```

The initializer parameter has a default value of Analytics.shared. This lets the view controller set the dependency, unless a call site passes in a different argument.

Try to build this by pressing ⌘-B. Below the initializer, Xcode will show the following error:

> ⊘ 'required' initializer 'init(coder:)' must be provided by subclass of 'UIViewController'

We can satisfy UIViewController requirements by selecting *Editor ▶ Fix All Issues* in the Xcode menu. Xcode will generate the following code:

HardDependencies/HardDependencies/InstanceInitializerViewController.swift
```
required init?(coder aDecoder: NSCoder) {
    fatalError("init(coder:) has not been implemented")
}
```

Finally, change viewDidAppear(_:) to use the analytics property instead of the Analytics.shared singleton:

HardDependencies/HardDependencies/InstanceInitializerViewController.swift
```
override func viewDidAppear(_ animated: Bool) {
    super.viewDidAppear(animated)
    analytics.track(event: "viewDidAppear - \(type(of: self))")
}
```

Now create a new test suite InstanceInitializerViewControllerTests with the following test case:

HardDependencies/HardDependenciesTests/InstanceInitializerViewControllerTests.swift
```
func test_viewDidAppear() {
    let sut = InstanceInitializerViewController(analytics: Analytics())
    sut.loadViewIfNeeded()

    sut.viewDidAppear(false)

    // Normally, assert something
}
```

The test creates the view controller, passing in an Analytics instance different from the singleton. We can change this to a mock object once we learn how to make one. For now, a different instance will do for our experiment.

Run tests. The test has no assertion, so check the console output (see Examine Console Output, on page 23) to confirm the tracking event, and that we avoided using the singleton.

Use Properties

Not all types let us change the initializer. In particular, we can't use constructor injection for storyboard-based view controllers. Instead, let's use *property injection.*

InstancePropertyViewController is a storyboard-based view controller. Let's give it a lazy property with Analytics.shared as its value:

HardDependencies/HardDependencies/InstancePropertyViewController.swift
```
lazy var analytics = Analytics.shared
```

By declaring it lazy, the property won't have an initial value. Once it's accessed, it will receive the value—but only if it doesn't already have one. This gives test code the opportunity to inject a different instance.

Then change viewDidAppear(_:) to use the analytics property instead of the Analytics.shared singleton:

HardDependencies/HardDependencies/InstancePropertyViewController.swift
```
override func viewDidAppear(_ animated: Bool) {
    super.viewDidAppear(animated)
➤   analytics.track(event: "viewDidAppear - \(type(of: self))")
}
```

Now create a new test suite InstancePropertyViewControllerTests with the following test case:

HardDependencies/HardDependenciesTests/InstancePropertyViewControllerTests.swift
```
func test_viewDidAppear() {
    let storyboard = UIStoryboard(name: "Main", bundle: nil)
    let sut: InstancePropertyViewController =
            storyboard.instantiateViewController(identifier:
                String(describing: InstancePropertyViewController.self))
    sut.analytics = Analytics()
    sut.loadViewIfNeeded()

    sut.viewDidAppear(false)

    // Normally, assert something
}
```

The test loads the view controller from the storyboard. Then it sets the value of the analytics property to an instance different from the singleton. Notice that it does this *before* calling loadViewIfNeeded() so that the replacement instance is ready before any view controller methods fire.

Run tests. The test has no assertion, so check the console output to confirm the tracking event, and that the test used something other than the singleton.

Inject Closures to Make New Instances

Injecting instances works well when the code outside knows what to pass in. But there are times when the code inside wants to create an instance of a difficult dependency. For example, it might be based on input from the user.

A good way to defer creation of new instances is by injecting closures. The closure acts as a small factory.

This technique is overkill for our analytics singleton example. But let's use it anyway to see what it looks like.

Use Initializers for Closures

ClosureInitializerViewController is a XIB-based view controller. We'll start by giving it a closure property set by its initializer. The initializer declares it as an @escaping closure so that it can store it in the property for later execution.

HardDependencies/HardDependencies/ClosureInitializerViewController.swift
```
private let makeAnalytics: () -> Analytics

init(makeAnalytics: @escaping () -> Analytics = { Analytics.shared }) {
    self.makeAnalytics = makeAnalytics
    super.init(nibName: nil, bundle: nil)
}
```

The initializer parameter has a default closure. This lets the view controller set its own closure, unless a call site passes one in.

Because we're defining a designated initializer, Swift will complain that our UIViewController needs to provide init(coder:). Select *Editor ▶ Fix All Issues* in the Xcode menu to generate the following code:

HardDependencies/HardDependencies/ClosureInitializerViewController.swift
```
required init?(coder aDecoder: NSCoder) {
    fatalError("init(coder:) has not been implemented")
}
```

Finally, change viewDidAppear(_:) to call the makeAnalytics closure instead of the Analytics.shared singleton:

HardDependencies/HardDependencies/ClosureInitializerViewController.swift
```
override func viewDidAppear(_ animated: Bool) {
    super.viewDidAppear(animated)
    makeAnalytics().track(event: "viewDidAppear - \(type(of: self))")
}
```

Now create a new test suite ClosureInitializerViewControllerTests with the following test case:

HardDependencies/HardDependenciesTests/ClosureInitializerViewControllerTests.swift
```
func test_viewDidAppear() {
    let sut = ClosureInitializerViewController { Analytics() }
    sut.loadViewIfNeeded()

    sut.viewDidAppear(false)

    // Normally, assert something
}
```

The test creates the view controller, passing in a closure returning an instance suitable for testing. Run tests. The test has no assertion, so check the console output (see Examine Console Output, on page 23) for the printout of the fake tracking event, and to check that we avoided using the singleton.

Use Properties for Closures

For types where we can't change the initializer, we can provide closures using property injection. This is necessary for storyboard-based view controllers.

ClosurePropertyViewController is a storyboard-based view controller. Let's give it a property with a closure:

HardDependencies/HardDependencies/ClosurePropertyViewController.swift
```
var makeAnalytics: () -> Analytics = { Analytics.shared }
```

Since the closure won't execute until it's called, there's no need to make it a lazy property. Simply assign it a suitable default closure. Test code can then replace it with a different closure.

Then change viewDidAppear(_:) to use the makeAnalytics closure instead of the Analytics.shared singleton:

HardDependencies/HardDependencies/ClosurePropertyViewController.swift
```
override func viewDidAppear(_ animated: Bool) {
    super.viewDidAppear(animated)
    makeAnalytics().track(event: "viewDidAppear - \(type(of: self))")
}
```

Now create a new test suite ClosurePropertyViewControllerTests with the following test case:

HardDependencies/HardDependenciesTests/ClosurePropertyViewControllerTests.swift
```
func test_viewDidAppear() {
    let storyboard = UIStoryboard(name: "Main", bundle: nil)
    let sut: ClosurePropertyViewController =
            storyboard.instantiateViewController(identifier:
                String(describing: ClosurePropertyViewController.self))
    sut.loadViewIfNeeded()

    sut.makeAnalytics = { Analytics() }
    sut.loadViewIfNeeded()

    sut.viewDidAppear(false)

    // Normally, assert something
}
```

The test loads the view controller from the storyboard. Then it sets the make-Analytics property to a closure returning an instance suitable for testing. Notice that it does this *before* calling loadViewIfNeeded() so the replacement closure is ready before any view controller methods fire.

Run tests. The test has no assertion, so check the console output for the fake tracking event, and that the test didn't use the singleton.

Key Takeaways

With experience, you'll begin distinguishing between problem-free dependencies and difficult dependencies. Use the FIRE rules to ask whether a dependency is fast, isolated, repeatable, and easy to test.

We discussed the following techniques for isolating difficult dependencies:

- Putting a singleton backdoor on a singleton you own. Use only for legacy code, not for new designs.

- Subclass and Override Method, using a test-specific subclass. Try to limit this to legacy code.

- Injecting dependencies through initializers—constructor injection

- Injecting dependencies through properties—property injection

The first two techniques are helpful for legacy code because they minimize changes to production code. But they minimize things that we *ought* to change. Sometimes I use Subclass and Override Method on new code when I haven't yet figured out how to design a replaceable dependency. But that's a temporary step. Once I know how to represent the dependency, I switch to a better technique.

Another form of Dependency Injection described in *Dependency Injection Principles, Practices, and Patterns [vS19]* is called *method injection*. This is where you add a new parameter to a function. It's useful for injecting values that change with each call. For example, instead of a function that directly retrieves the current time, we can sometimes pass the current time as an additional argument to that method.

Injecting closures gives us a way to extract creation of new instances. But injecting closures may show that there is a new type trying to break free. See if you can move the closures into a new type, changing them to methods.

Activities

To solidify this chapter, start with the first activity. You can try it on any file in your code. Get some practice identifying difficult dependencies. It's a good practice to use before attempting to write unit tests against any section of code.

The remaining activities 2–4 are for any code that already uses one of the dependency-isolating techniques.

1. Pick a file in your production code. Using the dependency rules and examples of Identify Difficult Dependencies, on page 75, try to list every dependency that will make it difficult to test what's in that file.

2. If you already use a singleton backdoor or Subclass and Override Method, try to shift to one of the other forms of explicit dependency injection.

3. If you already use property injection on a type that will let you change the initializer, try to shift to constructor injection.

4. If you already inject closures, see if you have a new type that's waiting to be discovered. This isn't always the case, but it's worth checking.

What's Next?

Now you have some idea of how to write unit tests for code with tricky dependencies. This concludes Part I, covering the foundations we need.

From here, we move to Part II, taking a tour of various things you may want to test in iOS apps. We'll learn various techniques, starting with how to test outlet connections.

Part II

iOS Testing Tips and Techniques

With foundations in place, how do we test specific behaviors of iOS apps?

Some of this requires tricks. You can test a button tap or navigation from one view controller to the next with a handful of tricks.

Some of it requires learning how to use test doubles to replace an actual component with a stand-in. This includes fakes, spies, and mocks.

And besides testing behavior, it's good to know how to test appearance.

This section offers a grab bag of tips and techniques that you can look up as needed.

CHAPTER 7

Testing Outlet Connections

Outlets give us a way to connect our code to storyboard and XIB objects. But sometimes we accidentally disconnect them. When this happens, it causes all sort of problems that can be hard to diagnose.

In this chapter, you'll learn how to write tests for outlet connections. These tests will serve as an early warning system. The next time someone disconnects an outlet, these tests will save you time.

Make a New Place to Play

Let's start a new experiment. Follow the steps for Create a Place to Play with Tests, on page 4, but name the project OutletConnections and delete the initial test file OutletConnectionsTests.swift.

Let's define a XIB-based view controller. Select the OutletConnections group in the Project Navigator. Make a new file, selecting Cocoa Touch Class and making it a subclass of UIViewController. Select the check box labeled "Also create XIB file." In the Save dialog, double-check that the app target is selected, not the test target.

Edit OutletConnectionsViewController.swift, and let's define a couple of outlets. Many people declare outlets to be private, so let's do that for this example:

OutletConnections/OutletConnections/OutletConnectionsViewController.swift
```
class OutletConnectionsViewController: UIViewController {
    @IBOutlet private var label: UILabel!
    @IBOutlet private var button: UIButton!
}
```

Now in OutletConnectionsViewController.xib, select *View ▸ Libraries ▸ Show Library* from the Xcode menu, or press Shift-⌘-L to bring up the Object Library. Click and drag a label onto the view in the main editor area. Do the same to add a button. For this experiment, don't worry about positioning them or setting any Auto Layout constraints.

Finally, wire these up to the outlets. (One way to do this is to show OutletConnectionsViewController.swift in the Assistant Editor. Click in the open circle next to each @IBOutlet and drag it to the appropriate view.) We now have a project that uses outlet connections. Let's see how to unit test this.

Test Outlet Connections

By using the foundations of Part I, we can write a test to confirm outlet connections. Let's start by adding a test suite OutletConnectionsViewControllerTests. Use Test Zero as temporary scaffolding to confirm that you hooked up the test suite. (See Start from Test Zero, on page 21.) Delete Test Zero once you see its expected failure message.

Add a test named test_outlets_shouldBeConnected() that starts by loading the view controller. (See Chapter 5, Load View Controllers, on page 61.) For our example, OutletConnectionsViewController is a XIB-based view controller.

OutletConnections/OutletConnectionsTests/OutletConnectionsViewControllerTests.swift
```
func test_outlets_shouldBeConnected() {
    let sut = OutletConnectionsViewController()

    sut.loadViewIfNeeded()
}
```

Run tests to confirm that you can successfully load the view controller.

Next, we need to make the outlets accessible to test code. They're currently private, which limits their visibility to the view controller alone. Recall from Hook Up Tests to Production Code, on page 22 that @testable import allows tests to access internal declarations. So let's soften the access control on the outlets from private to internal. Since internal is the default, we can omit it. But we can still restrict access to the setters with private(set). Combining these, the new outlet declarations are what you see here:

OutletConnections/OutletConnections/OutletConnectionsViewController.swift
```
@IBOutlet private(set) var label: UILabel!
@IBOutlet private(set) var button: UIButton!
```

Finally, let's add XCTAssertNotNil(_:) assertions. When testing optional values, we often unwrap them to check their properties. But to test outlet connections, we only want to see that the outlet is not nil:

OutletConnections/OutletConnectionsTests/OutletConnectionsViewControllerTests.swift
```
XCTAssertNotNil(sut.label, "label")
XCTAssertNotNil(sut.button, "button")
```

Run tests to confirm that they pass.

 When a test case has more than one assertion, it's helpful add a descriptive message to each assertion. This way, you don't even have to click on the failure message to know which assertion failed. See Add a Descriptive Message, on page 8.

Here's the new test in full:

OutletConnections/OutletConnectionsTests/OutletConnectionsViewControllerTests.swift
```
func test_outlets_shouldBeConnected() {
    let sut = OutletConnectionsViewController()

    sut.loadViewIfNeeded()

    XCTAssertNotNil(sut.label, "label")
    XCTAssertNotNil(sut.button, "button")
}
```

If you accidentally disconnect any outlets, you'll now know what went wrong immediately.

Check the Effectiveness of Failure Messages

Whenever you add a test case to existing code, it's best to see it fail once. We can do this by deliberately breaking the production code. Open OutletConnectionsViewController.xib and select the button. In the Xcode menu, select *View ▶ Inspectors ▶ Show Connections Inspector* or press ⌥-⌘-7. In the Connections Inspector on the right, the Referencing Outlets section shows the button's connection, as seen here:

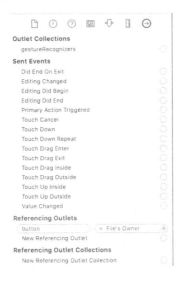

Click the little x to remove the connection. Then run tests. You will see this failure message:

```
XCTAssertNotNil failed - button
```

This proves that the test works. But it also gives us a chance to refine the failure message if it's not descriptive enough. In this case, the message clearly identifies the button outlet.

 When test code is written after production code, deliberately break the production code to watch the test fail. This is how we can test our tests.

Key Takeaways

There are several things you should take away from this chapter:

- Add tests to confirm outlet connections. Why bother if many things will fail without those outlets? Because the failures will be widespread and hard to diagnose. Writing outlet tests is quick, so they provide an early warning system for little cost. You'll still have a bunch of test failures, but the list of failure cases will include test_outlets_shouldBeConnected(), which will tell you the root cause.

- When a test case has more than one assertion, add short, descriptive messages to the assertions. The messages will help you identify the problem, even without clicking through to see the test code.

- You may need to relax access control so the test code can see a type's properties. For var properties, change them to private(set) so the getter is available, but the setter is still private. For let properties, just remove the private modifier.

- Always see a test case fail, even if you're adding tests to cover existing code. It helps you design the failure to be easy to understand.

- You can test your tests by deliberately breaking the production code.

Activities

To help your reading sink deeper, try this one activity, which has four steps. Of course, it only applies if your code uses outlets.

1. Find a view controller that has outlets.

2. Write a test that loads the view controller. If you face difficult dependencies in viewDidLoad(), move on to a different view controller for now.

3. Change the access control on the outlets to private(set).

4. Add XCTAssertNotNil(_:) assertions to check the outlets.

Repeat this for as many view controllers as you can. Then go back to any view controllers you skipped due to difficulties in viewDidLoad(). Try to isolate the dependencies using techniques from Chapter 6, Manage Difficult Dependencies, on page 73, then test their outlets.

What's Next?

Now you can rest assured if anyone disconnects an outlet, the test will report the problem. And you'll have made an important start on unit testing many of your view controllers.

In the next chapter, let's do more testing on the most fundamental outlet: a button that invokes an action.

CHAPTER 8

Testing Button Taps (Using Actions)

Tapping a button is one of the most basic things users do with controls. If we can write unit tests for button taps, we'll open up an entire world for your tests.

In this chapter, you'll learn how to write a unit test that taps a button. This will let you confirm the behavior of button taps on your view controllers without manual tests or even UI tests.

Make a Place to Play with a Button

As usual, let's make a new project. Follow the steps for Create a Place to Play with Tests, on page 4, but use the project name ButtonTap. Also delete the initial test file ButtonTapTests.swift.

Let's use the predefined storyboard-based view controller. Edit ViewController.swift, adding a button outlet. Many people declare outlets to be private, so let's do that for this example:

ButtonTap/ButtonTap/ViewController.swift
```
@IBOutlet private var button: UIButton!
```

Add an action, making it private. The action prints to the console to simulate doing something useful:

ButtonTap/ButtonTap/ViewController.swift
```
@IBAction private func buttonTap() {
    print(">> Button was tapped")
}
```

We need to do three things in the storyboard:

1. Add a button to the view controller.
2. Connect the button to its outlet.
3. Connect the button to its action.

First, let's add the button. Open Main.storyboard and drag a button onto the view controller. For this experiment, don't worry about positioning it or setting any Auto Layout constraints.

Second, let's connect it to the outlet. Show ButtonTapViewController.swift in the Assistant Editor, click in the open circle next to @IBOutlet, and drag it to the button on the storyboard.

Finally, connect it to the action. Click in the open circle next to @IBAction, and drag it to the button on the storyboard to connect them.

Let's confirm the button tap code with a manual test. Press ⌘-R to run the app. Then select *View* ▶ *Debug Area* ▶ *Activate Console* or press Shift-⌘-C to show the console on the bottom right. Tap the button in the running app. In the console, you'll see the following message:

```
>> Button was tapped
```

Now we're ready to see how to write a unit test that does the button tap.

Test Button Taps

Since buttons are UI elements, many assume you need UI tests to exercise them. But you can tap buttons using unit tests, which are much faster than UI tests.

Let's start by adding a test suite ViewControllerTests. Use Test Zero as temporary scaffolding to confirm that you hooked up the test suite. (See Start from Test Zero, on page 21.) Delete Test Zero once you see its expected failure message.

Add a test named test_tappingButton(). Recall from the tip in Add Tests for Existing Code, on page 40 that a good test name states the expected result. But this experimental test won't have any assertions, so we can skip the should clause. Instead, we'll check the console output for the printed message.

Inside the test, add code to load the view controller. (See Chapter 5, Load View Controllers, on page 61.) For our example, ViewController is a storyboard-based view controller. We'll use the simpler forced downcast approach:

```swift
ButtonTap/ButtonTapTests/ViewControllerTests.swift
func test_tappingButton() {
    let storyboard = UIStoryboard(name: "Main", bundle: nil)
    let sut: ViewController = storyboard.instantiateViewController(
            identifier: String(describing: ViewController.self))
    sut.loadViewIfNeeded()
}
```

Run the tests. Since this is a storyboard-based view controller, you'll see a failure message:

```
failed: caught "NSInvalidArgumentException", "Storyboard
    (<UIStoryboard: 0x6000001f08c0>) doesn't contain a view controller with
    identifier 'ViewController'"
```

Recall from Load a Storyboard-Based View Controller, on page 64 that for tests, we need to set the view controller's Storyboard ID. Open Main.storyboard and select the view controller. In the Xcode menu, select *View* ▶ *Inspectors* ▶ *Show Identity Inspector* or press ⌥-⌘-4. Then in the Identity Inspector on the right, copy and paste the Class name ViewController into the Storyboard ID field.

Run tests again to confirm that we can now load the view controller. So far, we've been following the principle *Take a small step, get feedback.*

To have a unit test tap a button, the button outlet must be accessible to test code. It's currently private, which limits its visibility to the view controller alone. Let's do the same thing we did for Test Outlet Connections, on page 96 and change the outlet's access to private(set):

ButtonTap/ButtonTap/ViewController.swift
```
@IBOutlet private(set) var button: UIButton!
```

Now we're ready to add code to tap the button. Add the following lines to the end of the test case:

ButtonTap/ButtonTapTests/ViewControllerTests.swift
```
sut.button.sendActions(for: .touchUpInside)

// Normally, assert something
```

Run tests and find the console output. (See Examine Console Output, on page 23.)

```
Test Case '-[ButtonTapTests.ViewControllerTests test_tappingButton]' started.
>> Button was tapped
Test Case '-[ButtonTapTests.ViewControllerTests test_tappingButton]' passed
    (0.014 seconds).
```

This shows that the unit test successfully did a button tap! All you need to do is make the outlet accessible, then call sendActions(for:). The event .touchUpInside is the correct event for button taps.

Of course, this means you can send any event to any control using the same trick.

Make a Test Helper for Button Taps

Tapping buttons is something we'll do quite a bit when unit testing view controllers. But sendActions(for: .touchUpInside) isn't very descriptive. We can improve the readability of our tests by extracting a helper to tap UIButtons.

Putting test helpers in a separate file makes it easier to find them. In the Project Navigator, select the ButtonTapTests group and press ⌘-N to make a new file. Select Swift File, name it TestHelpers.swift, and set its target to the test target. Give it the following code:

ButtonTap/ButtonTapTests/TestHelpers.swift
```
import UIKit

func tap(_ button: UIButton) {
    button.sendActions(for: .touchUpInside)
}
```

Change the test to use this new helper:

ButtonTap/ButtonTapTests/ViewControllerTests.swift
```
tap(sut.button)
```

Run the tests and confirm that the console output says Button was tapped.

UIBarButtonItems aren't UIControls, so we can't call sendActions(for:) on them. We can make a separate helper for them. We won't use it until the example in Chapter 17, Unleash the Power of Refactoring, on page 209, where we'll work through an example with a UIBarButtonItem. But for reference, here's a test helper to tap them:

ButtonTap/ButtonTapTests/TestHelpers.swift
```
func tap(_ button: UIBarButtonItem) {
    _ = button.target?.perform(button.action, with: nil)
}
```

Swift's function overloading lets us support the common abstraction of tap(_:) for two types. This also means that if we change a button type from UIButton to UIBarButton, the test code can stay the same.

Extract test helpers to make your tests more readable. They'll also make the tests less fragile.

Key Takeaways

The point of this chapter's exercise was to show you the following:

- That unit tests can send actions to controls.

- That doing so is simple. You just have to make controls non-private so tests can talk to them.

- That test helpers can make tests more readable.

But you may be wondering why I recommend writing unit tests to verify UI behavior such as button taps. Shouldn't we use Apple's UI testing to test UI?

It's helpful to know how the two testing paradigms differ. In UI testing, the tests run in a separate test runner app, sending UI events to the app under test. The app under test is a black box, revealing only the UI elements on the screen.

But in the unit testing paradigm, the tests can have full access to all code that isn't declared private. This brings many advantages:

- Unit tests don't have to start from your app's initial screen and navigate to specific screens. Instead, they create whatever view controllers they want.

- Unit tests can inject different dependencies to the system under test. These dependencies can provide canned inputs, or they can record outputs. For example, they can intercept network calls.

- Unit tests are orders of magnitude faster than UI tests.

So test behaviors (and even appearance, as we'll see in Chapter 16, Testing View Appearance (with Snapshots), on page 193) using unit tests as much as you can. They'll give you fast feedback you can incorporate into your coding workflow. Reserve UI testing for anything the unit tests don't already verify, especially end-to-end testing.

Activities

Try the following five-step activity to sink this chapter into your brain:

1. Find a view controller where tapping a button changes some state. If the action method contains difficult dependencies, skip it for now.

2. Write a test that loads the view controller. If you face difficult dependencies in viewDidLoad(), move on to a different view controller for now.

3. Change the access control of the button outlet to private(set).

4. Call sendActions(for:.touchUpInside) on the button. Use a test helper to make this easier.

5. Add an assertion to make a characterization test (see Add Tests for Existing Code, on page 40) for the changed state. Run tests to get the failure message. Update the assertion to match the actual value, and run tests again.

Repeat this for as many view controllers as you can. Then go back to any view controllers you skipped due to difficulties in either viewDidLoad() or the action method. Try to isolate their dependencies using techniques from Chapter 6, Manage Difficult Dependencies, on page 73.

What's Next?

Now you can test user input from button taps. This opens up much of your view controller code to tests. You can also begin testing other user events.

But what do we do when the user taps a button and we want the user to confirm the decision before proceeding with the action? In the next chapter, let's see how to test alerts.

CHAPTER 9

Testing Alerts

Alerts are another means of getting input from the user. But by their nature, alerts interrupt the flow of execution. This can complicate automated testing.

Let's just avoid the problem while making those alerts testable. In this chapter, you'll learn how to use the ViewControllerPresentationSpy framework to test alerts. You'll be able to test alerts using unit tests, which are faster and more reliable than UI tests.

Make a New Place to Play

Let's create a new project for this chapter. Follow the steps for Create a Place to Play with Tests, on page 4, naming the project Alert. Then delete the initial test file AlertTests.swift.

Let's use the predefined storyboard-based view controller. We'll trigger the alert from a button, so edit ViewController.swift to add a button outlet. Our tests will need access to the outlet, so declare it private(set):

Alert/Alert/ViewController.swift
```
@IBOutlet private(set) var button: UIButton!
```

Add an action for the button, making it private. This is where we'll present the alert. Give the alert Cancel and OK buttons, which print to the console to simulate doing something useful:

Alert/Alert/ViewController.swift
```
@IBAction private func buttonTap() {
    let alert = UIAlertController(
            title: "Do the Thing?",
            message: "Let us know if you want to do the thing.",
            preferredStyle: .alert
    )
```

```
    let cancelAction =
        UIAlertAction(title: "Cancel", style: .cancel) { _ in
          print(">> Cancel")
    }
    let okAction = UIAlertAction(title: "OK", style: .default) { _ in
        print(">> OK")
    }
    alert.addAction(cancelAction)
    alert.addAction(okAction)
    alert.preferredAction = okAction
    present(alert, animated: true)
  }
}
```

Follow the remaining steps from Make a Place to Play with a Button, on page 101 to add a button to the storyboard and connect it to the outlet and the action.

Now let's confirm our alert code manually. Make sure your destination is set to an iOS simulator, then press ⌘-R to run the app. Then select *View ▶ Debug Area ▶ Activate Console* or press Shift-⌘-C to show the console on the bottom right. Tap the button in the running app to present the alert, like this:

Tap one of the alert buttons and observe the message in the console output. Present the alert again and tap the other button.

Now we have a project that presents a simple test. In the rest of the chapter, let's see how to unit test this using a helper framework. We want to see whether an alert was presented. We want to see if the alert has the right message and the desired look. Finally, we want to simulate tapping the action buttons to trigger their closures.

Add the Helper Framework to the Project

Presenting an alert is normally a difficult dependency (see Identify Difficult Dependencies, on page 75). For unit tests, it's a side effect. For UI tests, it interrupts the flow of control, waiting for input. To make it easier to unit test alerts, I wrote a framework called ViewControllerPresentationSpy.

The framework is a collection of three verifiers. One is to capture alerts and action sheets, which we'll use here. The other two are to capture how view controllers are presented or dismissed.

Find the latest release by going to its GitHub page[1] and clicking "releases." Download the versioned zip file, which GitHub shows with a size. Drag ViewControllerPresentationSpy.framework to the open Xcode project, into the AlertTests group, as seen here:

In the "Choose options for adding these files" dialog, select the check box labeled "Copy items if needed" to copy the framework into the project folder. And make sure that "Add to targets" specifies the AlertTests target only.

For third-party frameworks to work, we often need to copy them to a place where the dynamic linker can find them. This is what we need to do with ViewControllerPresentationSpy. In the Project Navigator on the left, select the Alert project. Then select the AlertTests target. Within that, select the Build Phases tab. Click the + button at the top and select "New Copy Files Phase," as seen here:

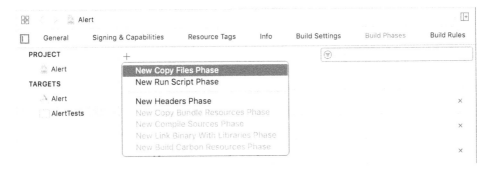

This creates a new Copy Files phase at the end of the list. In its Destination pop-up menu, select "Products Directory," as you'll see in the image on page 110. Click the + button at the bottom of the new Copy Files phase. In the "Choose items to add:" dialog, select ViewControllerPresentationSpy.framework and

1. https://github.com/jonreid/ViewControllerPresentationSpy

click Add. (Don't select the "Code Sign On Copy" check box because we're not shipping test code.)

Now the helper framework is ready for compiling against, and is also copied into place for dynamic linking at runtime.

Test Alerts Using the Alert Verifier

Now that we've added the ViewControllerPresentationSpy framework, we're ready to use it in tests.

Since our alert is triggered with a button tap, follow Test Button Taps, on page 102 to add a test suite ViewControllerTests with a test that taps the button. This also means editing Main.storyboard to give the view controller a Storyboard ID. Follow it through to Make a Test Helper for Button Taps, on page 104 to add the helper function for button taps:

Alert/AlertTests/TestHelpers.swift
```
func tap(_ button: UIButton) {
    button.sendActions(for: .touchUpInside)
}
```

This lets the test express the button tap as tap(sut.button). Run the tests, which should pass.

Next, edit ViewControllerTests.swift to import the new framework:

Alert/AlertTests/ViewControllerTests.swift
```
import ViewControllerPresentationSpy
```

This import provides a class named AlertVerifier. When test code instantiates an AlertVerifier, it patches UIKit to capture any alerts. (This works because the AlertVerifier initializer uses *method swizzling* to replace the UIViewController present(_:animated:completion:) method. Its deinitializer reverses the swizzling to restore the original method.)

To keep any tests from accidentally presenting real alerts, let's put the alert verifier in the test fixture—that is, we'll make it a property managed by setUp() and tearDown(). That way, we're patching alerts for all tests in the suite.

Alert/AlertTests/ViewControllerTests.swift

```
private var alertVerifier: AlertVerifier!

override func setUp() {
    super.setUp()
    alertVerifier = AlertVerifier()
}

override func tearDown() {
    alertVerifier = nil
    super.tearDown()
}
```

Rename the test to test_tappingButton_shouldShowAlert() and add the following assertions:

Alert/AlertTests/ViewControllerTests.swift

```
alertVerifier.verify(
        title: "Do the Thing?",
        message: "Let us know if you want to do the thing.",
        animated: true,
        actions: [
            .cancel("Cancel"),
            .default("OK"),
        ],
        presentingViewController: sut
)
XCTAssertEqual(alertVerifier.preferredAction?.title, "OK",
        "preferred action")
```

Run the tests, which should pass. The call to the verify() method checks quite a few things:

- That one alert was presented

- The alert title

- The alert message

- That the alert was presented with animation

- That the preferred style was UIAlertController.Style.alert. The verify() method takes this as a parameter, with .alert as the default value.

- The titles and styles of each action

- That the presenting view controller was the system under test

Our production code sets the preferredAction, so the final assertion after the long verify() checks that.

Move the SUT into the Test Fixture

As you can see, we're testing several aspects of the alert but not the alert buttons. Let's add separate tests for those. Since we want to load the view controller for each test, let's move that into the test fixture. (See Use setUp() and tearDown(), on page 31.)

First, define a new sut property as an implicitly unwrapped optional:

Alert/AlertTests/ViewControllerTests.swift
```
private var sut: ViewController!
```

Next, copy the code that loads the view controller into setUp(), with a change. Remove the let and the type so the view controller is assigned to the new property, not to a local variable:

Alert/AlertTests/ViewControllerTests.swift
```
override func setUp() {
    super.setUp()
    alertVerifier = AlertVerifier()
    let storyboard = UIStoryboard(name: "Main", bundle: nil)
    sut = storyboard.instantiateViewController(
            identifier: String(describing: ViewController.self))
    sut.loadViewIfNeeded()
}
```

In tearDown(), set the sut property to nil. Remember, anything you create in setUp() should be destroyed in tearDown().

Alert/AlertTests/ViewControllerTests.swift
```
override func tearDown() {
    alertVerifier = nil
    sut = nil
    super.tearDown()
}
```

Finally, remove the code in the test case that loads the view controller. This will change its references to sut from a local variable to the new property. Run tests to confirm this refactoring.

Add Tests for Alert Buttons

With the system under test now in the test fixture, we'll have an easier time adding more tests for the alert buttons. Let's add a test to execute the action for the OK button.

The AlertVerifier method executeAction(forButton:) throws an exception if it can't find a button with the given name. So we have to precede it with a try statement. For this to work in a test, mark the test method as throws:

Alert/AlertTests/ViewControllerTests.swift
```
func test_executeAlertAction_withOKButton() throws {
    tap(sut.button)

    try alertVerifier.executeAction(forButton: "OK")

    // Normally, assert something
}
```

 If you need a try in test code, mark the test case as a throwing function with throws. Then if the call ever throws an exception, XCTest will report it as a test failure.

For our experiment, this test has no assertions. Run tests and find the console output (See Examine Console Output, on page 23), where you will see the following.

```
Test Case '-[AlertTests.ViewControllerTests
    test_executeAlertAction_withOKButton]' started.
>> OK
Test Case '-[AlertTests.ViewControllerTests
    test_executeAlertAction_withOKButton]' passed (0.015 seconds).
```

Write another test to execute the action for the Cancel button.

Key Takeaways

This particular framework will help you test alerts and is good to know about. Besides that, though, there's a larger idea to take away from this chapter: there's usually a way to crack open things that look "untestable."

Parts of Apple's frameworks are black holes: we can pass data in, but tests can't access it to verify what we passed in. Alerts are one example of this. Moreover, alerts can interfere with UI testing.

Though we're coding in Swift these days, we depend on UIKit, which is written in Objective-C. One thing calls another in Objective-C by dynamic message passing. This gives us a way to intercept messages. ViewControllerPresentationSpy does this using method swizzling.

If you find a black hole that receives data with no way of getting it back out, search for helper libraries that intercept the data. For alerts, ViewController-PresentationSpy is one such solution.

Activities

To turn this chapter into something practical (and sink it deeper into your brain), try this one activity with six parts. Start at the top and go as far as you want to.

1. In your own code, find a view controller that presents an alert.

2. Determine what action triggers the alert. If it's a button tap, apply Chapter 8, Testing Button Taps (Using Actions), on page 101.

3. If the alert trigger is more complicated than a button tap, apply the "Extract to Method" Xcode refactoring. Do a manual test to confirm that the alert is still presented correctly. Then remove the fileprivate access control on the extracted function to make it internal. Now write a test that loads the view controller and calls the new function.

4. Copy the tests from this chapter but not the ones that execute button actions. Use the tests as characterization tests (see Add Tests for Existing Code, on page 40) by running them to get any failure messages. Update the assertions to match the actual values, and run tests again.

5. Check the production code, looking for any alert actions that change some state. If an action closure contains difficult dependencies, skip it for now. Add a test that executes the button action, with an assertion for the changed state. Apply the characterization test technique to get the test to fail, then update the assertion to match the actual state.

6. For a Cancel button, add a test that executes the action and confirms that the state doesn't change.

Repeat this for as many view controllers as you can.

What's Next?

Now your tests can handle user input from button taps and alerts. Remember, you're getting this with unit tests, which are faster than UI tests. Unit tests also give us opportunities to isolate difficult dependencies, which makes the tests easier to maintain.

Let's continue our tour of things to test in iOS apps. In the next chapter, we'll see how to test navigation between view controllers.

CHAPTER 10

Testing Navigation Between Screens

Most apps have more than one view controller. Besides interactions within a view controller, we ought to test navigation from one view controller to the next.

Going from one view controller to next is part of what we want to test. But what's even more interesting is that we can test the data the first view controller sends to the next one.

In this chapter, you'll learn how to write unit tests for code-based navigation and segue-based navigation. In fact, you'll be able to test this navigation without manual tests or UI tests.

Make a New Place to Play

Let's start as usual by making a new project, following Create a Place to Play with Tests, on page 4 but using the project name Navigation. And delete its initial test file NavigationTests.swift.

Open Main.storyboard. Since we'll be experimenting with push navigation (as well as modal navigation), we need to place the view controller within a navigation controller. Select the view controller scene. Then in the Xcode menu, select *Editor* ▶ *Embed In* ▶ *Navigation Controller*.

We're going to work with push navigation and modal presentation for both code-based and segue-based approaches. Let's add four buttons to trigger each form of navigation. Edit ViewController.swift to add four button outlets, declaring them private(set) so that tests can reach them:

Navigation/Navigation/ViewController.swift
```
@IBOutlet private(set) var codePushButton: UIButton!
@IBOutlet private(set) var codeModalButton: UIButton!
@IBOutlet private(set) var seguePushButton: UIButton!
@IBOutlet private(set) var segueModalButton: UIButton!
```

Back in the storyboard, open the Object Library and add four buttons to the view controller scene:

- Code Push
- Code Modal
- Segue Push
- Segue Modal

Position them as you like. Connect each to its @IBAction in ViewController.

Set Up Code-Based Navigation

Let's add a view controller for code-based navigation to go to. Select the Navigation group in the Project Navigator. Make a new file, selecting Cocoa Touch Class. Name it CodeNextViewController and make it a subclass of UIViewController. Leave the check box labeled "Also create XIB file" unselected. We want to demonstrate passing data from one view controller to the next, so let's pass a string. The next view controller will use it to set a label's text. For a code-based view controller, it's best to pass data through an initializer:

Navigation/Navigation/CodeNextViewController.swift
```
class CodeNextViewController: UIViewController {
    let label = UILabel()

    init(labelText: String) {
        label.text = labelText
        super.init(nibName: nil, bundle: nil)
    }
}
```

Xcode will complain that it doesn't have all required initializers. In the Xcode menu, select *Editor ▶ Fix All Issues* to generate the following code:

Navigation/Navigation/CodeNextViewController.swift
```
required init?(coder aDecoder: NSCoder) {
    fatalError("init(coder:) has not been implemented")
}
```

To center the label, we'll define Auto Layout constraints in viewDidLoad() using a helper method. We'll also set the background color:

Navigation/Navigation/CodeNextViewController.swift
```
override func viewDidLoad() {
    super.viewDidLoad()
    view.backgroundColor = .white
    view.addSubview(label)
    label.translatesAutoresizingMaskIntoConstraints = false
```

```
    activateEqualConstraints(.centerX, fromItem: label, toItem: view)
    activateEqualConstraints(.centerY, fromItem: label, toItem: view)
}

private func activateEqualConstraints(
        _ attribute: NSLayoutConstraint.Attribute,
        fromItem: UIView,
        toItem: UIView) {
    NSLayoutConstraint(
            item: fromItem,
            attribute: attribute,
            relatedBy: .equal,
            toItem: toItem,
            attribute: attribute,
            multiplier: 1,
            constant: 0
    ).isActive = true
}
```

Back in ViewController, let's add actions for the two code-based navigation buttons. This is where we'll either tell the navigation controller to push the next view controller, or we'll present a modal. Make the actions private.

Navigation/Navigation/ViewController.swift
```
@IBAction private func pushNextViewController() {
    let nextVC = CodeNextViewController(labelText: "Pushed from code")
    self.navigationController?
        .pushViewController(nextVC, animated: true)
}

@IBAction private func presentModalNextViewController() {
    let nextVC = CodeNextViewController(labelText: "Modal from code")
    self.present(nextVC, animated: true)
}
```

Finally, we need to connect these actions to their buttons. (You can show the storyboard in the Assistant Editor. Click in the open circle next to each @IBAction and drag it to the appropriate button on the storyboard to connect them.)

Now let's manually confirm the navigation we have so far. Run the app and tap Code Push. The label will say, "Pushed from code." Go back and tap the Code Modal button. The label will say, "Modal from code." (We're not going to add a Cancel button for this experiment, so just stop the app.)

Set Up Segue-Based Navigation

For segues, let's add another view controller to the storyboard, along with two segues to navigate to it. Let's start with the code. From the Project Navigator, make a subclass of UIViewController and give it the name SegueNextViewController.

In the code, let's define a settable property that determines the text of a label:

```
Navigation/Navigation/SegueNextViewController.swift
class SegueNextViewController: UIViewController {
    var labelText: String?

    @IBOutlet private(set) var label: UILabel!

    override func viewDidLoad() {
        super.viewDidLoad()
        label.text = labelText
    }
}
```

Back in the storyboard, open the Object Library and add a new view controller to the storyboard. Select the second view controller scene, which is the one we just added. In the Identity Inspector, set the Custom Class to SegueNextViewController.

In the main view controller scene, control-drag from the Segue Push button to the Segue Next View Controller. This brings up a pop-up menu of segue choices. From the Action Segue section, select "Show (e.g. Push)." Select the segue, then in the Identity Inspector, set its identifier to "pushNext."

Repeat to create a new segue from the Segue Modal button to the same Segue Next View Controller. This time, select "Present Modally" from the pop-up menu of segue choices. Now select the newly created segue. In the Identity Inspector, set its identifier to "modalNext."

Now add a label to the Segue Next View Controller. Position it where you like. Connect the label to its outlet. (You can show SegueNextViewController.swift in the Assistant Editor and drag from the @IBOutlet circle to the label.)

Finally, we need the code that prepares for each segue by setting the label text. Add the following method to ViewController:

```
Navigation/Navigation/ViewController.swift
override func prepare(for segue: UIStoryboardSegue, sender: Any?) {
    switch segue.identifier {
    case "pushNext"?:
        guard let nextVC = segue.destination as? SegueNextViewController
                else { return }
        nextVC.labelText = "Pushed from segue"
```

```
    case "modalNext"?:
        guard let nextVC = segue.destination as? SegueNextViewController
                else { return }
        nextVC.labelText = "Modal from segue"
    default:
        return
    }
}
```

Now let's manually confirm this navigation. Run the app. Tap the Segue Push button to show the next view controller. The label will say, "Pushed from segue." Go back, and tap the Segue Modal button to see it present a modal showing "Modal from segue."

We now have a project that does four styles of navigation from one view controller to the next. In the rest of the chapter, let's see how to unit test each style.

Test Code-Based Push Navigation

We'll start our testing with code-based navigation, taking push navigation first. Since all our navigation is triggered by button taps, follow Test Button Taps, on page 102 to add a test suite ViewControllerTests with a test named test_tappingCodePushButton_shouldPushCodeNextViewController(). This also means editing Main.storyboard to give the view controller a Storyboard ID. Also follow Make a Test Helper for Button Taps, on page 104 to add the tap(_:) helper. Have the test tap the codePushButton outlet. Run the tests, which should pass so far.

The @IBAction connected to codePushButton tells the view controller's navigationController to do a push. But since the test instantiates ViewController in isolation, it has no navigation controller at first. Let's prove this by adding an assertion to the end of the test.

Navigation/NavigationTests/ViewControllerTests.swift
```
XCTAssertNotNil(sut.navigationController)
```

Run the tests to see this fail. To get it to pass, we need to embed the view controller inside a navigation controller. Add the following line after load-ViewIfNeeded():

Navigation/NavigationTests/ViewControllerTests.swift
```
    sut.loadViewIfNeeded()
➤   let navigation = UINavigationController(rootViewController: sut)
```

Run the tests again. This time they should pass. Delete the XCTAssertNotNil(_:) assertion, which has served its purpose. We'll move forward with other assertions.

Since we pushed one view controller over another, the navigation controller should have two view controllers in its stack. The following assertion checks that:

Navigation/NavigationTests/ViewControllerTests.swift
```
XCTAssertEqual(navigation.viewControllers.count, 2, "navigation stack")
```

Finally, let's confirm that the last view controller in the stack is the right type:

Navigation/NavigationTests/ViewControllerTests.swift
```
let pushedVC = navigation.viewControllers.last
XCTAssertTrue(pushedVC is CodeNextViewController,
        "Expected CodeNextViewController, "
        + "but was \(String(describing: pushedVC))")
```

Run the tests but know that they'll fail. That's because some of UIKit's actions aren't immediate but add an event to the *run loop*. The run loop is a UIKit mechanism for handling events like mouse and keyboard input. UIKit also uses it for other things. Pushing onto a navigation controller is one example.

Before checking the stack of view controllers, we need to ask the run loop to execute one more time. This allows the push to take effect. To make this easier, let's create a test helper to execute the run loop. Add the following to TestHelpers.swift:

Navigation/NavigationTests/TestHelpers.swift
```
func executeRunLoop() {
    RunLoop.current.run(until: Date())
}
```

Then call executeRunLoop() before the first assertion and run the tests.

 If a unit test calls UIKit but you don't see the expected results, try executing the run loop.

This time, the tests will pass. What we're doing is asking the run loop to execute until Date(), which is the current time. So it nudges the run loop by telling it, "Run until I tell you. Now stop!" This gets us what we want while keeping the test duration short.

At this point, we know that pushedVC is a NextViewController. Most production code prepares the state of the next view controller and then pushes it. In test code, we can go beyond confirming only the type of the view controller. Instead of only asserting pushedVC is NextViewController, let's cast it. If the cast fails, we report the failure using XCTFail() and bail out of the test. Otherwise, we now have an instance of the correct type. Further assertions can check that we set the properties of NextViewController correctly. Here's the complete test case with a good test name:

Navigation/NavigationTests/ViewControllerTests.swift
```swift
func test_tappingCodePushButton_shouldPushCodeNextViewController() {
    let storyboard = UIStoryboard(name: "Main", bundle: nil)
    let sut = storyboard.instantiateViewController(
            withIdentifier: "ViewController") as! ViewController
    sut.loadViewIfNeeded()
    let navigation = UINavigationController(rootViewController: sut)

    tap(sut.codePushButton)

    executeRunLoop()
    XCTAssertEqual(navigation.viewControllers.count, 2, "navigation stack")
    let pushedVC = navigation.viewControllers.last
    guard let codeNextVC = pushedVC as? CodeNextViewController else {
        XCTFail("Expected CodeNextViewController, "
                + "but was \(String(describing: pushedVC))")
        return
    }
    XCTAssertEqual(codeNextVC.label.text, "Pushed from code")
}
```

We now have a way to test code-based push navigation, including the data sent to the next view controller.

How to Spy on the Animated Flag

We can ask the UINavigationController for its stack of view controllers. But is there a way to check whether the animated flag was set for pushViewController(_:animated:)? Yes, by using a *test spy*.[a] A test spy records information about how it's called. Normally, a test spy captures method arguments without doing actual work. But to test navigation, we want the real results of the view controller stack. We get both with a *subclassed test double* that overrides pushViewController(_:animated:) to capture the animated flag while still letting the superclass do its work.

Navigation/NavigationTests/SpyNavigationController.swift
```swift
class SpyNavigationController: UINavigationController {
    private(set) var pushViewControllerArgsAnimated: [Bool] = []

    override func pushViewController(
        _ viewController: UIViewController, animated: Bool) {
        super.pushViewController(viewController, animated: animated)
        pushViewControllerArgsAnimated.append(animated)
    }
}
```

A test would then create a SpyNavigationController instead of a UINavigationController. The test spy records the animated arguments passed to pushViewController(_:animated:) in the pushViewControllerArgsAnimated property, which tests can query.

---

a.   *xUnit Test Patterns [Mes07]*

Test Code-Based Modal Presentation

Let's continue to test code-based navigation, this time moving to modals. The view controller makes a present(_:animated:) call. How can we capture the result of this call?

If we had defined the main view controller outside of a storyboard, there's a useful trick we could have used. To intercept the call, we could make a test-specific subclass. It would provide its own implementation of the present(_:animated:completion:) method, including the optional completion handler.

Navigation/NavigationTests/ViewControllerTests.swift
```swift
// We can't use this for a view controller that comes from a storyboard.
private class TestableViewController: ViewController {
    var presentCallCount = 0
    var presentArgsViewController: [UIViewController] = []
    var presentArgsAnimated: [Bool] = []
    var presentArgsClosure: [(() -> Void)?] = []

    override func present(_ viewControllerToPresent: UIViewController,
                          animated flag: Bool,
                          completion: (() -> Void)? = nil) {
        presentCallCount += 1
        presentArgsViewController.append(viewControllerToPresent)
        presentArgsAnimated.append(flag)
        presentArgsClosure.append(completion)
    }
}
```

We first saw a test-specific subclass in Subclass and Override: A Legacy Code Technique, on page 83. Here, the subclass is a test spy, which captures method arguments without doing actual work. The idea is that tests can instantiate the TestableViewController instead of ViewController.

This works for view controllers that are code-based or XIB-based. Unfortunately, we can't use this approach for view controllers from storyboards. That's because the storyboard stores an instance of a particular class. We can't instantiate a ViewController from the storyboard and convert it to a subclass after it already exists.

Let's try a different approach. Create a new test case, giving it the name test_INCORRECT_tappingCodeModalButton_shouldPresentCodeNextViewController(). (As you can see from the name, we're going to experiment with an approach I don't recommend.) Load the view controller from the storyboard, and call loadViewIfNeeded(). Then supply the rest of the test case:

Navigation/NavigationTests/ViewControllerTests.swift
```
UIApplication.shared.windows.first?.rootViewController = sut

tap(sut.codeModalButton)

let presentedVC = sut.presentedViewController
guard let codeNextVC = presentedVC as? CodeNextViewController else {
    XCTFail("Expected CodeNextViewController, "
            + "but was \(String(describing: presentedVC))")
    return
}
XCTAssertEqual(codeNextVC.label.text, "Modal from code")
```

This test sets the view controller as the rootViewController inside a visible UIWindow. It gives the view controller a home in a larger ecosystem, allowing the present(_:animated:) call to work. Run the tests. They will pass. So what's the problem?

To see the problem, add the following diagnostic code to ViewController:

Navigation/Navigation/ViewController.swift
```
deinit {
    print(">> ViewController.deinit")
}
```

Add similar code to CodeNextViewController, changing the print statement so it identifies CodeNextViewController in the print() statement. Run the test by itself, and check the console output. You'll see that neither ViewController nor CodeNextViewController are deinitialized for this test.

This violates the clean room goals of Chapter 2, Manage Your Test Life Cycles, on page 19. The lingering objects from this memory leak may not cause trouble, but they have the potential to do so. We want to avoid this situation, if possible. It turns out, we can...for three out of four of our navigation scenarios.

To intercept the call to present, let's use the same helper framework we used for alerts. Follow the steps in Add the Helper Framework to the Project, on page 108 to add ViewControllerPresentationSpy to the project. Then edit View-ControllerTests.swift to import the new framework:

Navigation/NavigationTests/ViewControllerTests.swift
```
import ViewControllerPresentationSpy
```

Start a new test case named test_tappingCodeModalButton_shouldPresentCodeNextView-Controller(). At the top of the test, instantiate a PresentationVerifier:

Navigation/NavigationTests/ViewControllerTests.swift
```
let presentationVerifier = PresentationVerifier()
```

Like we did with the AlertVerifier in Test Alerts Using the Alert Verifier, on page 110, instantiating a PresentationVerifier uses method swizzling to intercept calls to present view controllers. When the PresentationVerifier goes out of scope, it reverses the swizzling to restore the original method.

The PresentationVerifier captures arguments, but without presenting anything. To finish the test, we call verify() on it to get an optional instance of the view controller type we want. We can then use that to check its properties:

Navigation/NavigationTests/ViewControllerTests.swift
```
tap(sut.codeModalButton)

let codeNextVC: CodeNextViewController? = presentationVerifier.verify(
        animated: true, presentingViewController: sut)
XCTAssertEqual(codeNextVC?.label.text, "Modal from code")
```

The verify() method checks several things:

- That one view controller was presented
- That it was presented with animation
- That the presenting view controller was the system under test
- That the type of the presented view controller is correct. And if so, it returns an instance of the correct type. (Otherwise, it returns nil.)

Run this test to see it pass. Then examine the console output. You'll see something like this:

```
Test Case '-[NavigationTests.ViewControllerTests
  test_tappingCodeModalButton_shouldPresentCodeNextViewController]' started.
>> CodeNextViewController.deinit
>> ViewController.deinit
Test Case '-[NavigationTests.ViewControllerTests
  test_tappingCodeModalButton_shouldPresentCodeNextViewController]' passed
  (0.021 seconds).
```

The presence of the deinit logging proves that this test successfully cleans up after itself.

Test Segue-Based Push Navigation

Segues are more of a black box than code-based navigation. But it turns out, part of what they do is to call present(_:animated:) to show the next view controller. This means we can use ViewControllerPresentationSpy framework as long as we do a little extra work.

We'll also want to keep an eye on the memory leak problem. Add the following diagnostic code to SegueNextViewController:

Navigation/Navigation/SegueNextViewController.swift

```
deinit {
    print(">> SegueNextViewController.deinit")
}
```

Before we write a third test, let's extract common Arrange code from the two tests we have. Follow Move the SUT into the Test Fixture, on page 112 but without an AlertVerifier. Move the common code up to sut.loadViewIfNeeded() into setUp(), and set sut = nil in tearDown(). Run the tests to confirm that they're still happy.

Now add the following test:

Navigation/NavigationTests/ViewControllerTests.swift

```
func test_tappingSeguePushButton_shouldShowSegueNextViewController() {
    let presentationVerifier = PresentationVerifier()

    tap(sut.seguePushButton)

    let segueNextVC: SegueNextViewController? = presentationVerifier.verify(
            animated: true, presentingViewController: sut)
    XCTAssertEqual(segueNextVC?.labelText, "Pushed from segue")
}
```

Run the tests. While we'd like this to pass, it fails with

```
failed - Expected SegueNextViewController, but was nil
```

To give the segue an environment that works, we need to load the view controller into a visible UIWindow. We managed to avoid this for code-based modals, but now we need this trick. Let's put the view controller into a window. We will use a slightly different way, adding a new helper function to TestHelpers.swift:

Navigation/NavigationTests/TestHelpers.swift

```
func putInWindow(_ vc: UIViewController) {
    let window = UIWindow()
    window.rootViewController = vc
    window.isHidden = false
}
```

For this to build, add import UIKit to the top of TestHelpers.swift.

Call this helper function in the "Arrange" section after setting up the PresentationVerifier:

Navigation/NavigationTests/ViewControllerTests.swift

```
    let presentationVerifier = PresentationVerifier()
➤   putInWindow(sut)
```

Run the tests again. This time, this test will pass. But check the console output for deinit logging. You'll find that the presented view controller SegueNextViewController is deinitialized. But the presenting view controller ViewController we put in a window isn't being cleaned up.

To give the window a chance to disappear, add a call to execute the run loop one more time at the top of tearDown():

Navigation/NavigationTests/ViewControllerTests.swift
```swift
override func tearDown() {
    executeRunLoop()
    sut = nil
    super.tearDown()
}
```

Run this test and check the console output. You can confirm that both view controllers are now deinitialized.

Test Segue-Based Modal Navigation

We've come to the last of our navigation types, the segue-based modal. Add the following test:

Navigation/NavigationTests/ViewControllerTests.swift
```swift
func test_tappingSegueModalButton_shouldShowSegueNextViewController() {
    let presentationVerifier = PresentationVerifier()

    tap(sut.segueModalButton)

    let segueNextVC: SegueNextViewController? = presentationVerifier.verify(
            animated: true, presentingViewController: sut)
    XCTAssertEqual(segueNextVC?.labelText, "Modal from segue")
}
```

Run the tests, which should pass.

Unfortunately, by peering into the console output, we can see that both view controllers still exist. There may be a trick I don't know yet, but as of this writing, I haven't found a way to clean them out. The presenting view controller and the presented view controller both live on past the life cycle of the test.

This violates our clean room goals. The best we can do is mitigate the effects. If either view controller has a persistent side effect, then provide a backdoor for tests to clean it up. Add a cleanup method wrapped in #if DEBUG ... #endif so that it's not included in your shipping app. Call this method at the end of your test or at the beginning of tearDown() if the view controller is in the test fixture.

It's not a perfect world. But we were able to test the modal presentation, so we'll take what we can get.

Key Takeaways

Sometimes tests need to downcast an object to a more specific type so it can query its properties. A force-cast as! is simple but will crash the test run if the type is wrong. Use the softer conditional cast as? with a guard let. If the guard fails, use an XCTFail() to report the desired type and the actual object.

"Execute the run loop" is a good trick to keep in your pocket. When things work in manual testing but not in unit testing, see if the trick works. Sometimes it gives UIKit that extra kick it needs.

To test code-based push navigation, follow these steps:

- Put the view controller inside a UINavigationController.

- Execute the run loop before any assertions. Then query the navigation controller.

To test code-based modal navigation, follow these steps:

- Add the ViewControllerPresentationSpy framework to your test target. Instantiate a PresentationVerifier.

- Call the PresentationVerifier's verify() method.

To test segue-based push navigation, follow these steps:

- Add the ViewControllerPresentationSpy framework to your test target. Instantiate a PresentationVerifier.

- Load the view controller into a visible UIWindow. You may wish to use putInWindow(_) for this.

- Call the PresentationVerifier's verify() method.

- Execute the run loop one more time at the end of tearDown() to clean everything up.

To test segue-based modal navigation, follow these steps:

- Add the ViewControllerPresentationSpy framework to your test target. Instantiate a PresentationVerifier.

- Call the PresentationVerifier's verify() method.

- Recognize that both the presenting view controller and the presented view controller will live on. Check both to see if this will leave any side effects, such as observing notifications or running a timer. If so, provide a backdoor cleanup method and call it from the test code.

Activities

To solidify this chapter in your head, find a simple point of navigation in your code. If you can, find navigation triggered by a button push. Then do the following:

1. Write a test case that triggers the navigation, testing the expected type of the next view controller.

2. If the presenting view controller passes any information along, look for a way to confirm that the presented view controller has this information. You may need to relax access control so tests can see this data.

What's Next?

Now your tests can confirm view navigation. Remember, you're getting this with unit tests, which are faster than UI tests.

In the next chapter, we'll look at testing UserDefaults. This will introduce us to replacing an actual type with a fake object.

CHAPTER 11

Testing UserDefaults (with Fakes)

The most basic form of persistence we have is UserDefaults. But we don't want unit tests to interact with real persistence. Otherwise, unit tests could end up affecting manual tests as well as each other. Instead, we can simulate persistence by using a fake object.

In this chapter you'll learn how to write a fake object that acts as a replacement for UserDefaults. In the process, you'll see how to use protocols to substitute testing objects in place of real ones, all while keeping Swift happy.

Make a New Place to Play

For this chapter, we want some code that writes to UserDefaults and other code that reads from it. We'll do that with an app that increments a counter when you tap a button. The counter will be persistent, so the app will show the last value when it launches.

We'll do this in a new project, following the steps for Create a Place to Play with Tests, on page 4 but using the project name UserDefaults. Create the project now and delete its initial test file UserDefaultsTests.swift.

Edit ViewController.swift to add outlets for a label and a button. Declare them private(set) so that our tests can reach them:

UserDefaults/UserDefaults/ViewController.swift
```
@IBOutlet private(set) var counterLabel: UILabel!
@IBOutlet private(set) var incrementButton: UIButton!
```

Add a private count property with a didSet observer. When the count changes, it updates the label and writes the value to UserDefaults:

UserDefaults/UserDefaults/ViewController.swift
```
private var count = 0 {
    didSet {
        counterLabel.text = "\(count)"
        UserDefaults.standard.set(count, forKey: "count")
    }
}
```

In viewDidLoad(), we'll read the value back from UserDefaults:

UserDefaults/UserDefaults/ViewController.swift
```
override func viewDidLoad() {
    super.viewDidLoad()
    count = UserDefaults.standard.integer(forKey: "count")
}
```

Finally, add an action for the button that increments the count:

UserDefaults/UserDefaults/ViewController.swift
```
@IBAction private func incrementButtonTapped() {
    count += 1
}
```

Follow the remaining steps from Make a Place to Play with a Button, on page 101 to add a button to the storyboard and connect it to the button outlet and the action. Also add a label and connect it to the label outlet.

Now let's manually confirm that we're successfully using UserDefaults. Run the app, observing the initial count. Tap the button to increment the count. Then rerun the app to see that the count persists across runs.

We now have a simple app that uses UserDefaults. This is a difficult dependency, so we'll start by isolating it. We'll extract a protocol so we can substitute something else in its place. Then we'll make a fake object, which will allow us to easily test this app.

Isolate UserDefaults with Dependency Injection

Recall from Identify Difficult Dependencies, on page 75 that UserDefaults is a difficult dependency because it uses persistent storage. We want to isolate it so we can replace it.

There's another way to handle persistence, though. That's to save the old value, overwrite it for testing, then restore the old value. But using real persistence can slow down test execution. And this approach carries the risk of leaving unwanted remains in the event of test crashes.

So let's take our first steps toward isolating this dependency. Since ViewController is a storyboard-based view controller, let's use property injection from Inject Instances Through Initializers or Properties, on page 85.

First, add the new property, giving it an initial value of the UserDefaults.standard singleton. Make it var, not let, so that a different value can be injected:

UserDefaults/UserDefaults/ViewController.swift
```
var userDefaults = UserDefaults.standard
```

Replace all other references to the UserDefaults.standard singleton with the userDefaults property:

UserDefaults/UserDefaults/ViewController.swift
```
private var count = 0 {
    didSet {
        counterLabel.text = "\(count)"
        userDefaults.set(count, forKey: "count")
    }
}

override func viewDidLoad() {
    super.viewDidLoad()
    count = userDefaults.integer(forKey: "count")
}
```

Use manual testing to confirm that the behavior hasn't changed.

Extract a Protocol to Support Test Doubles

The userDefaults property currently has an implicit type of UserDefaults. If we kept that type, then any replacement would have to be UserDefaults or a subclass. Subclassing is useful for allowing existing behavior to flow through, capturing extra information. (See How to Spy on the Animated Flag, on page 121.) But subclassing isn't useful when you want to stop some existing behavior. It also isn't useful when the type is a final class or a struct, or the type prevents you from creating your own instance of it.

What we need is a way to substitute an arbitrary type that honors a contract. In Swift, we can do this using protocols. Protocols give us a way to replace a concrete type with a *test double*.

 What's a test double? It's like a stunt double in filmmaking. We temporarily replace the real actor with someone that looks like that actor. Or in our case, something that looks like the original type as far as the calling code is concerned.

Start by defining a new protocol in production code. For lack of a better name, let's call it UserDefaultsProtocol. It'll be empty to start with:

UserDefaults/UserDefaults/ViewController.swift
```
protocol UserDefaultsProtocol {
}
```

Now add an explicit type to the userDefaults property, specifying the protocol.

UserDefaults/UserDefaults/ViewController.swift
```
var userDefaults: UserDefaultsProtocol = UserDefaults.standard
```

Xcode will show a Swift error:

```
Value of type 'UserDefaults' does not conform to specified type
    'UserDefaultsProtocol'
```

Since Swift allows us to extend existing types, we can declare an extension saying that UserDefaults *does* conform to our new protocol:

UserDefaults/UserDefaults/ViewController.swift
```
extension UserDefaults: UserDefaultsProtocol {}
```

That fixes the first error. But we still have errors at the places the code calls userDefaults:

```
Value of type 'UserDefaultsProtocol' has no member 'set'
Value of type 'UserDefaultsProtocol' has no member 'integer'
```

Note which line shows the first error about set. We want to get the original definition of the function it's calling. Change the type of the userDefaults property from UserDefaultsProtocol to UserDefaults. Go to the line that was showing the first error and place the cursor within set. Then in the Xcode menu, select *Navigate ▶ Jump to Definition* or press ^-⌘-J. Take a few breaths while Xcode determines the correct definition.

Eventually, Xcode will show you the interface of UserDefaults, highlighting this method:

```
/// -setInteger:forKey: is equivalent to -setObject:forKey: except that the
/// value is converted from an NSInteger to an NSNumber.
open func set(_ value: Int, forKey defaultName: String)
```

There are several definitions of set(_:forKey:). Make sure you have the version where the first argument is of type Int. Copy that line and paste it into UserDefaultsProtocol. Delete the open attribute since that doesn't apply to protocols.

Do the same for the call to integer(forKey:). You'll end up with a protocol with the following definition:

UserDefaults/UserDefaults/ViewController.swift
```
protocol UserDefaultsProtocol {
    func set(_ value: Int, forKey defaultName: String)
    func integer(forKey defaultName: String) -> Int
}
```

Finally, change the type of the userDefaults property from UserDefaults back to UserDefaultsProtocol. Confirm the changes by pressing ⌘-B to build.

We've done two things:

- Used an extension to declare that UserDefaults conforms to a new protocol
- Copied the declarations of two methods from UserDefaults into the protocol

Since UserDefaults already implements these methods, the extension is empty. Swift nods its head and says, "Sure, the type conforms to that extension."

Benefits to Protocols Beyond Testing

There are benefits to protocols beyond making the code testable. What we're doing is implementing the *interface segregation principle*.[a] This principle states that clients shouldn't depend on methods it doesn't use. If the entire UserDefaults interface is a cut diamond, we've reduced the dependency to a small facet.

This makes it easier to write test doubles. But we don't have to limit use of this protocol to testing. We can substitute any type that meets the contract of the protocol. This would let us shift the underlying persistence model to anything we want. We could even defer the question of how we're going to handle persistence until later.

---

a. *Agile Software Development, Principles, Patterns, and Practices [Mar02]*

Make a Fake Object

A *fake object* offers limited functionality like the real object. But the implementation is lightweight. In our case, we don't need (or want) actual persistence. We only need a way to associate an integer with a key and retrieve it using that key. We can do this using a dictionary.

Let's make a fake object in the test target. Select the UserDefaultsTest group in the Project Navigator and press ⌘-N to make a new file. Click the iOS selector at the top, select Swift File, and press Next.

In the dialog, enter FakeUserDefaults.swift as the name of the file. In the Save dialog, double-check that the test target is selected, not the app target. Press Create, then define a class that conforms to the UserDefaultsProtocol protocol:

UserDefaults/UserDefaultsTests/FakeUserDefaults.swift

```
@testable import UserDefaults

class FakeUserDefaults: UserDefaultsProtocol {
}
```

Xcode will show a Swift error:

```
Type 'FakeUserDefaults' does not conform to protocol 'UserDefaultsProtocol'
```

In the Xcode menu, select *Editor* ▶ *Fix All Issues*. Xcode will generate stubs for the protocol methods. Fill in the rest as shown here:

UserDefaults/UserDefaultsTests/FakeUserDefaults.swift

```
var integers: [String: Int] = [:]

func set(_ value: Int, forKey defaultName: String) {
    integers[defaultName] = value
}

func integer(forKey defaultName: String) -> Int {
    integers[defaultName] ?? 0
}
```

This gives us a simple implementation, backed by a dictionary of integers. In the Xcode menu, select *Product* ▶ *Build For* ▶ *Testing* or press Shift-⌘-U to confirm our work so far.

Test UserDefaults

Now we're ready to use our fake object to test the app. Let's start by adding a test suite ViewControllerTests. Use Test Zero as temporary scaffolding to confirm that you hooked up the test suite. (See Start from Test Zero, on page 21.) Delete Test Zero once you see its expected failure message.

For our first test case, let's test viewDidLoad(). That method gets the integer for the key "count" from userDefaults and stores this in the count property. The didSet observer on that property takes the count and updates the counter label. These are the things we'll test. (It also happens to write the count back to userDefaults, which is a little wasteful but not a big deal. It's not a requirement, so we shouldn't test it.) To invoke viewDidLoad(), our test will call loadViewIfNeeded(). Let's think about how to set up the test and how to confirm the result. We want to do the following:

- Instantiate the view controller from the storyboard.
- Create an instance of FakeUserDefaults but leave its dictionary blank.
- Inject the FakeUserDefaults into the view controller *before* viewDidLoad() is called.
- Call loadViewIfNeeded() to trigger viewDidLoad().
- Confirm that the counter label is displaying 0.

Following the test naming tip from Observe Object Life Cycles to Learn the Phases of a Test, on page 26, here's a name that expresses the test:

```
test_viewDidLoad_withEmptyUserDefaults_shouldShow0InCounterLabel
```

Create a test with that name, and follow Load a Storyboard-Based View Controller, on page 64 to load ViewController from the storyboard. Remember that this also means editing Main.storyboard to give the view controller a Storyboard ID. Run the tests, which should pass.

Here's the rest of the test. Notice that we inject the fake object into place before loadViewIfNeeded():

UserDefaults/UserDefaultsTests/ViewControllerTests.swift
```
let defaults = FakeUserDefaults()
sut.userDefaults = defaults

sut.loadViewIfNeeded()

XCTAssertEqual(sut.counterLabel.text, "0")
```

Run the tests to confirm they pass.

Since we need more tests that load the fake object into the system under test, let's move both into the test fixture. Define properties for them as implicitly unwrapped optionals. Copy the code to set them up, but remove each let to assign them to the properties. Also change as! to as? to silence a Swift warning. Remember to tear them down.

UserDefaults/UserDefaultsTests/ViewControllerTests.swift
```
private var sut: ViewController!
private var defaults: FakeUserDefaults!

override func setUp() {
    super.setUp()
    let storyboard = UIStoryboard(name: "Main", bundle: nil)
    sut = storyboard.instantiateViewController(
            identifier: String(describing: ViewController.self))
    defaults = FakeUserDefaults()
    sut.userDefaults = defaults
}

override func tearDown() {
    sut = nil
    defaults = nil
    super.tearDown()
}
```

Press Shift-⌘-U to build tests. Then delete the corresponding lines from the test case so the test uses the properties. Run tests to confirm this refactoring.

Now we want a second test much like the first, except that we'll preload FakeUserDefaults with some integer. The test will confirm that the counter label reflects this value.

UserDefaults/UserDefaultsTests/ViewControllerTests.swift

```
func test_viewDidLoad_with7InUserDefaults_shouldShow7InCounterLabel() {
    defaults.integers = ["count": 7]

    sut.loadViewIfNeeded()

    XCTAssertEqual(sut.counterLabel.text, "7")
}
```

Run tests to confirm.

That takes care of reading from UserDefaults. Let's write a test that confirms that tapping the button writes the incremented count to UserDefaults. First, follow Make a Test Helper for Button Taps, on page 104 to create TestHelpers.swift with the helper for button taps. Then add the following test:

UserDefaults/UserDefaultsTests/ViewControllerTests.swift

```
func test_tappingButton_with12InUserDefaults_shouldWrite13ToUserDefaults() {
    defaults.integers = ["count": 12]
    sut.loadViewIfNeeded()

    tap(sut.incrementButton)

    XCTAssertEqual(defaults.integers["count"], 13)
}
```

Run tests to confirm.

 Reusing the same input values across tests makes those tests weaker. Production code could pass all tests but happen to work only for that one input. To reduce the chances of this happening, it's best to vary your test inputs. (Here, we're varying the "count" value we load into FakeUserDefaults.)

Finally, one last test confirms that tapping the button increments the value shown in the counter label:

UserDefaults/UserDefaultsTests/ViewControllerTests.swift

```
func test_tappingButton_with42InUserDefaults_shouldShow43InCounterLabel() {
    defaults.integers = ["count": 42]
    sut.loadViewIfNeeded()

    tap(sut.incrementButton)

    XCTAssertEqual(sut.counterLabel.text, "43")
}
```

Run the tests to confirm. To see how effective the tests are, try breaking the production code to see what happens. (See Check the Effectiveness of Failure Messages, on page 97.)

> **Why Not Combine Similar Tests?**
>
> Why not combine the button tap tests, using multiple assertions? In Test Alerts Using the Alert Verifier, on page 110, we got by with multiple assertions. *But those assertions were all checking properties of the same object.* Here, we want to check the fake object but also check the counter label.
>
> By keeping these in separate tests, we're following the principle that a good unit test should fail for one reason. It takes only a little more work on the test side but is much easier to diagnose when a failure occurs.

Key Takeaways

Let's review the main things from this chapter that you should carry with you:

- Centralize direct references to a difficult dependency by putting that dependency into a property.

- You can replace a concrete type with a protocol because Swift lets us attach protocols to existing types. The protocol should have only the parts of the type's interface that you need.

- Once you express a dependency as a protocol, you can inject anything that conforms to that protocol. This brings extra flexibility while still preserving type safety. Tests can provide test doubles in place of the real types.

- A fake object is a test double with a lighter-weight implementation. The fake object avoids the complications that make the real thing a difficult dependency. Besides FakeUserDefaults, examples include fake databases and fake web services.

- Avoid reusing the same input values across tests. Vary the input. This reduces the chances that the production code "happens to work" for some inputs but not others.

Activities

If you have any code that uses UserDefaults, it's time to apply what you've learned. Here's one activity with four steps:

1. Find a class that uses UserDefaults.

2. Replace direct references to UserDefaults.standard. Instead, use a property with UserDefaults.standard as the default value.

3. Extract the UserDefaults methods you use into a protocol. (See Extract a Protocol to Support Test Doubles, on page 131.) Set the property's type to this protocol.

4. Define a fake object that conforms to the protocol. (See Make a Fake Object, on page 133.) Inject it from test code and use it to write test cases.

What's Next?

Now you can create fake objects that simulate UserDefaults. This works for several persistence mechanisms, not only UserDefaults. (But don't use this technique for core data, where you can avoid persistence by using an in-memory store.)

Fake objects are one type of test double. What about mock objects? In the next chapter, we'll move on to testing networking and how to write and use mock objects.

CHAPTER 12

Testing Network Requests (with Mocks)

Most iOS apps communicate with a web service. How can we unit test such communication? This crosses a clear architectural boundary, making unit testing impractical.

When a piece of functionality is too big for effective unit testing, break it into smaller pieces. Instead of testing an entire chain, test the individual links that make up the chain. For networking, this means we'll start by testing the request content. Testing networking without doing any actual networking makes tests fast and consistent. You'll be able to run your tests, even when you have no network connection.

In this chapter, you'll see how to test network requests. Along the way, we'll introduce test spies and mock objects. You'll see how to write effective mock objects in Swift.

Make a New Place to Play

For this chapter, we want some code that communicates with a web service. We'll do that with an app that communicates with the iTunes Search API[1] when you tap a button. We'll hard-code the search to get information about a particular book. For now, we'll print the response to the console.

Let's work in a new project named NetworkRequest. Follow the steps for Create a Place to Play with Tests, on page 4 using the new name, and delete the initial test file NetworkRequestTests.swift.

Edit ViewController.swift to add an outlet for a button. Declare it private(set) so our tests can reach it. Also declare a property to remember the current data task:

---

1. https://affiliate.itunes.apple.com/resources/documentation/itunes-store-web-service-search-api/

NetworkRequest/NetworkRequest/ViewController.swift
```swift
@IBOutlet private(set) var button: UIButton!
private var dataTask: URLSessionDataTask?
```

Declare an action for the button that initiates the search. It'll call a new method, passing the search terms.

NetworkRequest/NetworkRequest/ViewController.swift
```swift
@IBAction private func buttonTapped() {
    searchForBook(terms: "out from boneville")
}
```

Finally, add the method that performs the search. It does this with a URLSessionDataTask. When the data task begins, it disables the button so the user can't stack up network calls in parallel. When the task completes, it enables the button again.

NetworkRequest/NetworkRequest/ViewController.swift
```swift
private func searchForBook(terms: String) {
    guard let encodedTerms = terms.addingPercentEncoding(
            withAllowedCharacters: .urlQueryAllowed),
        let url = URL(string: "https://itunes.apple.com/search?" +
                "media=ebook&term=\(encodedTerms)") else { return }
    let request = URLRequest(url: url)
    dataTask = URLSession.shared.dataTask(with: request) {
        [weak self] (data: Data?, response: URLResponse?, error: Error?)
                    -> Void in
        guard let self = self else { return }

        let decoded = String(data: data ?? Data(), encoding: .utf8)
        print("response: \(String(describing: response))")
        print("data: \(String(describing: decoded))")
        print("error: \(String(describing: error))")

        DispatchQueue.main.async { [weak self] in
            guard let self = self else { return }
            self.dataTask = nil
            self.button.isEnabled = true
        }
    }
    button.isEnabled = false
    dataTask?.resume()
}
```

Follow the remaining steps from Make a Place to Play with a Button, on page 101 to add a button to the storyboard, connecting it to the button outlet and the action.

Let's do a manual test to confirm this networking code. Press ⌘-R to run the app. Then select *View ▶ Debug Area ▶ Activate Console* or press Shift-⌘-C to show the console on the bottom right. Tap the button in the running app to search for the book. The console will show you the results of the network call.

Now we have code that calls an actual web service. This is a difficult dependency, so we'll start by isolating it and extracting a protocol. Then we'll create a test spy that records how it's called. This will give us a way to write tests that confirm the call to the web service.

Isolate URLSession with Dependency Injection

Recall from Identify Difficult Dependencies, on page 75 that calls to web services are difficult dependencies. For unit testing, we want to isolate these calls so we can replace them.

Isolated unit tests aren't the only automated testing game in town, though. Another way to handle network calls is to fake the entire networking layer. OHHTTPStubs[2] is an example of a library that does this, letting you provide fake network data. This is quite useful when doing automated UI testing. A fake network makes UI tests faster and more reliable.

But back to unit tests...let's take our first steps toward isolating the URLSession.shared singleton. Since ViewController is a storyboard-based view controller, we'll use property injection from Inject Instances Through Initializers or Properties, on page 85.

First, add the new property, giving it an initial value of the URLSession.shared singleton. Make it var, not let, so a different value can be injected:

NetworkRequest/NetworkRequest/ViewController.swift
```
var session = URLSession.shared
```

Replace the reference to the URLSession.shared singleton with the session property:

NetworkRequest/NetworkRequest/ViewController.swift
```
dataTask = session.dataTask(with: request) {
```

Use manual testing to confirm that the behavior hasn't changed.

Extract a URLSession Protocol for Test Doubles

The session property currently has an implicit type of URLSession. Let's follow the same steps we used for Extract a Protocol to Support Test Doubles, on page 131. Start by defining a new protocol in production code. It'll start out empty:

NetworkRequest/NetworkRequest/ViewController.swift
```
protocol URLSessionProtocol {
}
```

Now add an explicit type to the session property, specifying the protocol:

---

2. https://github.com/AliSoftware/OHHTTPStubs

NetworkRequest/NetworkRequest/ViewController.swift
```
var session: URLSessionProtocol = URLSession.shared
```

Xcode will show a Swift error:

```
Value of type 'URLSession' does not conform to specified type
    'URLSessionProtocol'
```

Since Swift allows us to extend existing types, we can declare an extension saying that URLSession *does* conform to our new protocol:

NetworkRequest/NetworkRequest/ViewController.swift
```
extension URLSession: URLSessionProtocol {}
```

That fixes the first error. But we still have an error where the code calls session:

```
Value of type 'URLSessionProtocol' has no member 'dataTask'
```

We want to get the original definition of the function it's calling. Change the type of the session property from URLSessionProtocol to URLSession. Go to the line that had the error and place the cursor within dataTask. Then in the Xcode menu, select *Navigate ▶ Jump to Definition* or press ^-⌘-J. Xcode will show you the interface of URLSession, highlighting this method:

```
open func dataTask(
        with request: URLRequest,
        completionHandler: @escaping (Data?, URLResponse?, Error?) -> Void
) -> URLSessionDataTask
```

Copy that line and paste it into URLSessionProtocol. Delete the open attribute since that doesn't apply to protocols. You'll end up with a protocol with the following definition:

NetworkRequest/NetworkRequest/ViewController.swift
```
protocol URLSessionProtocol {
    func dataTask(
            with request: URLRequest,
            completionHandler: @escaping (Data?, URLResponse?, Error?) -> Void
    ) -> URLSessionDataTask
}
```

Finally, change the type of the session property from URLSession back to URLSessionProtocol. Confirm the changes by pressing ⌘-B to build.

We've now decoupled the session property from URLSession, which is a difficult dependency for unit tests. Changing its type to a protocol means tests can supply a different implementation. Next, let's see how to write a test spy that implements the protocol.

Make a Test Spy

A test spy records calls to its methods. Tests can then confirm whether the system under test made the expected calls.

For network requests, we want to intercept any calls to URLSession. The spy can stop calls from doing any actual networking. There's no need to test URLSession itself. We can trust that if we ask it to fetch data for a given URL, it'll do that. What we want to test is how many data tasks we asked for and whether the URL is correct.

Let's make a test spy in the test target. The difference between a test spy and a mock object is subtle. Most developers lump them together, calling them all mocks. Let's skirt around the difference for now, and give the test spy a "mock" name. (Later, we're going to evolve it into a full mock object.) Select the NetworkRequestTests group in the Project Navigator and press ⌘-N to make a new file. Give it the name MockURLSession.swift. In the Save dialog, double-check that the test target is selected, not the app target. Press Create. Inside, let's define a class that conforms to the URLSessionProtocol protocol:

NetworkRequest/NetworkRequestTests/MockURLSession.swift
```
import Foundation
@testable import NetworkRequest

class MockURLSession: URLSessionProtocol {
}
```

Xcode will show a Swift error:

```
Type 'MockURLSession' does not conform to protocol 'URLSessionProtocol'
```

In the Xcode menu, select *Editor* ▶ *Fix All Issues*. Xcode will generate a stub for the protocol method. It has to return a URLSessionDataTask, so just initialize one for now. We'll see in Design the Test Case, on page 144 that this won't work in practice, but it'll satisfy the Swift compiler so that we can make progress.

NetworkRequest/NetworkRequestTests/MockURLSession.swift
```
func dataTask(
        with request: URLRequest,
        completionHandler: @escaping (Data?, URLResponse?, Error?) -> Void
) -> URLSessionDataTask {
    return URLSessionDataTask()
}
```

Now let's capture the number of calls, and the request argument. (Ignore the completionHandler argument for now. We'll get to it in Chapter 13, Testing Network Responses (and Closures), on page 153.)

NetworkRequest/NetworkRequestTests/MockURLSession.swift

```
class MockURLSession: URLSessionProtocol {
    var dataTaskCallCount = 0
    var dataTaskArgsRequest: [URLRequest] = []

    func dataTask(
            with request: URLRequest,
            completionHandler: @escaping (Data?, URLResponse?, Error?) -> Void
    ) -> URLSessionDataTask {
        dataTaskCallCount += 1
        dataTaskArgsRequest.append(request)
        return URLSessionDataTask()
    }
}
```

 For each method in a test spy, capture the call count by increment-
ing an integer. Capture any arguments by appending them to
arrays.

Design the Test Case

Now we can try using our test spy to test the app. Let's start by adding a test
suite ViewControllerTests. Use Test Zero as temporary scaffolding to confirm that
you hooked up the test suite. (See Start from Test Zero, on page 21.) Delete
Test Zero once you see its expected failure message.

Let's test that tapping the button creates a data task with the expected request.
Think for a moment about how to set up the test and how to confirm the
result. We want to do the following:

- Instantiate the view controller from the storyboard.

- Create an instance of MockURLSession.

- Inject the MockURLSession into the view controller. Following what we learned
  in Test UserDefaults, on page 134, let's make sure to do this *before* loading
  the view. We do this to avoid having any methods use the real URLSession.

- Simulate the button tap.

- Confirm that the test spy was called once, with the expected request.

Following the test naming tip from Observe Object Life Cycles to Learn the
Phases of a Test, on page 26, here's a name that expresses the test:

```
test_tappingButton_shouldMakeDataTaskToSearchForEBookOutFromBoneville()
```

Create a test with that name, and follow Load a Storyboard-Based View
Controller, on page 64 to load ViewController from the storyboard. Remember

that this also means editing Main.storyboard to give the view controller a Storyboard ID. Run the tests, which should pass.

Since we're going to tap a button, follow Make a Test Helper for Button Taps, on page 104 to add the tap(_:) helper.

Here's more of the test, up to the button tap. Notice that we inject the test spy into place before loadViewIfNeeded():

NetworkRequest/NetworkRequestTests/ViewControllerTests.swift
```
let mockURLSession = MockURLSession()
sut.session = mockURLSession
sut.loadViewIfNeeded()

tap(sut.button)
```

Run the tests. You'll get "1 unexpected failure" with the following message:

```
failed: caught "NSInvalidArgumentException", "*** -resume cannot be sent to
    abstract instance of class NSURLSessionDataTask"
```

This tells us that the Objective-C implementation of URLSessionDataTask is an abstract base class. We can make a subclass that provides a do-nothing version of the resume() method:

NetworkRequest/NetworkRequestTests/MockURLSession.swift
```
private class DummyURLSessionDataTask: URLSessionDataTask {
    override func resume() {
    }
}
```

This is a *dummy object*.[3] It's something we need to satisfy the compiler, but it has no effect on the test. Update MockURLSession to return an instance of the dummy.

NetworkRequest/NetworkRequestTests/MockURLSession.swift
```
return DummyURLSessionDataTask()
```

Run the tests. This time we won't get any failures. (This does result in a warning that URLSessionDataTask's init() was deprecated in iOS 13.0. That's a sensible warning for production code, but for test code, we need to create our own instance directly.)

Finally, let's add two assertions of the data captured by the test spy. The first checks that the method was called once:

NetworkRequest/NetworkRequestTests/ViewControllerTests.swift
```
XCTAssertEqual(mockURLSession.dataTaskCallCount, 1, "call count")
```

---

3. *xUnit Test Patterns [Mes07]*

The second is a characterization test we'll use to get the request argument:

NetworkRequest/NetworkRequestTests/ViewControllerTests.swift
```
XCTAssertEqual(
        mockURLSession.dataTaskArgsRequest.first,
        URLRequest(url: URL(string: "http://FOO")!),
        "request")
```

Run the tests. You'll get the following failure message.

```
XCTAssertEqual failed: ("Optional(
  https://itunes.apple.com/search?media=ebook&term=out%20from%20boneville)")
  is not equal to ("Optional(http://FOO)") - request
```

The failure message from the characterization test tells us the actual behavior. Copy and paste the URL from the failure back into the assertion:

NetworkRequest/NetworkRequestTests/ViewControllerTests.swift
```
XCTAssertEqual(
        mockURLSession.dataTaskArgsRequest.first,
        URLRequest(url: URL(string: "https://itunes.apple.com/search?" +
                "media=ebook&term=out%20from%20boneville")!),
        "request")
```

Run the tests, which will pass. We now have a test that checks the network request without starting the download.

 This isn't the only way to test requests. In fact, it's simpler to extract the creation of web requests into their own types. Then you can test the results of different inputs without using test spies at all. But you'll still want a test somewhere that intercepts networking, to confirm that the code sends the request.

We now have a test that confirms the contents of the network request, using a test spy. In the rest of this chapter, we'll give our spy some more smarts, turning it into a mock object. This can simplify the test code, making it easier to write (and read). It can also give more helpful information in the event of a test failure.

Promote the Test Spy into a Mock Object

Our test case makes two assertions against the test spy:

NetworkRequest/NetworkRequestTests/ViewControllerTests.swift
```
XCTAssertEqual(mockURLSession.dataTaskCallCount, 1, "call count")
XCTAssertEqual(
        mockURLSession.dataTaskArgsRequest.first,
        URLRequest(url: URL(string: "https://itunes.apple.com/search?" +
                "media=ebook&term=out%20from%20boneville")!),
        "request")
```

It's saying, "Confirm that system under test called the dataTask method once, with this request as the argument." Let's get a sense for how these assertions report failures. Go to the production code for the button tap action:

NetworkRequest/NetworkRequest/ViewController.swift
```
@IBAction private func buttonTapped() {
    searchForBook(terms: "out from boneville")
}
```

Try altering the production code in these three ways:

1. Comment out the searchForBook(terms:) line. Run tests and check the failure messages. Undo.

2. Duplicate the line. Run tests and check the failure messages. Undo.

3. Go back to one line, but change the URL. Run tests and check the failure messages. Undo.

The call count is important. We don't want to fire off any redundant network calls by mistake. And the test spy works pretty well. But if more than one test uses the spy, each test case will end up duplicating the assertion that the call count is 1. Can we avoid this duplication?

Now at last we come to mock objects. The difference between a test spy and a *mock object* is where the assertions live. Let's create a verification method inside the test double that calls the assertions for us.

NetworkRequest/NetworkRequestTests/MockURLSession.swift
```
func verifyDataTask(with request: URLRequest) {
    XCTAssertEqual(dataTaskCallCount, 1, "call count")
    XCTAssertEqual(dataTaskArgsRequest.first, request, "request")
}
```

For this to build, add an import XCTest statement to the top of the file. Then in the Xcode menu, select *Product* ▶ *Build For* ▶ *Testing* or press Shift-⌘-U.

Now let's change the test to use this verification method. In the test case, replace the assertions with the following:

NetworkRequest/NetworkRequestTests/ViewControllerTests.swift
```
mockURLSession.verifyDataTask(
    with: URLRequest(url: URL(string: "https://itunes.apple.com/search?" +
        "media=ebook&term=out%20from%20boneville")!))
```

Run the tests, which will pass. But now introduce a bug in the production code. Change the URL argument and run tests to get a failure. In the Xcode menu, select *View* ▶ *Navigators* ▶ *Show Report Navigator* (or press ⌘-9).

Double-click on the test failure message. Xcode will take you to the failing XCTAssertEqual() in MockURLSession, not to the test case that failed.

We can fix this so that test failures point to the test cases instead of to the emerging mock object. Every XCTest assertion has two more parameters with default arguments. They capture the file name and line number of the call site. We can add these same parameters to the verification method:

NetworkRequest/NetworkRequestTests/MockURLSession.swift
```
func verifyDataTask(with request: URLRequest,
                    file: StaticString = #file, line: UInt = #line) {
```

Then pass these file and line arguments down to each assertion.

NetworkRequest/NetworkRequestTests/MockURLSession.swift
```
XCTAssertEqual(dataTaskCallCount, 1, "call count", file: file, line: line)
XCTAssertEqual(dataTaskArgsRequest.first, request, "request",
       file: file, line: line)
```

Run the failing test again. Double-click on the failure message. This time, Xcode will take you to where the failing test case calls the verification method.

Now we have a mock object. By adding more smarts to MockURLSession, we've made it easier to write more tests that use it. And the test code is more expressive.

> Any time you call an XCTest assertion from a helper function, get the file name and line number in arguments. Pass them on to any assertions. This way, test failures will report the calling line in the test, not the helper.

XCTest Assertions Work Differently in Objective-C

In Swift, XCTest assertions are free functions. Any type can call them, which makes it easier to write test helpers.

But in Objective-C, assertions are methods. We can only invoke them from within the running XCTestCase subclass. Don't worry, though. Objective-C mocking libraries like OCMockito[a] mean you shouldn't have to write any mock objects by hand.

---

a.   https://github.com/jonreid/OCMockito

Improve Mock Object Reporting

We can improve the reporting from our mock object in different ways. Right now, the verify method checks the call count is 1. It goes on to check the first URL argument, regardless of the call count.

Let's see the current failure reporting by introducing errors to ViewController. First, in the buttonTapped() method, comment out the call to searchForBook(terms:). Run tests. You'll see two errors:

```
XCTAssertEqual failed: ("0") is not equal to ("1") - call count
XCTAssertEqual failed: ("nil") is not equal to  ("Optional(
  https://itunes.apple.com/search?media=ebook&term=out%20from%20boneville)")
  - request
```

When the method is never called, it's kind of odd to report a mismatch on the URL argument.

Next, restore the original call to searchForBook(terms:). But add a second call below it, with different search terms—for example:

NetworkRequest/NetworkRequest/ViewController.swift
```
searchForBook(terms: "out from boneville")
searchForBook(terms: "the great cow race")
```

Run tests. This time, the error log shows:

```
XCTAssertEqual failed: ("2") is not equal to ("1") - call count
```

When the method is called more than once, we're throwing away information. The first URL argument matches. But it would be useful to know the URL arguments from other calls. The added information would make it easier to pinpoint what's going wrong. Let's add some helpers to the mock object to help us improve the reporting. Edit MockURLSession.swift and add the following standalone function *outside* of the class definition:

NetworkRequest/NetworkRequestTests/MockURLSession.swift
```
func verifyMethodCalledOnce(
        methodName: String,
        callCount: Int,
        describeArguments: @autoclosure () -> String,
        file: StaticString = #file,
        line: UInt = #line) -> Bool {
    if callCount == 0 {
        XCTFail("Wanted but not invoked: \(methodName)",
                file: file, line: line)
        return false
    }
    if callCount > 1 {
        XCTFail("Wanted 1 time but was called \(callCount) times. " +
                "\(methodName) with \(describeArguments())",
                file: file, line: line)
        return false
    }
    return true
}
```

Make sure to put this function outside of any type so it's available to all mock objects. Then inside MockURLSession, write a method that uses this function:

NetworkRequest/NetworkRequestTests/MockURLSession.swift
```
private func dataTaskWasCalledOnce(
        file: StaticString = #file, line: UInt = #line) -> Bool {
    verifyMethodCalledOnce(
            methodName: "dataTask(with:completionHandler:)",
            callCount: dataTaskCallCount,
            describeArguments: "request: \(dataTaskArgsRequest)",
            file: file,
            line: line)
}
```

Make sure this builds. In the Xcode menu, select *Product ▶ Build For ▶ Testing* or press Shift-⌘-U.

Finally in the verify method, replace the call count assertion with a guard clause that calls this new helper method. If the helper returns false, we do an early return to skip the rest of the test.

NetworkRequest/NetworkRequestTests/MockURLSession.swift
```
func verifyDataTask(with request: URLRequest,
                    file: StaticString = #file, line: UInt = #line) {
    guard dataTaskWasCalledOnce(file: file, line: line) else { return }
    XCTAssertEqual(dataTaskArgsRequest.first, request, "request",
            file: file, line: line)
}
```

Run tests with that call to searchForBook(terms:) commented out. This time, the error log says:

```
failed - Wanted but not invoked: dataTask(with:completionHandler:)
```

Now run tests with not one but two searches. The error log shows this:

```
failed - Wanted 1 time but was called 2 times.
  dataTask(with:completionHandler:) with request:
  [https://itunes.apple.com/search?media=ebook&term=out%20from%20boneville,
  https://itunes.apple.com/search?media=ebook&term=the%20great%20cow%20race]
```

Notice how much clearer the error messages can become with a little work. For the second case, the message lists each request to give a clearer picture of what's going on. Logging this information in the test results can cut down on the amount of time you spend in the debugger.

This scratches the surface of ways to improve error reports from mock objects. If you use a mock object in only one place, it may not be worth spending too much time on it. But the more often it's used, the more it pays off to improve its reporting.

> ### Making Tests Insensitive to Things That Don't Matter
>
> Using XCTAssertEqual(_:_:) is a quick way to compare two Equatable objects. But equality can be overkill.
>
> For example, the order of queries doesn't matter in a URL. If we made a change that switched the media and term query items, the new URL would still work. But the test would fail. Such tests inhibit refactoring.
>
> We want tests that are sensitive to things that matter and insensitive to things that don't. To examine a URL, consider constructing URLComponents from it. Then you can test that the components' queryItems contains each query you expect, regardless of their order.

Key Takeaways

As we finish this chapter, here are the main things you should hold on to:

- A test spy records the method calls it receives. This lets us test that the system under test called it as expected. It lets us verify the communication between components.

- Don't use a Boolean flag to record when the test spy receives a call. That's throwing away information about the communication. Instead, increment a call count so you can tell how many times a method was called.

- A mock object is a test spy that does its own assertions. This simplifies test code. It also gives us opportunities to improve failure reporting.

- Helper methods can call the XCTest assertions. Get the file name and line number of the call site as function arguments. Pass them along to the assertions.

- Tests should be sensitive to things that matter and insensitive to things that don't. For data where the order doesn't matter, avoid using equality assertions. Otherwise tests can reject valid results, giving you false negatives.

Activities

Almost every app does some networking. Try this activity, following steps 1–4. Pause to celebrate. Then try step 5 to see how it simplifies the test.

1. Find a place in your code that calls a simple web service. Whether you use URLSession or a networking library, replace direct references to singletons. Instead, use a property with the singleton as the default value.

2. Extract the methods you call on this networking property into a protocol. (See Extract a Protocol to Support Test Doubles, on page 131.) Set the property's type to this protocol.

3. Define a test spy that conforms to the protocol. (See Make a Test Spy, on page 143.) For each method, record the call count and collect the arguments.

4. Inject the test spy from test code and use it to write one test case.

5. Convert the test spy into a mock object by giving it a verify method that does its own assertions. (See Promote the Test Spy into a Mock Object, on page 146.) Remember to get the file name and line number as parameters, passing them down to any assertions. Check error reporting by deliberately introducing errors.

What's Next?

Now you can test the first half of networking. The trick is to go right up to the boundary of real networking and stop. Then test everything about the request.

You've learned how to create effective test spies that record their call counts and arguments. You know how to move assertions, promoting test spies into mock objects. And you've seen how doing so simplifies test code and lets you create clearer failure messages.

But what about handling the responses? In the next chapter, let's tackle the second half of networking. And since we tend to write response handling using Swift closures, let's learn how to test those closures.

CHAPTER 13

Testing Network Responses (and Closures)

In the previous chapter, we saw a way to test network requests. These tests confirm that we're sending the expected network calls. But we also want to test how to handle network responses, from the "happy path" to error cases.

Response handling is commonly done with closures. Since closures are like code hidden inside of code, how can we test them?

In this chapter you'll learn how to test closures. This will give you a way to test all kinds of network responses, including errors that are normally hard to reproduce. You'll also learn how to test asynchronous code that crosses threads.

Make a New Place to Play

If you worked through the example from Chapter 12, Testing Network Requests (with Mocks), on page 139, you can continue with that code and skip to Parse the Response, on page 155. Otherwise, let's set up code that communicates with a web service. It happens to be the iTunes Search API.

If you want a new project, follow the steps for Create a Place to Play with Tests, on page 4, but use the project name NetworkResponse. As usual, delete the initial test file NetworkResponseTests.swift.

Edit ViewController.swift to define a protocol containing one method copied from URLSession. Declare an empty protocol extension that says URLSession conforms to this protocol. This is what we arrived at in Extract a URLSession Protocol for Test Doubles, on page 141:

NetworkResponse/NetworkResponse/ViewController.swift
```
protocol URLSessionProtocol {
    func dataTask(
            with request: URLRequest,
            completionHandler: @escaping (Data?, URLResponse?, Error?) -> Void
    ) -> URLSessionDataTask
}

extension URLSession: URLSessionProtocol {}
```

Inside the ViewController class, add an outlet for a button, a property to remember the current data task, and a replaceable property that holds the URLSession using the new protocol. Declare the outlet private(set) so that our tests can reach it. Also declare an action for the button that initiates the search. It'll call a new method, passing the search terms:

NetworkResponse/NetworkResponse/ViewController.swift
```
@IBOutlet private(set) var button: UIButton!
private var dataTask: URLSessionDataTask?
var session: URLSessionProtocol = URLSession.shared

@IBAction private func buttonTapped() {
    searchForBook(terms: "out from boneville")
}
```

Add the method that performs the search. It uses the technique from Isolate URLSession with Dependency Injection, on page 141 of calling the session property instead of directly calling URLSession.shared. It also disables the button when it issues the network request, and enables the button again upon receiving the response:

NetworkResponse/NetworkResponse/ViewController.swift
```
private func searchForBook(terms: String) {
    guard let encodedTerms = terms.addingPercentEncoding(
            withAllowedCharacters: .urlQueryAllowed),
        let url = URL(string: "https://itunes.apple.com/search?" +
                "media=ebook&term=\(encodedTerms)") else { return }
    let request = URLRequest(url: url)
    dataTask = session.dataTask(with: request) {
        [weak self] (data: Data?, response: URLResponse?, error: Error?)
                    -> Void in
        guard let self = self else { return }

        let decoded = String(data: data ?? Data(), encoding: .utf8)
        print("response: \(String(describing: response))")
        print("data: \(String(describing: decoded))")
        print("error: \(String(describing: error))")
```

```
        DispatchQueue.main.async { [weak self] in
            guard let self = self else { return }
            self.dataTask = nil
            self.button.isEnabled = true
        }
    }
    button.isEnabled = false
    dataTask?.resume()
}
```

Finally, follow the remaining steps from Make a Place to Play with a Button, on page 101 to add a button to the storyboard, connecting it to the button outlet and the action.

Let's confirm this networking code by tapping the button manually and checking the logs. Press ⌘-R to run the app. Then select *View* ▶ *Debug Area* ▶ *Activate Console* or press Shift-⌘-C to show the console on the bottom right. Tap the button in the running app to search for the book. The console will show you the results of the network call.

Parse the Response

The production code is now up to date with Chapter 12, Testing Network Requests (with Mocks), on page 139. Let's continue by adding some parsing. Add the following decodable structures to ViewController.swift:

NetworkResponse/NetworkResponse/ViewController.swift
```
struct Search: Decodable {
    let results: [SearchResult]
}

struct SearchResult: Decodable, Equatable {
    let artistName: String
    let trackName: String
    let averageUserRating: Float
    let genres: [String]
}
```

Define SearchResult so that it conforms to the Equatable protocol. This will make it simple to test with an XCTAssertEqual() assertion.

Now in the ViewController class, add a property to hold an array of search results. Let's also give it a didset observer to print the results in the console.

NetworkResponse/NetworkResponse/ViewController.swift
```
private(set) var results: [SearchResult] = [] {
    didSet {
        print(results)
    }
}
```

Finally, in searchForBook(terms:), replace the lines that printed the data, response, and error closure arguments. If data is present, let's parse it with a JSONDecoder. And if that's successful, let's save the results in the results property. We'll do so back on the main thread as a simple approach to thread safety. If there's any sort of error (which can happen in several ways), let's show an alert:

NetworkResponse/NetworkResponse/ViewController.swift
```swift
private func searchForBook(terms: String) {
    guard let encodedTerms = terms.addingPercentEncoding(
            withAllowedCharacters: .urlQueryAllowed),
        let url = URL(string: "https://itunes.apple.com/search?" +
                "media=ebook&term=\(encodedTerms)") else { return }
    let request = URLRequest(url: url)
    dataTask = session.dataTask(with: request) {
        [weak self] (data: Data?, response: URLResponse?, error: Error?)
                    -> Void in
        guard let self = self else { return }

        var decoded: Search?
        var errorMessage: String?
        if let error = error {
            errorMessage = error.localizedDescription
        } else if let response = response as? HTTPURLResponse,
                response.statusCode != 200 {
            errorMessage = "Response: " +
                    HTTPURLResponse.localizedString(
                            forStatusCode: response.statusCode)
        } else if let data = data {
            do {
                decoded = try JSONDecoder().decode(Search.self, from: data)
            } catch {
                errorMessage = error.localizedDescription
            }
        }

        DispatchQueue.main.async { [weak self] in
            guard let self = self else { return }
            if let decoded = decoded {
                self.results = decoded.results
            }
            if let errorMessage = errorMessage {
                self.showError(errorMessage)
            }
            self.dataTask = nil
            self.button.isEnabled = true
        }
    }
    button.isEnabled = false
    dataTask?.resume()
}
```

If errorMessage is non-nil, we call a showError(_:) method. Let's define that method so it shows an alert. It also prints the error to the console:

NetworkResponse/NetworkResponse/ViewController.swift
```
private func showError(_ message: String) {
    let title = "Network problem"
    print("\(title): \(message)")
    let alert = UIAlertController(
            title: title,
            message: message,
            preferredStyle: .alert
    )
    let okAction = UIAlertAction(title: "OK", style: .default)
    alert.addAction(okAction)
    alert.preferredAction = okAction
    present(alert, animated: true)
}
```

Now we're ready to do some manual testing to confirm this parsing code. First, turn off your network connection to force an error. Run the app with ⌘-R. Then select *View* ▸ *Debug Area* ▸ *Activate Console* or press Shift-⌘-C to show the console on the bottom right.

While disconnected from your network, tap the button in the running app. You should see an alert with the title "Network problem" and the message "The Internet connection appears to be offline." (If you don't get an alert, then you may have tapped the button already, and the network layer cached the results. Delete the NetworkResponse app from the simulator, then try again with no network.)

Now reconnect to your network, and tap the button again to make the network call. The console will show you the results, this time parsed into an array of SearchResult.

 This isn't meant to be an example of good code. Rather, it's an example of a typical view controller with too many responsibilities. Once we bring such code under test, we can clean it up. That's why this book has Part III.

Now we have code that calls a real web service, parses the response, and saves the result into a property if successful. Let's use a test spy to record the call, only this time the spy will also capture the completion handler. We'll use this to write various tests of the completion handler. We'll look at how to test the asynchronous call from the completion handler back to the main thread. And we'll test one of the error scenarios.

Start with a Fresh Test Spy

If you didn't work through Chapter 12, Testing Network Requests (with Mocks), on page 139, the full-fledged mock object we developed would be a confusing starting point for learning closure techniques. To simplify this example, let's set that MockURLSession aside and start over with a fresh test spy. (If you're continuing with last chapter's code, when you see NetworkResponse or NetworkResponse-Tests below, mentally convert to NetworkRequest and NetworkRequestTests.)

Select the NetworkResponseTests group in the Project Navigator and press ⌘-N to make a new file. Click the iOS selector at the top, select Swift File, and press Next. In the dialog, enter SpyURLSession.swift as the name of the file. In the Save dialog, double-check that the test target is selected, not the app target. Press Create and enter the following code:

NetworkResponse/NetworkResponseTests/SpyURLSession.swift

```
@testable import NetworkResponse
import Foundation

private class DummyURLSessionDataTask: URLSessionDataTask {
    override func resume() {
    }
}

class SpyURLSession: URLSessionProtocol {
}
```

Xcode will show a Swift error:

```
Type 'SpyURLSession' does not conform to protocol 'URLSessionProtocol'
```

In the Xcode menu, select *Editor ▶ Fix All Issues*. Xcode will generate a stub for the protocol method. Fill in the rest as shown here to increment the call count, capture the arguments, and return a DummyURLSessionDataTask:

NetworkResponse/NetworkResponseTests/SpyURLSession.swift

```
var dataTaskCallCount = 0
var dataTaskArgsRequest: [URLRequest] = []
var dataTaskArgsCompletionHandler:
        [(Data?, URLResponse?, Error?) -> Void] = []

func dataTask(
        with request: URLRequest,
        completionHandler: @escaping (Data?, URLResponse?, Error?) -> Void
) -> URLSessionDataTask {
    dataTaskCallCount += 1
    dataTaskArgsRequest.append(request)
    dataTaskArgsCompletionHandler.append(completionHandler)
    return DummyURLSessionDataTask()
}
```

This is identical to Make a Test Spy, on page 143 except that now we're capturing the completionHandler argument.

Design the Test Case

Now we have the tools we need to start testing the network response. Let's start by adding a test suite ViewControllerTests. Use Test Zero as temporary scaffolding to confirm that you hooked up the test suite. (See Start from Test Zero, on page 21.) Delete Test Zero once you see its expected failure message.

We want to test how the code handles different network responses. This could include error scenarios, but for now let's concentrate on the happy path. Think for a moment about how to set up such a test. We want to do the following:

- Instantiate the view controller from the storyboard.

- Create an instance of SpyURLSession.

- Inject the SpyURLSession into the view controller. Make sure to do this *before* loading the view to avoid having any methods use the real URLSession.

- Simulate the button tap to start the network call. This will call the test spy, which will capture the arguments—including the closure.

- Call the captured closure with any arguments we want for testing. For the happy path, this will include JSON data and a response with the "OK" status code. We can test that the data was decoded into the results property.

Following the test naming tip from Observe Object Life Cycles to Learn the Phases of a Test, on page 26, here's a name that expresses the test:

```
test_searchForBookNetworkCall_withSuccessResponse_shouldSaveDataInResults()
```

Create a test with that name, and follow Load a Storyboard-Based View Controller, on page 64 to load ViewController from the storyboard. Remember that this also means editing Main.storyboard to give the view controller a Storyboard ID. Run the tests, which should pass.

Also follow Make a Test Helper for Button Taps, on page 104 to create the tap(_:) helper. Then add the following to the test. It creates the test spy, injects it, loads the view, and taps the button.

```
NetworkResponse/NetworkResponseTests/ViewControllerTests.swift
let spyURLSession = SpyURLSession()
sut.session = spyURLSession
sut.loadViewIfNeeded()
tap(sut.button)
```

We need some test JSON. Let's do that by defining a multiline string, then converting it to Data. Do this in a helper function so we can use the same data in a couple of tests:

NetworkResponse/NetworkResponseTests/ViewControllerTests.swift
```
private func jsonData() -> Data {
    """
    {
        "results": [
            {
                "artistName": "Artist",
                "trackName": "Track",
                "averageUserRating": 2.5,
                "genres": [
                    "Foo",
                    "Bar"
                ]
            }
        ]
    }
    """.data(using: .utf8)!
}
```

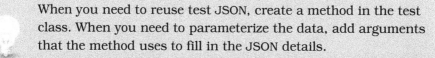

If test JSON is small, define it using a string inside test code. This keeps the input close to the assertions, making their relationship clearer.

When you need to reuse test JSON, create a method in the test class. When you need to parameterize the data, add arguments that the method uses to fill in the JSON details.

When test JSON is large, store it in a file to make it easier to copy and paste from an actual response. Stored JSON files also give you an opportunity to periodically check that they still match real server responses. You can write *contract tests*[1] that do this work.

To test a successful network response, we should supply an HTTPURLResponse with a status code of 200 for HTTP "OK." Let's add a helper method to make a response:

NetworkResponse/NetworkResponseTests/ViewControllerTests.swift
```
private func response(statusCode: Int) -> HTTPURLResponse? {
    HTTPURLResponse(url: URL(string: "http://DUMMY")!,
            statusCode: statusCode, httpVersion: nil, headerFields: nil)
}
```

---

1.   https://martinfowler.com/bliki/ContractTest.html

Now we can call the closure the test spy captured. For the happy path, we supply JSON data, an HTTP response with status code 200, and no error:

NetworkResponse/NetworkResponseTests/ViewControllerTests.swift
```
spyURLSession.dataTaskArgsCompletionHandler.first?(
        jsonData(), response(statusCode: 200), nil
)
```

For our first attempt, let's assert that the decoded results match the JSON input:

NetworkResponse/NetworkResponseTests/ViewControllerTests.swift
```
XCTAssertEqual(sut.results, [
    SearchResult(artistName: "Artist", trackName: "Track",
            averageUserRating: 2.5, genres: ["Foo", "Bar"])
])
```

This would work if the closure stayed on the same thread. But run tests, and you'll see a failure message. We need to account for multithreading.

Test Asynchronous Code

Swift makes closures so pleasant to read, you may forget they're there. We have a good start on testing the data task completion handler. But inside that closure, there's another closure hiding. It's DispatchQueue.main.async. The part in braces is a closure, scheduled to run on the main thread.

In real life, Cocoa Touch calls the data task completion handler on a background thread. This lets us parse the response without causing the UI to stutter. We can use different approaches for this. I've chosen a simple strategy of keeping the decoding in the background, then saving the results on the main thread because that's what operates the UI.

But be aware that test code executes on the main thread. And when any code schedules a closure for asynchronous execution, life gets tricky. We need to find a way to resynchronize it back to the main thread. A *Test Expectation* can usually help us.

XCTestCase provides methods that wait for one or more test expectations to be fulfilled. If a test waits on an XCTestExpectation, the "wait" method stops. It continues as soon as fulfill() is called on the expectation. If the expectation isn't fulfilled before a given timeout period, the test fails.

To show an XCTestCaseExpectation example, we need a way for the test code to provide a closure to the production code. A natural point to do this is on the didset observer for the results property. It's where we currently print the results

> ### How Do You Wait If There's No Completion Closure?
>
> A test expectation works as long as the test code has an opportunity to provide a completion closure. Then the closure can call the expectation's fulfill() method.
>
> But sometimes, we want to wait for something to happen when the code doesn't provide a completion closure. In that case, we need a way to check for the condition in periodic intervals. If the condition isn't met within a timeout, the test should fail.
>
> The Nimble matcher framework[a] is one example of a library that provides a simple way to do this, with its toEventually matcher.
>
> _____
>
> a.   https://github.com/Quick/Nimble

as a substitute for the real work an app might do. Let's move that work into a new handleResults closure property:

NetworkResponse/NetworkResponse/ViewController.swift
```
var handleResults: ([SearchResult]) -> Void = { print($0) }

private(set) var results: [SearchResult] = [] {
    didSet {
        handleResults(results)
    }
}
```

Run the app, tap the button, and check the console to confirm that the parsed results are still printed.

Now we have a place for the test to provide its own closure. Before the test calls the data task completion handler, create an XCTestCaseExpectation using the expectation(description:) method. Provide a closure that calls fulfill() on the expectation. After calling the data task completion handler, add a wait(timeout:):

NetworkResponse/NetworkResponseTests/ViewControllerTests.swift
```
let handleResultsCalled = expectation(description: "handleResults called")
sut.handleResults = { _ in
    handleResultsCalled.fulfill()
}
spyURLSession.dataTaskArgsCompletionHandler.first?(
        jsonData(), response(statusCode: 200), nil
)
waitForExpectations(timeout: 0.01)
```

Run tests again. This time, the test passes! (If the test doesn't pass, check the console output before the assertion failure message. The showError(_:) method prints to the console in addition to showing an alert, so it may give you a clue.)

Many examples of waiting for an XCTestCaseExpectation specify a timeout of 1 second. I've even seen 10 seconds. But for unit testing where there is no actual networking, that's an eternity. Try to use 0.01 seconds (10 milliseconds) or less, as shown in the preceding example.

Keeping Assertions Out of Closures

When a test provides a closure for asynchronous testing, most online examples stick XCTest assertions right inside the closure. The problem with this style is it mixes up the Arrange, Act, and Assert sections of a test. We end up with part of the Assert living inside the Arrange section.

Instead, I recommend that test-supplied closures do two things for asynchronous tests:

1. Capture the arguments we want to test.
2. Call fulfill() to escape the wait condition.

Once we have escaped the wait condition, the rest of the test can check the captured arguments. This gives us asynchronous tests with assertions at the end. Being able to read tests top-down makes them easier to understand and maintain.

Keep Asynchronous Code in Its Closure

We can now test the code that goes from the background thread back to the main thread to save the results. But there's a weakness in having that test by itself. If someone made a mistake and moved that code to save the results outside the DispatchQueue.main.async closure, the tests would still pass.

To prevent this from happening, we need a second test that skips the async closure. This test will prove that without the closure, the results aren't saved.

Duplicate the first test. Change the test case name of the copy to test_searchFor-BookNetworkCall_withSuccessBeforeAsync_shouldNotSaveDataInResults(). Remove everything that has to do with test expectations. Change the assertion so that the expected results are an empty array. Here's the body of the new test:

NetworkResponse/NetworkResponseTests/ViewControllerTests.swift
```
tap(sut.button)

spyURLSession.dataTaskArgsCompletionHandler.first?(
        jsonData(), response(statusCode: 200), nil
)

XCTAssertEqual(sut.results, [])
```

Run the tests to see them pass. Let's also see what this particular test guards against. Find the lines that save the result:

```
NetworkResponse/NetworkResponse/ViewController.swift
if let decoded = decoded {
    self.results = decoded.results
}
```

Temporarily move them outside the async closure and run the tests again. The first test will continue to pass, but the one we just added will fail.

 Whenever you write a test of asynchronous code, write a second test without the test expectations. It shows what happens without the asynchronous code. This helps keep the asynchronous part from creeping outside its closure.

Test an Error Scenario

Once we have a test that calls the data task completion closure, testing error scenarios isn't hard. We know how to capture the closure, call it with some arguments, and handle asynchronous code. For errors, all we need to do is change the arguments we pass to the completion closure.

When our parsing code detects an error, it displays an alert to the user. We know from Chapter 9, Testing Alerts, on page 107 how to test alerts and that we need the helper framework. Follow Add the Helper Framework to the Project, on page 108 to add ViewControllerPresentationSpy to the test target. Then import ViewControllerPresentationSpy it in ViewControllerTests.swift.

Since we're adding new tests, let's move the system under test and the test spy, adding the AlertVerifier spy. Follow Move the SUT into the Test Fixture, on page 112 to set up the text fixture and tear it down:

```
NetworkResponse/NetworkResponseTests/ViewControllerTests.swift
private var alertVerifier: AlertVerifier!
private var sut: ViewController!
private var spyURLSession: SpyURLSession!

override func setUp() {
    super.setUp()
    alertVerifier = AlertVerifier()
    let storyboard = UIStoryboard(name: "Main", bundle: nil)
    sut = storyboard.instantiateViewController(
            identifier: String(describing: ViewController.self))
    spyURLSession = SpyURLSession()
    sut.session = spyURLSession
    sut.loadViewIfNeeded()
}
```

```
override func tearDown() {
    alertVerifier = nil
    sut = nil
    spyURLSession = nil
    super.tearDown()
}
```

Remove the beginning lines of the test case, which are now handled by setUp().
So the first line of the test will be tap(sut.button). Run tests to confirm that
everything still passes.

In ViewController, the first error scenario is when the closure receives an Error
argument. Since Error is a protocol, let's define a simple implementation for
testing purposes. Create a new file in the NetworkResponseTests group with
the name TestError.swift:

NetworkResponse/NetworkResponseTests/TestError.swift
```
import Foundation

struct TestError: LocalizedError {
    let message: String

    var errorDescription: String? { message }
}
```

We're going to be testing alerts. To simplify the test code, let's make a helper
method in ViewControllerTests to verify that the code showed an alert. Each alert
will be the same, except for the message, so the helper has a message
parameter:

NetworkResponse/NetworkResponseTests/ViewControllerTests.swift
```
private func verifyErrorAlert(
        message: String, file: StaticString = #file, line: UInt = #line) {
    alertVerifier.verify(
            title: "Network problem",
            message: message,
            animated: true,
            actions: [
                .default("OK"),
            ],
            presentingViewController: sut,
            file: file,
            line: line
    )
    XCTAssertEqual(alertVerifier.preferredAction?.title, "OK",
            "preferred action", file: file, line: line)
}
```

Since these assertions live outside of a test case method, the helper takes the
file name and line number of the call site. We pass these arguments down to

each assertion. That way, if there's a failure, the assertion will identify the call site, not the helper.

With our helpers in place, we can write our first error test:

NetworkResponse/NetworkResponseTests/ViewControllerTests.swift
```swift
func test_searchForBookNetworkCall_withError_shouldShowAlert() {
    tap(sut.button)
    let alertShown = expectation(description: "alert shown")
    alertVerifier.testCompletion = {
        alertShown.fulfill()
    }

    spyURLSession.dataTaskArgsCompletionHandler.first?(
            nil, nil, TestError(message: "oh no")
    )

    waitForExpectations(timeout: 0.01)
    verifyErrorAlert(message: "oh no")
}
```

The first line of the Arrange section is the button tap to trigger the data task. This sets up the completion handler, which spyURLSession captures.

In the rest of the Arrange section, we set up an XCTestExpectation that an alert was shown. We need this because the alert is created and presented inside the DispatchQueue.main.async closure. To fulfill the expectation, we set up a testCompletion closure on the alertVerifier. The ViewControllerPresentationSpy framework calls this closure when an alert is presented.

The middle Act section calls the captured completion handler. This time, we pass in a TestError with an arbitrary message.

The final Assert section waits a short time for the expectation. It then uses our big helper to verify that an alert was presented with the given message. Change the message temporarily and run the tests. You'll see a failure for the alert message. And by doing all that work to pass on the file name and line number of the call site, the failure will point to the verifyErrorAlert(message:) call.

Change the message back and run the tests again to see them pass.

This is good. But we need one more test for this error case. Since tests run on the main thread, someone might move the alert stuff out of async closure. test_searchForBookNetworkCall_withError_shouldShowAlert() would still pass, but it would fail in real life because the closure is run on a background thread. We need to do what we did for Keep Asynchronous Code in Its Closure, on page 163 by adding another test that ignores the async closure:

NetworkResponse/NetworkResponseTests/ViewControllerTests.swift
```swift
func test_searchForBookNetworkCall_withErrorPreAsync_shouldNotShowAlert() {
    tap(sut.button)

    spyURLSession.dataTaskArgsCompletionHandler.first?(
            nil, nil, TestError(message: "DUMMY")
    )

    XCTAssertEqual(alertVerifier.presentedCount, 0)
}
```

There's no XCTestExpectation in this test and no waiting. So it blazes through without invoking the DispatchQueue.main.async closure.

The two error tests show that if the data task completion handler receives an error argument, it will show an alert. But it won't attempt to show this alert from its own thread (which will be a background thread in real life).

Key Takeaways

To test closures, make a test spy that captures the closure. The test should trigger the call that sends the closure, which the test spy captures. The test can then invoke the closure with any arguments it wants.

For network responses, testing the closure with various inputs will let you exercise all sorts of scenarios, including the following:

- Success responses with valid data
- Success responses but with incomplete or malformed data
- Responses with HTTP status codes other than 200 "OK"
- Errors

Unit testing makes it possible to test scenarios that would be hard to simulate in real life.

You've also seen how to use test expectations to test asynchronous code. Be warned that there are cases that can cause expectations to crash your tests. For details and workarounds, read Jeremy Sherman's "XCTestExpectation Gotchas."[2]

Tests of asynchronous code should generally come in pairs. One test should use a test expectation to wait until the asynchronous code is called. Another test should skip the test expectations, avoiding the asynchronous code. The second test shows that the desired outcome happens because it's in an async closure.

---

2. https://jeremywsherman.com/blog/2016/03/19/xctestexpectation-gotchas/

Activities

To help solidify this chapter in your head, pick one of the following activities. (The first three have sample solutions in this book's accompanying source code.)

1. Test another error scenario: What if the JSON is incomplete? Write a test to call the data task completion handler with a 200 "OK" response, but remove a field from the JSON data. Test the resulting alert.

2. Here's yet another error scenario: What if we receive a response from the server, but the HTTP status code is something other than a 200 "OK" response? Test the alert.

3. Add tests showing how the button is disabled when searchForBook(terms:) is called and is enabled again by the async closure.

4. In the Activities, on page 151 for testing network requests, did you find places in your code that call simple web services? Build on the foundation of those tests by adding tests for network responses. Start with the happy paths of processing successful responses. Then build on those, testing error scenarios.

What's Next?

Now you can test the second half of networking. The trick is to use a test spy to capture the closure. Then call the closure with various arguments.

You've also seen how to use test expectations to test asynchronous code. Create an expectation, fulfill it in a completion closure, and wait for it.

In the next chapter, let's get back to handling user input. We'll explore text fields, which will show us how to test delegate methods.

CHAPTER 14

Testing Text Fields (and Delegate Methods)

Text fields are another common means of user input. We can customize the behavior of text fields using delegates. Delegate methods give us a way to insert our own code into Cocoa Touch's flow of control.

In this chapter you'll learn how to test text fields. You'll be able to write tests for delegate methods in a way that makes refactoring them easier, not harder. Along the way, you'll learn how to assert against Objective-C enumerations and against optional Bools. You'll also pick up a trick we need to test which text field has input focus.

Make a Place to Play

You know the drill. Create a new project by following the steps for Create a Place to Play with Tests, on page 4, but give it the name TextField. Delete its initial test file.

Let's use the predefined storyboard-based view controller. Edit ViewController.swift, adding two text field outlets. We'll use them to enter the username and password for a simple login simulation. Declare these outlets private(set) so that our tests can reach them:

TextField/TextField/ViewController.swift
```
@IBOutlet private(set) var usernameField: UITextField!
@IBOutlet private(set) var passwordField: UITextField!
```

We need something to serve as the delegate for the text fields. Let's follow the common practice of using the view controller. (In a later chapter, we'll see how to move away from this practice.) Add a declaration to ViewController that it conforms to the UITextFieldDelegate protocol:

TextField/TextField/ViewController.swift
```
class ViewController: UIViewController, UITextFieldDelegate {
```

Now let's add these text fields to the storyboard. Open Main.storyboard and select *View ▶ Libraries ▶ Show Library* from the Xcode menu or press Shift-⌘-L. This will bring up the Object Library. Click and drag "Text Field" onto the view controller in the main editor area. For this experiment, don't worry about positioning the label or setting any Auto Layout constraints. Do this twice to create two text fields.

Now connect these text fields to their outlets. (You can show ViewController.swift in the Assistant Editor, and drag from the @IBOutlet circles to their respective text fields.)

Let's switch back to viewing one source file. Select *View ▶ Standard Editor ▶ Show Standard Editor* from the Xcode menu or press ⌘-↵.

Since we want to use ViewController as the delegate for the text fields, let's make those connections. Show the Connections Inspector by selecting *View ▶ Inspectors ▶ Show Connections Inspector* from the Xcode menu or press ⌥-⌘-6. Select the first text field. From the Outlets section of the Connection Inspector, click in the open circle next to "delegate" and drag it to the View Controller, as you can see in the image. Repeat this for the second text field.

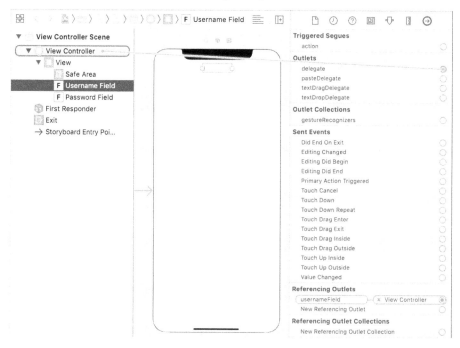

For our last settings in the storyboard, let's set the attributes of the text fields. Show the Attributes Inspector by selecting *View ▶ Inspectors ▶ Show Attributes*

Inspector from the Xcode menu or press ⌥-⌘-4. Select the first text field. In the Text Input Traits section of the Attributes Inspector, make these changes:

- Content Type: Username
- Correction: No
- Return Key: Next

For the second text field, set these attributes:

- Content Type: Password
- Return Key: Go
- Secure Text Entry: Checked

Finally, let's add some delegate methods. Add the following method to the ViewController class. It prevents the user from entering spaces into the username field:

TextField/TextField/ViewController.swift

```
func textField(_ textField: UITextField,
              shouldChangeCharactersIn range: NSRange,
              replacementString string: String) -> Bool {
    if textField === usernameField {
        return !string.contains(" ")
    } else {
        return true
    }
}
```

Let's add one more delegate method. UIKit calls this next method when the user presses the return key. When that happens from usernameField, we shift the keyboard input focus to the password field. When the user presses the return key from passwordField, we hide the keyboard. Then we perform some sort of login. The return value of this only matters in rare cases, so let's return false. We won't bother to test it:

TextField/TextField/ViewController.swift

```
func textFieldShouldReturn(_ textField: UITextField) -> Bool {
    if textField === usernameField {
        passwordField.becomeFirstResponder()
    } else {
        guard let username = usernameField.text,
            let password = passwordField.text else {
            return false
        }
        passwordField.resignFirstResponder()
        performLogin(username: username, password: password)
    }
    return false
}
```

(If you haven't seen === before, this is not the same as checking that two values are equal. Instead, this is checking whether the textField argument *is* usernameField or not.)

Our pretend login method will just print the fields to the console:

TextField/TextField/ViewController.swift

```
private func performLogin(username: String, password: String) {
    print("Username: \(username)")
    print("Password: \(password)")
}
```

Let's manually confirm that the text fields function correctly. Press ⌘-R to run the app. Then select *View ▶ Debug Area ▶ Activate Console* or press Shift-⌘-C to show the console on the bottom right.

Tap into the first text field. The keyboard should appear. (If it doesn't, deselect *Hardware ▶ Keyboard ▶ Connect Hardware Keyboard* in the simulator menu.) Enter any username. Make sure that it doesn't allow you to enter spaces. Tap Next. This will move input focus to the second field.

Enter any password. iOS will conceal the input behind text bullets. Tap Go. The keyboard will disappear, and our pretend login will show what you entered in the console.

Now we have some fairly complex behavior. Part of it is specified in the storyboard. Let's start our testing there. We'll check the outlets, then the storyboard attributes. And we'll add extensions to improve test failure reporting when comparing UIKit types.

Test the Outlets

Before we approach the delegate methods, let's lay down some tests of the storyboard settings. Start by adding a test suite ViewControllerTests. Use Test Zero as temporary scaffolding to confirm that you hooked up the test suite. (See Start from Test Zero, on page 21.) Delete Test Zero once you see its expected failure message.

Following Chapter 7, Testing Outlet Connections, on page 95, add a test named test_outlets_shouldBeConnected(). Begin the test by following Load a Storyboard-Based View Controller, on page 64 to load ViewController from the storyboard. Remember that this also means editing Main.storyboard to give the view controller a Storyboard ID. Run the tests, which should pass.

Finish off this test by asserting that the outlets aren't nil:

TextField/TextFieldTests/ViewControllerTests.swift
```
XCTAssertNotNil(sut.usernameField, "usernameField")
XCTAssertNotNil(sut.passwordField, "passwordField")
```

Recall from Test Outlet Connections, on page 96 that when a test case has more than one assertion, it helps to add descriptive messages to identify them. Run the tests, which should pass.

Test Attributes and Wrangle UIKit Descriptions

Next, let's add a test to confirm the attributes of the username text field. But testing every single attribute is overkill. Let's only test the attributes we changed from their default settings. Add a test named test_username-Field_attributesShouldBeSet(). Copy and paste the content of the outlet test, except for its assertions. Then add the following assertions and run the tests:

TextField/TextFieldTests/ViewControllerTests.swift
```
let textField = sut.usernameField!
XCTAssertEqual(textField.textContentType, .username, "textContentType")
XCTAssertEqual(textField.autocorrectionType, .no, "autocorrectionType")
XCTAssertEqual(textField.returnKeyType, .next, "returnKeyType")
```

The tests pass. But let's see what the failure messages look like. We'll do this by following Check the Effectiveness of Failure Messages, on page 97 and breaking the production code on purpose. Open Main.storyboard. Show the Attributes Inspector by selecting *View ▶ Inspectors ▶ Show Attributes Inspector* from the Xcode menu or press ⌥-⌘-4. Select the first text field. In the Text Input Traits section of the Attributes Inspector, change "Content Type" from "Username" to "Password." Run the tests, and you'll see this failure message:

```
XCTAssertEqual failed:
  ("Optional(__C.UITextContentType(_rawValue: password))") is not equal to
  ("Optional(__C.UITextContentType(_rawValue: username))") - textContentType
```

This is pretty noisy. Let's see if we can improve on it by digging into the underlying type. Place your cursor in textContentType, then select *Navigate ▶ Jump to Definition* from the Xcode menu or press ^-⌘-J. This will show you UIKit's definition of the property.

```
@available(iOS 10.0, *)
optional public var textContentType: UITextContentType! { get set }
  // default is nil
```

Now place your cursor in UITextContentType and jump to its definition. Here's what you'll see:

```
public struct UITextContentType : Hashable, Equatable, RawRepresentable
```

We can see that UITextContentType doesn't conform to CustomStringConvertible. Recall from Describe Objects upon Failure, on page 10 that CustomStringConvertible defines how a type describes itself in assertions. So let's extend UITextContentType to conform to this protocol. We'll make a separate file for test helpers.

In the Project Navigator, select the TextFieldTests group and press ⌘-N to make a new file. Select Swift File, name it TestHelpers.swift, and set its target to the test target. Add an import UIKit declaration to the top, then add the following empty extension:

TextField/TextFieldTests/TestHelpers.swift
```
extension UITextContentType: CustomStringConvertible {
}
```

Because we haven't implemented anything yet, Swift will complain that the type doesn't conform to the protocol. Select *Editor ▶ Fix All Issues* in the Xcode menu. This will generate the stub. Fill in the rest as shown here:

TextField/TextFieldTests/TestHelpers.swift
```
public var description: String { rawValue }
```

Run the tests again. This time, we'll get the following message:

```
XCTAssertEqual failed: ("Optional(password)") is not equal to
  ("Optional(username)") - textContentType
```

That's better. Let's reset the storyboard and move on to the next assertion. Go back to Main.storyboard and press ⌘-Z to undo the change. Select the first text field again. This time, change "Correction" from "No" to "Yes." Run the tests and look at the failure message:

```
XCTAssertEqual failed: ("UITextAutocorrectionType") is not equal to
  ("UITextAutocorrectionType") - autocorrectionType
```

Oh dear. This tells us the type but nothing about the values.

Swift knows how to describe enumerations written in Swift but stumbles over enumerations written in Objective-C. This is especially noticeable for the Cocoa Touch frameworks, which have Objective-C interfaces.

Let's dig into the underlying type. Place your cursor in autocorrectionType, then select *Navigate ▶ Jump to Definition* from the Xcode menu or press ^-⌘-J. Here is UIKit's definition of the property:

```
optional public var autocorrectionType: UITextAutocorrectionType { get set }
  // default is UITextAutocorrectionTypeDefault
```

Now place your cursor in UITextAutocorrectionType and jump to its definition:

```
public enum UITextAutocorrectionType : Int {
    case `default`
    case no
    case yes
}
```

Once again, we can see that this type doesn't conform to the CustomStringConvertible protocol. Let's add an empty extension to our test code:

TextField/TextFieldTests/TestHelpers.swift
```
extension UITextAutocorrectionType: CustomStringConvertible {
}
```

This results in the following error:

```
Type 'UITextAutocorrectionType' does not conform to protocol
  'CustomStringConvertible'
```

Select *Editor ▶ Fix All Issues* in the Xcode menu to generate the method stub. Since we want a description for each case, let's switch on self:

TextField/TextFieldTests/TestHelpers.swift
```
public var description: String {
    switch self {
    }
}
```

Now we get this error:

```
Switch must be exhaustive
```

Again, select *Editor ▶ Fix All Issues* in the Xcode menu. This gives us all the case statements for the enumeration. For each case (except for Swift 5's @unknown default), return a string:

TextField/TextFieldTests/TestHelpers.swift
```
public var description: String {
    switch self {
    case .default:
        return "default"
    case .no:
        return "no"
    case .yes:
        return "yes"
    @unknown default:
        fatalError("Unknown UITextAutocorrectionType")
    }
}
```

Run the tests again. This time, we'll get the following message:

```
XCTAssertEqual failed: ("yes") is not equal to ("no") - autocorrectionType
```

Now that is a useful failure message.

 Be careful when using XCTAssertEqual with types declared in Objective-C. Introduce an error to check the failure message. Where needed, add an extension to make the type conform to the CustomStringConvertible protocol.

Let's move on to the last assertion in test_usernameField_attributesShouldBeSet(). Undo the previous change in the storyboard and select the first text field. This time, change Return Key from "Next" to "Join." Run the tests and look at the failure message:

```
XCTAssertEqual failed: ("UIReturnKeyType") is not equal to
  ("UIReturnKeyType") - returnKeyType
```

Following the preceding steps, create an extension so that UIReturnKeyType conforms to CustomStringConvertible, describing each case. Run the tests to confirm the improved failure message:

```
XCTAssertEqual failed: ("join") is not equal to ("next") - returnKeyType
```

We now have duplicate code between the tests to load the view controller. Following Move the SUT into the Test Fixture, on page 112, let's extract this. For storyboard-based view controllers, remember to change the type cast from as! to as? to silence the warning about assigning to an optional:

```
TextField/TextFieldTests/ViewControllerTests.swift
private var sut: ViewController!

override func setUp() {
    super.setUp()
    let storyboard = UIStoryboard(name: "Main", bundle: nil)
    sut = storyboard.instantiateViewController(
            identifier: String(describing: ViewController.self))
    sut.loadViewIfNeeded()
}

override func tearDown() {
    executeRunLoop()
    sut = nil
    super.tearDown()
}
```

Finally, we can test the attributes of the password text field. Let's do this in another test case. We check each text field in its own test case instead of combining the tests, as explained in Why Not Combine Similar Tests?, on page 137.

TextField/TextFieldTests/ViewControllerTests.swift
```swift
func test_passwordField_attributesShouldBeSet() {
    let textField = sut.passwordField!
    XCTAssertEqual(textField.textContentType, .password, "textContentType")
    XCTAssertEqual(textField.returnKeyType, .go, "returnKeyType")
    XCTAssertTrue(textField.isSecureTextEntry, "isSecureTextEntry")
}
```

Run tests to confirm that this passes. We've already improved the types used, so these tests will report useful error messages.

With this, we've tested the text field attributes as defined in the storyboard. In the rest of this chapter, let's see how to test the code. We'll look at delegate methods, and finish by testing input focus—that is, the first responder.

Test Delegate Methods

Delegate methods are the classic way for Cocoa Touch to call back to our code. Thankfully, we don't have to try to coax this to happen in test code. For unit tests, it doesn't matter what calls a delegate method. We only have to mimic the arguments and call the method directly. So what Cocoa Touch would call, the test calls.

Let's consider how to test the first delegate method, textField(_:shouldChangeCharactersIn:replacementString:). To test with a naive approach, we do two things:

- First, test that the delegate of the text field is the view controller.
- Second, call the delegate method directly on the view controller.

The problem with this approach is that it locks down who gets to be the delegate. Programmers earlier in their Cocoa Touch experience will always use the view controller. This results in a view controller that conforms to several delegate protocols. The common joke in iOS circles is that MVC stands for "Massive View Controller."

But there's nothing about the delegate pattern that says you have to do this. A good way to slim down a Massive View Controller is to extract delegates into their own types. With a little care, we can move delegation around without changing any tests. Ideally, tests should strive to check behavior (like what a delegate method does). Tests shouldn't care about implementation details (like where a delegate method lives). Here's how to write tests that stay ignorant of the location of delegate methods:

- First, test that the delegate of the text field is set. It doesn't matter what it is, as long as it's not nil.

- Second, call the delegate method on the delegate. We do so by asking the text field for its delegate, then calling the method we want.

In theory, we could do without the first type of test, since the second type of test will fail if the delegate is nil. But it would be trickier to diagnose. Just as we test outlets with Chapter 7, Testing Outlet Connections, on page 95, we can save time by testing that we've assigned those delegates. Add the following test to check that they're not nil:

TextField/TextFieldTests/ViewControllerTests.swift
```swift
func test_textFieldDelegates_shouldBeConnected() {
    XCTAssertNotNil(sut.usernameField.delegate, "usernameField")
    XCTAssertNotNil(sut.passwordField.delegate, "passwordField")
}
```

Run the tests, which should pass.

Next, let's test the first delegate method. The job of textField(_:shouldChangeCharactersIn:replacementString:) is to determine whether to replace some text in a text field. It takes a replacement string instead of a single character since the user can paste text. The code prevents the entry of spaces in the username field. We need at least three tests:

- Don't allow spaces in the username.
- Do allow text without spaces in the username.
- Allow any text in the password.

(This isn't intended to be a prescription for how to code your entry fields. I'm just describing what this example does so we can test its behavior.)

Add the following test. Run tests to confirm that it passes:

TextField/TextFieldTests/ViewControllerTests.swift
```swift
func test_shouldChangeCharacters_usernameWithSpaces_shouldPreventChange() {
    let allowChange = sut.usernameField.delegate?.textField?(
            sut.usernameField,
            shouldChangeCharactersIn: NSRange(),
            replacementString: "a b")

    XCTAssertEqual(allowChange, false)
}
```

To reach the text field delegate, we're *not* simply calling the view controller. Instead, we ask the username text field for its delegate. This way, the test will continue to work, even if we switch the delegate to another object.

For this test, the replacement string contains a space, as if the user pasted it. We don't want to allow it to enter this text field.

Since the call uses optional chaining, the result is an optional Bool. So it may be true, false, or nil. We can't use XCTAssertFalse(_:), which requires a Bool. Instead, we used XCTAssertEqual(_:_:) to assert that the result is false.

 To assert that a Bool? value is true or false, use XCTAssertEqual(_:_:). If there's a mismatch, it'll report the actual value.

The test works, but it's cumbersome to get the text field delegate and then pass that same text field as the first argument. Let's extract a helper to make the tests more readable. Put this, and other helpers, in a separate file, like TestHelpers.swift, so it'll be available to other suites:

TextField/TextFieldTests/TestHelpers.swift
```
func shouldChangeCharacters(in textField: UITextField,
                            range: NSRange = NSRange(),
                            replacement: String) -> Bool? {
    textField.delegate?.textField?(
        textField,
        shouldChangeCharactersIn: range,
        replacementString: replacement)
}
```

Since the range of characters to replace will often (but not always) be empty, it's handy to give that parameter an empty range as a default value. This simplifies the test code:

TextField/TextFieldTests/ViewControllerTests.swift
```
let allowChange = shouldChangeCharacters(in: sut.usernameField,
        replacement: "a b")
```

Run the tests to confirm that everything is still happy with these changes. Now it's easy to add a new test that the username field allows text without spaces:

TextField/TextFieldTests/ViewControllerTests.swift
```
func test_shouldChangeCharacters_usernameWithoutSpaces_shouldAllowChange() {
    let allowChange = shouldChangeCharacters(in: sut.usernameField,
            replacement: "abc")

    XCTAssertEqual(allowChange, true)
}
```

Run the tests, which should pass. Finally, we need to test the password field. It should accept all text changes. Since it's going through the same method that handles the username field, let's add tests of two replacement strings: one with a space, and one without:

TextField/TextFieldTests/ViewControllerTests.swift
```
func test_shouldChangeCharacters_passwordWithSpaces_shouldAllowChange() {
    let allowChange = shouldChangeCharacters(in: sut.passwordField,
            replacement: "a b")

    XCTAssertEqual(allowChange, true)
}
func test_shouldChangeCharacters_passwordWithoutSpaces_shouldAllowChange() {
    let allowChange = shouldChangeCharacters(in: sut.passwordField,
            replacement: "abc")

    XCTAssertEqual(allowChange, true)
}
```

We now have tests fully covering the text field delegate method textField(_:shouldChangeCharactersIn:replacementString:).

Test Input Focus

We have one more delegate method, textFieldShouldReturn(_:). It does two things:

- When the user presses the return key in the username field, the input focus should move to the password field.

- When the user presses the return key in the password field, the keyboard should be dismissed, and the login process should start.

Let's start with the second behavior (logging in) before moving to the challenge of testing keyboard input focus. Add a test that populates the text fields, and confirms that pressing the return key in the password field starts the login process. As we did in Test Delegate Methods, on page 177, we'll ask the text field for its delegate and talk to it:

TextField/TextFieldTests/ViewControllerTests.swift
```
func test_shouldReturn_withPassword_shouldPerformLogin() {
    sut.usernameField.text = "USERNAME"
    sut.passwordField.text = "PASSWORD"

    _ = sut.passwordField.delegate?.textFieldShouldReturn?(sut.passwordField)

    // Normally, assert something
}
```

Run the tests. Our pretend login method only prints to the console, so we'll check that instead of asserting as we normally would. Following Examine Console Output, on page 23, drill down in the test results until you find the output for this test. You should see this:

```
Username: USERNAME
Password: PASSWORD
```

Next, let's extract a helper for this delegate method. Most tests can ignore this delegate method's return value, so declare this helper with @discardableResult:

TextField/TextFieldTests/TestHelpers.swift
```
@discardableResult func shouldReturn(in textField: UITextField) -> Bool? {
    textField.delegate?.textFieldShouldReturn?(textField)
}
```

Using this helper, it's easier to write tests that check the return key behavior:

TextField/TextFieldTests/ViewControllerTests.swift
```
func test_shouldReturn_withPassword_shouldPerformLogin() {
    sut.usernameField.text = "USERNAME"
    sut.passwordField.text = "PASSWORD"

    shouldReturn(in: sut.passwordField)

    // Normally, assert something
}
```

With this test in place, let's now try to test the input focus. Pressing the return key in the username field should move the focus to the password field by calling becomeFirstResponder(). So you'd think we'd be able to test the isFirstResponder property as follows:

TextField/TextFieldTests/ViewControllerTests.swift
```
func test_shouldReturn_withUsername_shouldMoveInputFocusToPassword() {
    shouldReturn(in: sut.usernameField)

    XCTAssertTrue(sut.passwordField.isFirstResponder)
}
```

Run the tests...but this one will fail. Unfortunately, this test won't work without some extra help. For changes to the first responder to take effect, UIKit needs the view to live inside a view hierarchy. Add the following helper:

TextField/TextFieldTests/TestHelpers.swift
```
func putInViewHierarchy(_ vc: UIViewController) {
    let window = UIWindow()
    window.addSubview(vc.view)
}
```

Let's put the view controller in a view hierarchy in the test's Arrange section:

TextField/TextFieldTests/ViewControllerTests.swift
```
func test_shouldReturn_withUsername_shouldMoveInputFocusToPassword() {
    putInViewHierarchy(sut)

    shouldReturn(in: sut.usernameField)

    XCTAssertTrue(sut.passwordField.isFirstResponder)
}
```

Run the tests. This time, the latest test passes.

To test keyboard input focus, add the view controller's view to a UIWindow beforehand.

To test that a text field resigns the first responder, we need to make it the first responder in the Arrange section. Now we can write a test that puts the focus on the password field and confirms that pressing the return key removes that focus:

TextField/TextFieldTests/ViewControllerTests.swift
```
func test_shouldReturn_withPassword_shouldDismissKeyboard() {
    putInViewHierarchy(sut)
    sut.passwordField.becomeFirstResponder()
    XCTAssertTrue(sut.passwordField.isFirstResponder, "precondition")

    shouldReturn(in: sut.passwordField)

    XCTAssertFalse(sut.passwordField.isFirstResponder)
}
```

It's sometimes helpful to put an assertion in the Arrange section to confirm a precondition. This essentially acts as a test of the putFocusOn(textField:) helper method. By mirroring the opposite assertion at the end, we can clearly see that the lines in between caused this state to change.

Unfortunately, adding a view controller's view to a window keeps it in memory past the lifetime of the test. To see this, add the following to ViewController:

TextField/TextField/ViewController.swift
```
deinit {
    print("ViewController.deinit")
}
```

Run all tests, then check the console output. You'll see ViewController.deinit sprinkled here and there. But check the very bottom of the output after all test have completed.

```
Test Suite 'All tests' passed at 2019-05-30 17:13:17.930.
   Executed 11 tests, with 0 failures (0 unexpected) in 0.035 (0.041) seconds
ViewController.deinit
```

As you can see, a stray view controller has managed to stay alive past the end of all tests. This violates the clean room goal of Chapter 2, Manage Your Test Life Cycles, on page 19. Drill into the console output for test_shouldReturn_withPassword_shouldDismissKeyboard() and you'll see that it's missing the expected deinit logging.

As we did with Test Segue-Based Push Navigation, on page 124, UIKit will clean up the window if we give the run loop a kick. To make it easier to execute the run loop one time, add the following helper:

TextField/TextFieldTests/TestHelpers.swift
```
func executeRunLoop() {
    RunLoop.current.run(until: Date())
}
```

Then execute the run loop in tearDown() after setting everything in the test fixture to nil.

TextField/TextFieldTests/ViewControllerTests.swift
```
override func tearDown() {
    executeRunLoop()
    sut = nil
    super.tearDown()
}
```

We need to do this whenever any test code calls the putInViewHierarchy() helper. Run tests one more time to confirm that this fixes the memory problem.

Key Takeaways

Let's review the main points from this chapter:

- To test delegate methods, don't directly call the object that implements it. That would lock down that particular class as the delegate. Instead, request the delegate (whatever it is) and call through it. This allows the delegate to move in future refactoring without breaking tests.

- Getting an object's delegate and passing that same object as an argument makes for clumsy test code. You've seen how extracting helper functions (sometimes with default arguments) can go a long way to making test code easy to write and easy to read.

- Some types written in Objective-C need help describing themselves, especially enumerations. Add extensions so these types conform to the CustomStringConvertible protocol. And you've learned that to assert against a Bool? value, you can use XCTAssertEqual(_:_:).

- To test the first responder, the view needs to be in a view hierarchy for input focus to take effect.

- If you add anything to a temporary UIWindow, execute the run loop in tearDown() so that UIKit releases the window. This avoids memory leaks.

Activities

To solidify your learning from this chapter, try one or more of these activities. Start with the first one and work down as far as you want to.

1. Search your code for any classes that conform to UITextFieldDelegate or UITextViewDelegate. Add tests that the fields using these classes as delegates have non-nil delegates.

2. Choose a simple delegate method with no references to the first responder, and write one test for it. Make sure not to directly call the object that provides the method but to call through the delegate.

3. Extract a helper function to simplify the test. Put this helper in a file of test helpers so you can use them across your test suites.

4. Expand your testing into delegate methods that set or resign the first responder.

What's Next?

Now you can test delegate methods. You know not to directly call the object that implements it since that locks it down as the delegate.

Perhaps the most common delegates are those of table views. In the next chapter, we'll look at an example of testing a UITableView.

CHAPTER 15

Testing Table Views

In the previous chapter, we saw how to test delegate methods, focusing our example on text fields. But the most common use of delegates is probably for table views.

Though the principles are the same as Chapter 14, Testing Text Fields (and Delegate Methods), on page 169, let's work through a table view example. A table view has two delegates: one focusing on content, and the other on actions. In this chapter, you'll learn how to test table views. You'll be able to test table view output (displaying cells) and input (cell selection).

Make a Place to Play

It's time for another project. Copy the steps from Create a Place to Play with Tests, on page 4, but use TableView as the project name. Delete its initial test file as usual.

In the Project Navigator, select the TableView group. Create a new file, selecting Cocoa Touch Class, and make it a subclass of UITableViewController.

With this new file in place, delete the old file ViewController.swift.

Next, let's put this in the storyboard. Edit Main.storyboard, select "View Controller Scene," and press ⌫ to delete it. Select *View ▸ Libraries ▸ Show Library* from the Xcode menu or press Shift-⌘-L to bring up the Object Library. Double-click "Table View Controller" to add it to the storyboard. Now let's modify it. In the storyboard, select "Table View Controller Scene." Then in the Xcode menu, select *View ▸ Inspectors ▸ Show Identity Inspector* or press ⌥-⌘-3. In the Identity Inspector on the right, in the Custom Class section, click the Class pull-down menu. Select the class we just made, TableViewController, like you see in the image on page 186.

Show the Attributes Inspector by selecting *View ▶ Inspectors ▶ Show Attributes Inspector* from the Xcode menu or press ⌥-⌘-5. In the View Controller section, shown here, select "Is Initial View Controller."

Xcode still shows a warning symbol. Click on the symbol, or select *View ▶ Navigators ▶ Show Issue Navigator*, or press ⌘-5. Under "Unsupported Configuration," click the warning that says the following:

```
Prototype table cells must have reuse identifiers
```

This will select "Table View Cell." In the Attributes Inspector on the right, in the Table View Cell section (shown in the following image), enter cell as the identifier.

Before we work on the code, let's make sure this shows an empty table. Set your destination to an iOS simulator, then press ⌘-R to run the app. You should see a table with empty rows.

Now delete the generated contents of the TableViewController class. Define the following property, which will serve as our simple model:

TableView/TableView/TableViewController.swift
```
private let model = [
    "One",
    "Two",
    "Three"
]
```

Add these methods to display this model:

TableView/TableView/TableViewController.swift
```
override func tableView(_ tableView: UITableView,
                        numberOfRowsInSection section: Int) -> Int {
    model.count
}

override func tableView(_ tableView: UITableView,
                        cellForRowAt indexPath: IndexPath)
            -> UITableViewCell {
    let cell = tableView.dequeueReusableCell(
        withIdentifier: "cell", for: indexPath)
    cell.textLabel?.text = model[indexPath.row]
    return cell
}
```

And when a row is selected, we'll print the selected row to the console:

TableView/TableView/TableViewController.swift
```
override func tableView(_ tableView: UITableView,
                        didSelectRowAt indexPath: IndexPath) {
    print(model[indexPath.row])
}
```

Let's make sure this table works. Run the app. You should see three rows, showing "One," "Two," and "Three." Select *View ▶ Debug Area ▶ Activate Console* or press Shift-⌘-C to show the console on the bottom right. Tap each row to confirm that the app prints the selected row in the console.

Now that we have a table view, let's see how to write tests for it. In most cases, all we need to do is test that each delegate method does what we want.

Test Table Views

You've already learned how to test delegate methods in Chapter 14, Testing Text Fields (and Delegate Methods), on page 169. Testing table views isn't much more complicated. All we have to do is manage two delegates, not one: the UITableViewDataSource and the UITableViewDelegate.

Add a new test suite, TableViewControllerTests, using the Test Zero technique from Start from Test Zero, on page 21. Once it reports the expected failure, delete Test Zero.

Let's now test that the table view's delegates exist. Though a UITableViewController serves as its own delegates by default, we may want to change that in the future. The following test ensures that we have the connections we need. Add an empty test case named test_tableViewDelegates_shouldBeConnected().

Inside this test, follow Load a Storyboard-Based View Controller, on page 64 to load TableViewController from the storyboard. Remember that this also means editing Main.storyboard to give the view controller a Storyboard ID. Run the tests, which should pass.

Finish off this test by asserting that the view controller's table view has both delegates:

TableView/TableViewTests/TableViewControllerTests.swift
```
XCTAssertNotNil(sut.tableView.dataSource, "dataSource")
XCTAssertNotNil(sut.tableView.delegate, "delegate")
```

Run the tests, which should pass. Next, let's start testing those delegate methods. The first method tableView(_:numberOfRowsInSection:) is a data source method. Add a new test named test_numberOfRows_shouldBe3(). To load the view controller, copy and paste that part from the previous test. Then add the following assertion, and run the tests:

TableView/TableViewTests/TableViewControllerTests.swift
```
XCTAssertEqual(sut.tableView.dataSource?.tableView(
        sut.tableView, numberOfRowsInSection: 0), 3)
```

Note that we're calling the method indirectly through the dataSource delegate. As we did in Chapter 14, Testing Text Fields (and Delegate Methods), on page 169, avoid calling delegate methods directly against the view controller. This gives you the possibility of moving the delegate methods to another object. The tests don't need to know where they're implemented.

Most of the time, tests should provide their own models to view controllers. But here, we rely on our knowledge that the built-in model has three entries.

Since the code to load the view controller is duplicated, let's follow Move the SUT into the Test Fixture, on page 112 to extract it. Remember to change the type cast from as! to as? to silence the warning about assigning to an optional:

TableView/TableViewTests/TableViewControllerTests.swift
```
private var sut: TableViewController!

override func setUp() {
    super.setUp()
    let storyboard = UIStoryboard(name: "Main", bundle: nil)
    sut = storyboard.instantiateViewController(
            identifier: String(describing: TableViewController.self))
    sut.loadViewIfNeeded()
}

override func tearDown() {
    sut = nil
    super.tearDown()
}
```

Run the tests to make sure they still pass. Now let's clean up that awkward call to the delegate method. Again, let's make a separate file for test helpers. Name it TestHelpers.swift and set its target to the test target. Add an import UIKit declaration to the top.

Add the following helper function. Many table views have just one section, so declaring 0 as the default for section can be helpful:

TableView/TableViewTests/TestHelpers.swift
```
func numberOfRows(in tableView: UITableView, section: Int = 0) -> Int? {
    tableView.dataSource?.tableView(
        tableView, numberOfRowsInSection: section)
}
```

This simplifies our test:

TableView/TableViewTests/TableViewControllerTests.swift
```
func test_numberOfRows_shouldBe3() {
    XCTAssertEqual(numberOfRows(in: sut.tableView), 3)
}
```

Next, let's test tableView(_:cellForRowAt:). Any helper function is best when there's more than one example driving it, so let's start with two tests:

TableView/TableViewTests/TableViewControllerTests.swift
```
func test_cellForRowAt_withRow0_shouldSetCellLabelToOne() {
    let cell = sut.tableView.dataSource?.tableView(
            sut.tableView, cellForRowAt: IndexPath(row: 0, section: 0))

    XCTAssertEqual(cell?.textLabel?.text, "One")
}
func test_cellForRowAt_withRow1_shouldSetCellLabelToTwo() {
    let cell = sut.tableView.dataSource?.tableView(
            sut.tableView, cellForRowAt: IndexPath(row: 1, section: 0))

    XCTAssertEqual(cell?.textLabel?.text, "Two")
}
```

Run the tests, which should pass. Now we can see that the value that's varying between the tests is row. Let's create a helper that hides the IndexPath, using 0 for the section by default:

TableView/TableViewTests/TestHelpers.swift
```
func cellForRow(in tableView: UITableView, row: Int, section: Int = 0)
    -> UITableViewCell? {
    tableView.dataSource?.tableView(
        tableView, cellForRowAt: IndexPath(row: row, section: section))
}
```

Using this new helper, let's clean up our two tests and add the third. Run the tests to see them pass.

TableView/TableViewTests/TableViewControllerTests.swift
```
func test_cellForRow_withRow0_shouldSetCellLabelToOne() {
    let cell = cellForRow(in: sut.tableView, row: 0)

    XCTAssertEqual(cell?.textLabel?.text, "One")
}

func test_cellForRow_withRow1_shouldSetCellLabelToTwo() {
    let cell = cellForRow(in: sut.tableView, row: 1)

    XCTAssertEqual(cell?.textLabel?.text, "Two")
}

func test_cellForRow_withRow2_shouldSetCellLabelToThree() {
    let cell = cellForRow(in: sut.tableView, row: 2)

    XCTAssertEqual(cell?.textLabel?.text, "Three")
}
```

Finally, let's test tableView(_:didSelectRowAt:), which handles row selection. The only thing we need to be careful about is that we talk to the correct delegate. While the dataSource provides cell content, the delegate handles cell selection.

In our example, tapping a row prints to the console instead of doing actual work. Here's a test that taps row 1 (the second row, counting from row 0):

TableView/TableViewTests/TableViewControllerTests.swift
```
func test_didSelectRow_withRow1() {
    sut.tableView.delegate?.tableView?(
            sut.tableView, didSelectRowAt: IndexPath(row: 1, section: 0))

    // Normally, assert something
}
```

Run the tests and follow Examine Console Output, on page 23 to drill down to the test results. You should see something like this:

Two

Now we can extract a helper function. Once again, it hides the IndexPath and uses a section of 0 unless told otherwise:

TableView/TableViewTests/TestHelpers.swift
```
func didSelectRow(in tableView: UITableView, row: Int, section: Int = 0) {
    tableView.delegate?.tableView?(
        tableView, didSelectRowAt: IndexPath(row: row, section: section))
}
```

Then we can clean up the test to use this helper:

TableView/TableViewTests/TableViewControllerTests.swift
```
func test_didSelectRow_withRow1() {
    didSelectRow(in: sut.tableView, row: 1)

    // Normally, assert something
}
```

Run all tests to confirm that everything passes. We don't have an assertion on this last test, so drill down into the test results again to confirm that it prints Two. We've now successfully opened the door to testing this table view. The rest would be assertions confirming the behavior of tapping different rows.

Key Takeaways

Testing table views is a continuation of testing delegate methods. So the same techniques from Chapter 14, Testing Text Fields (and Delegate Methods), on page 169 apply, except that table views have two delegates instead of one.

- Write a test to confirm that the table view's dataSource and delegate aren't nil. Remember to call methods through the appropriate delegate.

- There's a lot of opportunity to extract test helpers for table view delegate methods. Doing so will lead to simpler test code, especially if you give the section number a default value of 0.

Activities

You can use the following activities to sink this chapter into your brain. Start with the first. Work down as far as you want to go.

1. Search your code for any classes that use table views. Add tests to ensure that their data sources and delegates are non-nil.

2. Choose a simple table with one kind of cell. Write a test that creates a data model, then checks the number of rows.

3. Write another test that gets a cell. Use a guard let to cast the cell to your cell subclass. If the cast is unsuccessful, report the failure with XCTFail() and do an early return. Otherwise, test that the cell contents are correct.

4. Extract helper functions to simplify the data source tests. Put these helpers in a file of test helpers you can use across your test suites.

5. Expand your testing into table view delegate methods that handle cell selection. For example, if selecting a cell pushes another view controller, apply Chapter 10, Testing Navigation Between Screens, on page 115 (as long as you're not using segues).

What's Next?

Now you can test table views. As you can see, they're not very different from testing other delegate methods. Since table views have two delegates, direct your calls through the right delegate.

As you did with Chapter 14, Testing Text Fields (and Delegate Methods), on page 169, extract helper functions to keep your tests clean.

We've now tested the behavior of various view controllers. But what about their appearance? In the next chapter, we explore a way to test how views look.

CHAPTER 16

Testing View Appearance (with Snapshots)

Until now, we've focused on unit testing the behavior of view controllers. But view controllers don't just manage input and output. They lay out views, and we want those views to look good. How do we test their appearance?

In this chapter, you'll learn how to write *snapshot tests* to compare views with reference images. We'll use the FBSnapshotTestCase library for our example.[1] By writing snapshot tests for your views, you'll be able to make changes to view layouts and test the results.

Because you won't have to manually navigate through your view controllers and then do visual comparisons, this is a huge time saver. It's also good for testing custom views.

Make a Place to Play

Let's make a new project for this chapter's learning experience. Follow the steps for Create a Place to Play with Tests, on page 4 to create a new project, but give it the name Snapshot. Delete its initial test file.

We'll use the predefined storyboard, adding some visual elements. Edit Main.storyboard. Feel free to add any UI elements you want using correct Auto Layout constraints with no warnings.

If you arranged your own elements with no warnings, you can proceed to the next section. Or you can follow along with this example. Open Main.storyboard and select *View ▶ Libraries ▶ Show Library* from the Xcode menu or press Shift-⌘-L. This will bring up the Object Library. Drag a label, a slider, and a button into the View Controller Scene.

---

1. https://github.com/uber/ios-snapshot-test-case

Select the label. In the bottom right of the storyboard editor, hover your mouse cursor over the icon showing a square between two margins. This will reveal the help tag "Add New Constraints." Click the icon. In the following image, it's the middle icon:

In the pop-over, enter 20 for the top, left, and right constraints. Keep the bottom constraint unselected. Press "Add 3 Constraints," as shown here:

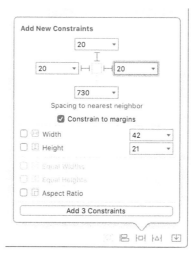

Let's relax that right edge. With the label still selected, show the Size Inspector by selecting *View ▶ Inspectors ▶ Show Size Inspector* from the Xcode menu or press ⌥-⌘-6. In the Constraints section of the Size Inspector, find the "Align Trailing to: Safe Area" constraint and click Edit. Change the Constant from = to ≤, and its Priority from Required (1000) to Low (250), like this:

Next, select the slider, and set the following constraints:

- Top Space to Label Equals 20
- Align Leading to Safe Area Equals 20
- Align Trailing to Safe Area Equals 20

Finally, select the button and add these constraints:

- Top Space to Horizontal Slider Equals 20
- Align Leading to Safe Area >= 20 with Priority 250
- Align Trailing to Safe Area Equals 20
- Height Equals 44

With these layout constraints in place, the storyboard should look something like this:

Confirm that Xcode is showing you no warnings. If you like, you can run the app to see what it feels like to manipulate the controls.

Now we have a view controller with a few subviews. Let's see how we can capture its layout in a test. This way, the test will catch us if the layout ever changes unintentionally. In order to do this, we will add a helper library to our test code.

Add FBSnapshotTestCase to a Test Target

To test how a view appears, we can do the following:

1. Render a view to an image.
2. Save this image to disk.

The saved image acts as a reference image. Once we have a reference image, then we can:

1. Read the reference image from disk.
2. Render the view to a new image.
3. If the new image matches the reference image, the test passes. Otherwise, the test fails.

This is characterization testing applied to images. The reference image captures the appearance of a view. As long as the view continues to generate the same pixels, the test doesn't care. Such tests are often called snapshot tests.

In the past, I wrote such tests by hand. I would switch a test between record mode and test mode using #if conditional compilation. There's nothing stopping you from developing your own test helpers to do this work. But you can use third-party libraries to make it easier. One of them is FBSnapshotTestCase.[2]

FBSnapshotTestCase supports the dependency managers CocoaPods and Carthage. If you want to use either, feel free to skip ahead to Set the Location for Reference Images, on page 198. Otherwise, let's add a pre-built library to the project by hand.

On GitHub, go to the Releases page for ios-snapshot-test-case to check if the latest release has a zip file for your version of Xcode.[3] If there is one, download FBSnapshotTestCase.framework.zip. This will expand to a folder named Carthage. Navigate through its subfolders Build and iOS until you find FBSnapshotTestCase.framework.

If the releases on GitHub are out of date, then download the source code for this book[4] and look in the TestFrameworks folder.

---

2.   https://github.com/uber/ios-snapshot-test-case
3.   https://github.com/uber/ios-snapshot-test-case/releases
4.   https://pragprog.com/titles/jrlegios/source_code

Drag the framework into the SnapshotTests group in the Xcode project, as shown here:

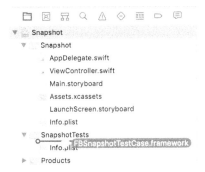

In the "Choose options for adding these files" dialog, select the check box labeled "Copy items if needed" to copy the folder into your project files. And make sure that "Add to targets" specifies the SnapshotTests target only.

Let's check if the downloaded framework works with your version of Swift. In the Xcode menu, select *Product ▶ Build For ▶ Testing*. If Xcode complains that a module compiled with a certain version of Swift cannot be imported, see if you can find a build that matches. Otherwise, you'll need to build the framework yourself or use a dependency manager.

For third-party frameworks to work, we often need to copy them to a place where the dynamic linker can find them. This is what we need to do with the snapshot library. In the Project Navigator on the left, select the Snapshot project. Then select the SnapshotTests target. Within that, select the Build Phases tab. Click the + button at the top and select "New Copy Files Phase" like this:

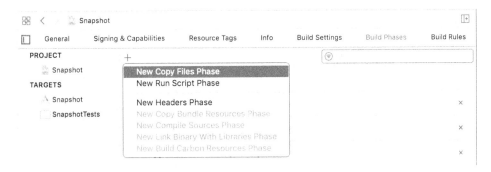

This creates a new Copy Files phase at the end of the list. In its Destination pop-up menu, select "Products Directory" as shown here:

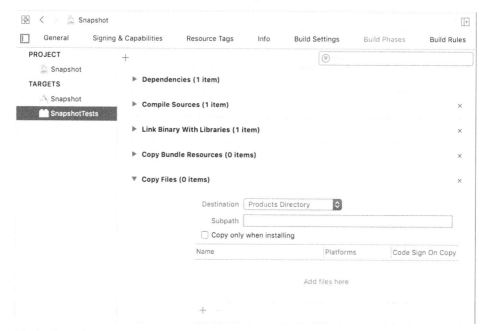

Click the + button at the bottom of the new Copy Files phase. In the "Choose items to add:" dialog, select FBSnaphotTestCase.framework and click Add. (Don't select the "Code Sign On Copy" check box because we're not shipping test code.)

Now the snapshot framework is ready for compiling against and is also copied into place for dynamic linking.

Set the Location for Reference Images

FBSnapshotTestCase is ready to use. Next, we need to tell it where to put the reference images. The simplest way is to add an environment variable to the run scheme. In the Xcode menu, select *Product ▶ Scheme ▶ Edit Scheme...* or press ⌘-<.

In the scheme editor, select Run in the left column. Then from the tabs, select Arguments. In the Environment Variables section, click the + button to create a new entry. In the figure on page 199, the new entry is filled with the name and value we'll describe next:

- For Name, enter FB_REFERENCE_IMAGE_DIR.
- For Value, enter $(SOURCE_ROOT)/SnapshotImages. (Of course, you can specify any location in your own projects.)

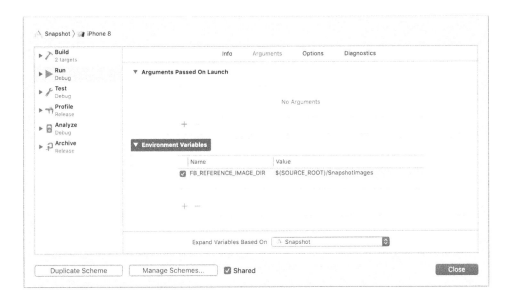

Finally, make sure to select the "Shared" check box at the very bottom. This allows your teammates to use the same scheme. Press Close to save your changes.

Write a Snapshot Test

Now we're ready to create a snapshot test. Let's start by adding a test suite ViewControllerSnapshotTests. Use Test Zero as temporary scaffolding to confirm that you hooked up the test suite. (See Start from Test Zero, on page 21.) Delete Test Zero once you see its expected failure message.

Now instead of import XCTest, change that to import FBSnapshotTestCase. Change the superclass of ViewControllerSnapshotTests from XCTestCase to FBSnapshotTestCase. Make sure this builds so far. In the Xcode menu, select *Product* ▶ *Build For* ▶ *Testing* or press Shift-⌘-U.

Add a special setUp() method to set the record mode of the snapshot tests in this suite:

Snapshot/SnapshotTests/ViewControllerSnapshotTests.swift
```
override func setUp() {
    super.setUp()
    recordMode = false
}
```

Now create a test named test_example(). Follow Load a Storyboard-Based View Controller, on page 64 to load ViewController from the storyboard. Remember that this also means editing Main.storyboard to give the view controller a Storyboard ID. Run the tests, which should pass.

Finally, add the call to verify a snapshot of the view controller:

Snapshot/SnapshotTests/ViewControllerSnapshotTests.swift
```
FBSnapshotVerifyViewController(sut)
```

Here's what the whole file looks like:

Snapshot/SnapshotTests/ViewControllerSnapshotTests.swift
```
@testable import Snapshot
import FBSnapshotTestCase

class ViewControllerSnapshotTests: FBSnapshotTestCase {

    override func setUp() {
        super.setUp()
        recordMode = false
    }

    func test_example() {
        let storyboard = UIStoryboard(name: "Main", bundle: nil)
        let sut: ViewController = storyboard.instantiateViewController(
                identifier: String(describing: ViewController.self))

        FBSnapshotVerifyViewController(sut)
    }
}
```

Run the tests again. This time, you'll see a failure beginning with the message:

```
failed - Snapshot comparison failed
```

The whole failure message is wordy, describing several objects. But buried in the failure text is the following explanation:

```
Reference image not found. You need to run the test in record mode
```

To run the test in record mode, temporarily change recordMode to true in setUp(). Then set your destination to the iOS simulator you want to use for snapshots, and run the tests. This time, you'll get a different test failure:

```
failed - Test ran in record mode. Reference image is now saved. Disable
record mode to perform an actual snapshot comparison!
```

Based on the location you set for reference images (see Set the Location for Reference Images, on page 198), look for a new folder. If the simulator you chose is for a 64-bit device, it'll append _64 to the name, so look for SnapshotImages_64. Inside that folder is another folder for the test suite, SnapshotTests.ViewControllerSnapshotTests. And inside that folder is the new reference image, named for the test case. Examine the reference image.

Finally, set recordMode back to false and run the tests again. This time the snapshot verification will pass.

What If the Snapshot Doesn't Look Right?

Sometimes a reference image won't look right. This can happen because tests normally create view controllers without surrounding context. In such cases, it's good to try creating a container for the view controller that's closer to what it has in a real app. For example, you can try creating a UIWindow to hold the view controller's view:

```
let window = UIWindow(frame: UIScreen.main.bounds)
window.addSubview(sut.view)
```

Just remember from Test Input Focus, on page 180 that you need to execute the run loop to clean up window memory.

Now we have a test that records how the view controller looks, capturing it in a reference image. As long as the test continues to generate that same image, it passes. In the rest of this chapter, let's look at ways to work effectively with snapshot tests.

See the Difference in a Snapshot Failure

Now we have a passing snapshot test. But what happens when the test fails? Let's find out by changing the layout.

Open Main.storyboard and select the button. Show the Size Inspector by selecting *View ▶ Inspectors ▶ Show Size Inspector* from the Xcode menu or press ⌥-⌘-6. In the Constraints section, find the "Align Trailing to: Safe Area" constraint as shown here:

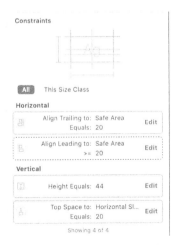

Click Edit and change the constant to 25. Run the tests. The snapshot will report a failure. If you go to the test case, you'll see the test failure annotation:

FBSnapshotVerifyViewController(sut) ◇ failed - Snapshot comparison failed: Optional(Error...

But there's more information that's not visible in the failure annotation, even if you click to expand it. Let's find the console output by following *Examine Console Output*, on page 23. The log icon, which is hidden for passing tests, is shown to the right of the failing test. Click the log icon to expand the log. It will look something like this, with different details:

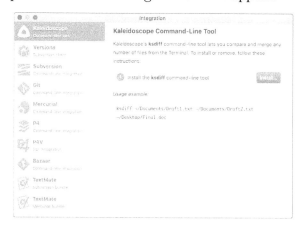

The failure highlighted in the screenshot says, "Images different." But the most important information comes at the very beginning and isn't highlighted. After the line showing that the test case started, it says:

```
If you have Kaleidoscope installed you can run this command to see an
image diff:
```

This is followed by a ksdiff command. Kaleidoscope[5] is a commercial Mac app that does file comparison. You can download a fourteen-day free trial. If you download the Mac app and launch it, select *Kaleidoscope ▶ Integration...* from the Kaleidoscope menu. The following window will appear:

With "Kaleidoscope Command-line tool" selected on the left, click Install on the right to install the ksdiff command-line tool.

---

5.   https://www.kaleidoscopeapp.com

Now open a new terminal shell. You can find the terminal by selecting *Go* ▶ *Utilities* from the Finder menu. Go back to Xcode and find the ksdiff command in the test log. Copy and paste that line into your terminal shell. Pressing ↵ will run the command, which will compare the images in Kaleidoscope in a window like this:

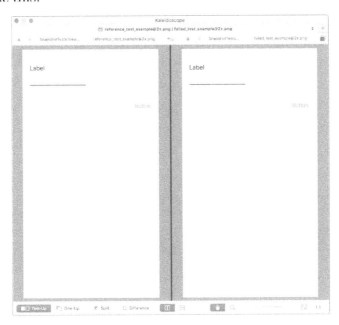

You may not be able to spot subtle differences in Two-Up mode. But they pop out if you select the Difference mode at the bottom.

If you don't want to use Kaleidoscope, you can use a different tool as long as it has a command-line interface. Just make a shell function named ksdiff that passes its arguments to the tool you like.

Manage Your Snapshot Tests

To get the most out of your snapshot tests, you should know that these tests are slow, and somewhat touchy. Also, you don't have to wait until you've finished coding the views for them to be useful.

Slow Snapshots: Keep Them in Their Own Corner

When you first discover snapshot tests, it's tempting to use them to test all kinds of visible state. But compared to a normal unit test, a snapshot test is an order of magnitude slower. That is, in the time it takes to run one snapshot test, you can run ten to twenty unit tests.

The speed of one snapshot may not seem like much. But they accumulate quickly. To keep snapshot tests from slowing down rapid feedback, I keep snapshots in their own corner. Here's how:

First, don't mix unit tests and snapshot tests in the same test suite. Create separate suites. That's why we named the test suite for this chapter ViewControllerSnapshotTests. Any unit tests can go in ViewControllerTests instead. This gives us a way to run them separately, because Xcode lets us run a single test suite. To the left of a test suite, Xcode shows an empty lozenge icon:

```
◇ class ViewControllerSnapshotTests: FBSnapshotTestCase {
```

Hover your mouse cursor over the icon. It changes to a play button:

```
▶ class ViewControllerSnapshotTests: FBSnapshotTestCase {
```

Clicking this will run all the tests in that class.

Second, keep these snapshot tests in separate files. That is, don't group ViewControllerSnapshotTests together with ViewControllerTests in the same file. Eventually, you'll have quite a few snapshot tests. To get fast feedback on my local machine, I like to either run all unit tests, or run one set of snapshots. This is easier if you create separate test targets: one for unit tests, and one for snapshot tests. So I have one unit testing bundle for unit tests and another for snapshots.

Finally, keep your snapshots limited. Snapshot the appearance of small custom views in different states. With those tests in place, another snapshot can capture the overall layout of a view controller. Getting larger snapshots that repeat the same smaller state changes is a waste of time. Instead, use faster unit tests to confirm combinations of state.

Touchy Snapshots: One Device, One iOS Version

Be sure to capture and run snapshots using the same simulator. Given enough developers, there's bound to be some confusion about which simulator to use. You may want to write your own FBSnapshotTestCase subclass. It can have a setUp() method that checks UIDevice.current and fails if the device doesn't match.

Capturing view layouts with one device in one orientation can feel limiting. You may wish to investigate other open-source libraries that extend FBSnapshotTestCase. But capturing every device combination is overkill. Remember, snapshot tests are inherently slower. Be selective, and try to limit yourself to tests that add value.

Pixel-perfect image comparison is touchy. Different versions of iOS often use slightly different math to render images. So your team will also have to agree on a single iOS version to use across all snapshots. You can enforce this in the setUp method of your custom FBSnapshotTestCase subclass.

To adopt a new version of iOS, you'll need to update all reference images for your snapshots. You can do this in one shot with a global find-and-replace to set recordMode = true. You could also set recordMode using an environment variable.

Use Snapshots to Write View Code

Characterization tests capture the existing behavior of code. Since snapshot tests are a type of characterization test, it'd be easy to assume they always come after the finished code. But snapshots can also give you feedback about views and view controllers *as you write them.*

One of the best things about unit testing view controllers is that you don't have to navigate through your app to reach the screen you want. So if your app has a login screen, an accounts tab, and a screen you can reach from that tab, you don't have to do any of that manual tapping. Instead, unit tests create the objects they need, including view controllers. The time saved by not navigating adds up quickly.

The same applies to snapshot tests. Instead of slow, manual navigation, the tests create what they need. But on top of that, you don't need to stare at a screen wondering if a button shifted five points to the left. If the test passes, you know view's appearance is identical to the reference image. This saves you even more time.

But now imagine that you're starting work on a new view controller or on a new custom view. What if the first thing you did was create a new snapshot test with recordMode set to true? Then every time you run the test, you could see what the view looks like—without navigating to it. In fact, there may not even be a way to navigate to it yet!

This lets you observe the view as it grows. The generated reference image will be closer to real life than what you see in Interface Builder. And the benefits are even greater if you write code-based view controllers. The reference image shows the result of using Auto Layout constraints to lay out views. By keeping recordMode on, you can visually confirm each step you take.

Key Takeaways

Find a way to render views from XCTest without using UI tests. FBSnap-shotTestCase is just one of many libraries that do this. The important thing is that your tests should be able to create any view or view controller, and render it to a file.

Snapshots are good for capturing aspects of appearance that would be hard to express by checking properties. But they become tempting to overuse. Because snapshot tests are slower than normal unit tests, try to limit their use to layout. Use normal unit tests to check behavior and simple state change. For example, use a normal unit test to check whether a control is enabled by checking its isEnabled property.

Snapshot tests are useful not only to record a "known good" baseline, but to also provide quick feedback to power iterative development. You can make a change, run the test, and see how the view looks—without firing up the app and navigating to that screen.

Activities

Take action to give your reading concrete benefits. If you don't already use a library to render view for testing, do the first activity.

1. Add FBSnapshotTestCase to your own project. Use CocoaPods, Carthage, or direct integration by hand.

2. Add some snapshot tests, starting from the smallest custom views. Work up to entire view controllers, trying to limit the total number of snapshots.

3. Create a custom subclass of FBSnapshotTestCase. Use its setUp() method to enforce the type of simulator and the version of iOS your team uses for snapshots. You can call fatalError() from setUp() if anyone strays from your standard to put an immediate stop to any testing on the wrong device type.

4. The next time you create a new view or view controller, start with a new snapshot test that has recordMode on. Use the captured image to give you feedback as you design the Auto Layout constraints.

What's Next?

Now you can capture the appearance of views in snapshot tests. This will help you save time by alerting you whenever any rendered views change. It'll also save you time while you're actively developing custom views or changing the layout of any view controllers.

This concludes our tour of iOS testing techniques. You now have the means to transform legacy code into tested code.

But what does all this testing enable? Starting in the next chapter, let's begin looking at the refactoring possibilities that open up to you thanks to having well-tested code.

Part III

Using Your New Power

Why is all this unit testing useful? The speed of unit test feedback empowers powerful styles of development.

Fast feedback is the engine that powers disciplined refactoring: working in small, verified steps. Refactoring gives us a way to change the design of code without changing its behavior. We'll see an example of refactoring a view controller's design from MVC to MVVM, then on to MVP.

And if we flip conventional coding-then-testing on its head, we get test-driven development. We will see how TDD combines a test-first approach with refactoring. The result is a powerful way to develop code.

CHAPTER 17

Unleash the Power of Refactoring

Now you're able to bring much of your app under test. But adding unit tests is a lot of work. What purpose do they serve? Tests validate that the code does what the tests say it does, and unit tests are fast by definition. This fast validation makes refactoring possible. But refactoring is widely misunderstood.

In this chapter, you'll learn what refactoring is and you'll see some of the most common refactoring moves. Learning these moves will help you make changes to your own code safely and with confidence.

What Is Refactoring?

The term "refactoring" has become quite popular in the workplace. We developers say, "I need to refactor this thing," then proceed to rewrite a large chunk of code. From a big-picture view, this use of the term carries the same intent as its proper definition: we want to change the way the code does its work without changing its behavior. This matches the definition from the book *Refactoring: Improving the Design of Existing Code, 2nd Edition [Fow18]*:

> Refactoring is the process of changing a software system in a way that does not alter the external behavior of the code yet improves its internal structure.

But the common use of the word ignores both the methodology and the mechanics shown in the book. We get no further than page 5 before the book explains:

> Whenever I do refactoring, the first step is always the same. I need to ensure that I have a solid set of tests for that section of code. The tests are essential...

The reason tests are essential is that changing things around is risky. We can reduce the risk of breaking things by testing the changed code. The better the tests are, the safer the change becomes. The faster the tests are, the more often we can run them. And the more often we can run them, the smaller the steps we can take become.

Working in small, verified steps is a game changer. Many developers like to work with large changes. But if we practice refactoring as described in the book, the changes are very small. Let me summarize it this way: *disciplined refactoring is changing code in small steps, with automated verification of each step.*

Why do we want to change the internal structure of the code in the first place? Because this can make the code easier to read, understand, and modify. Often, adding new functionality will be faster and safer if we make other changes first. Kent Beck writes:

> for each desired change, make the change easy (warning: this may be hard), then make the easy change[1]

In a fast-moving world, we strive to follow the Agile Manifesto[2] by valuing "responding to change." (This is one of the four points of the manifesto.) But to accommodate these changes safely, our software must be malleable, not brittle. We need the freedom to restructure the internals of our code without breaking anything. This is why disciplined refactoring is important.

So unit testing has a tight connection with refactoring. Unit tests form the safety net that makes disciplined refactoring possible. Part III of this book focuses on the practical steps of what that kind of refactoring looks like.

Lay Out the Views for Our Practice App

In Parts I and II, each chapter pretty much had its own project. But for Part III, each chapter will build on the previous work. This means you won't be able to cherry-pick chapters but instead will need to progress through them if you want to work through the examples.

The project we'll use across Part III is an interface for changing a password. Start a new project as we've done before by copying the steps from Create a Place to Play with Tests, on page 4. Use Refactoring as the project name.

Edit Main.storyboard, adding a button in the center of the View Controller Scene. Give it a title like "Change My Password." Give it the following layout constraints:

- Height Equals 44
- Align Center X to Safe Area
- Align Center Y to Safe Area

---

1. https://twitter.com/kentbeck/status/250733358307500032
2. https://agilemanifesto.org

That's the layout of the starting view. Next, let's lay out the change password view controller. Still in Main.storyboard, select *View* ▶ *Libraries* ▶ *Show Library* from the Xcode menu, or press Shift-⌘-L to bring up the Object Library. Drag a new view controller onto the storyboard. Then drag a navigation bar to the top of the new view controller.

Set the constraints of the navigation bar:

- Align Top to Safe Area
- Align Leading to Safe Area
- Align Trailing to Safe Area

Show the Attributes Inspector by selecting *View* ▶ *Inspectors* ▶ *Show Attributes Inspector* from the Xcode menu or press ⌥-⌘-5. In the Attributes Inspector in the Navigation Bar section, deselect "Translucent."

Adding a navigation bar also creates an embedded navigation item. Double-click on its title, renaming it to "Change Password."

Next, drag a bar button item to the left of the navigation title.

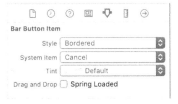

In the Attributes Inspector in the Bar Button Item section, set System Item to Cancel, like this:

Now for the main part. Drag a text field below the navigation bar. Click Add New Constraints at the bottom right of the storyboard editor. Set the top, left, and right constraints to 20, and the height to 44. Using the Attributes

Inspector, in the Text Field section, set the Placeholder to "Current Password." Then in the Text Input Traits section, set the following:

- Content Type: Password
- Auto-enable Return Key: Selected
- Secure Text Entry: Selected

Drag another text field below the first one. For the layout constraints, set the top to 8, left and right to 20, and height to 44. Set its placeholder to "New Password." Do this again with a third text field. Use the same constraints, and set its placeholder to "Confirm New Password."

Now select the bottom two text fields. In the Attributes Inspector in the Text Input Traits section, set the following:

- Content Type: New Password
- Auto-enable Return Key: Selected
- Secure Text Entry: Selected

Drag a button below the text fields. For its layout constraints, set the top to 16, left and right to 20, and height to 44. Double-click the button's title and change it to "Submit."

Finally, let's add a segue to go from the button on the initial view controller to the Change Password view. Control-drag from the "Change My Password" button onto the Change Password Scene. This brings up a pop-up menu of segue choices, as you can see here:

From the Action Segue section, select "Present Modally." This concludes the layout of our views. Look at what we've done so far by running the app and clicking that first button.

Add the Code to Our Practice App

In real life, we would make a type that communicates with some password changing API. But for our example, we don't have an actual web service. Instead, we will just print its arguments to the console. To simulate the time it would take to do network communication, it will call either the success closure or the failure closure after 1 second. Additonally, we will be able to alternate between both success and failure so that we are able to try both.

Select the Refactoring group in the Project Navigator and press ⌘-N to make a new file. Select Swift File and name it PasswordChanger.swift:

Refactoring/Refactoring/PasswordChanger.swift

```swift
import Foundation

final class PasswordChanger {
    private static var pretendToSucceed = false
    private var successOrFailureTimer: SuccessOrFailureTimer?

    func change(securityToken: String,
                oldPassword: String,
                newPassword: String,
                onSuccess: @escaping () -> Void,
                onFailure: @escaping (String) -> Void) {
        print("Initiate Change Password:")
        print("securityToken = \(securityToken)")
        print("oldPassword = \(oldPassword)")
        print("newPassword = \(newPassword)")
        successOrFailureTimer = SuccessOrFailureTimer(
                onSuccess: onSuccess,
                onFailure: onFailure,
                timer: Timer.scheduledTimer(
                        withTimeInterval: 1,
                        repeats: false
                ) { [weak self] _ in self?.callSuccessOrFailure() }
        )
    }

    private func callSuccessOrFailure() {
        if PasswordChanger.pretendToSucceed {
            successOrFailureTimer?.onSuccess()
        } else {
            successOrFailureTimer?.onFailure("Sorry, something went wrong.")
        }
        PasswordChanger.pretendToSucceed.toggle()
        successOrFailureTimer?.timer.invalidate()
        successOrFailureTimer = nil
    }
}
```

```
private struct SuccessOrFailureTimer {
    let onSuccess: () -> Void
    let onFailure: (String) -> Void
    let timer: Timer
}
```

The change() method takes a security token, the old password, and a new password. Upon success, it calls the onSuccess closure. Upon failure, it calls the onFailure closure with a failure message.

The helper method callSuccessOrFailure() alternates between failure and success. The pretendToSucceed flag is a static property, so it persists across PasswordChanger instances. The change() method calls it after a 1-second timer to simulate network lag.

Next, let's write the code for the Change Password view. Similar to Set Up a Storyboard-Based View Controller for Experiments, on page 62, make a new Cocoa Touch file that's a subclass of UIViewController but with the name ChangePasswordViewController. Define the following outlets in the new class:

Refactoring/Refactoring/ChangePasswordViewController.swift
```
@IBOutlet private(set) var cancelBarButton: UIBarButtonItem!
@IBOutlet private(set) var oldPasswordTextField: UITextField!
@IBOutlet private(set) var newPasswordTextField: UITextField!
@IBOutlet private(set) var confirmPasswordTextField: UITextField!
@IBOutlet private(set) var submitButton: UIButton!
```

Edit Main.storyboard and select the Change Password Scene. In the Identity Inspector, set the Custom Class to ChangePasswordViewController. Connect all the new outlets to their corresponding storyboard objects. Then add the following additional properties:

Refactoring/Refactoring/ChangePasswordViewController.swift
```
private var passwordChanger = PasswordChanger()
var securityToken = ""
private let blurView = UIVisualEffectView(effect: UIBlurEffect(style: .dark))
private let activityIndicator = UIActivityIndicatorView(style: .large)
```

Now let's define viewDidLoad(). It adds a rounded border around the button. It prepares for Auto Layout constraints on blurView and activityIndicator. It also sets the color of activityIndicator. Add this method, then run the app to see what the button looks like now:

Refactoring/Refactoring/ChangePasswordViewController.swift
```
override func viewDidLoad() {
    super.viewDidLoad()
    submitButton.layer.borderWidth = 1
    submitButton.layer.borderColor = UIColor(
            red: 55/255.0, green: 147/255.0, blue: 251/255.0, alpha: 1
```

```
    ).cgColor
    submitButton.layer.cornerRadius = 8
    blurView.translatesAutoresizingMaskIntoConstraints = false
    activityIndicator.translatesAutoresizingMaskIntoConstraints = false
    activityIndicator.color = .white
}
```

Add the following action and connect the Cancel bar button to it. Then run
the app and try the Cancel button.

Refactoring/Refactoring/ChangePasswordViewController.swift

```
@IBAction private func cancel() {
    oldPasswordTextField.resignFirstResponder()
    newPasswordTextField.resignFirstResponder()
    confirmPasswordTextField.resignFirstResponder()
    dismiss(animated: true)
}
```

Next is a big one. Add the following action. Don't worry that it's one big glob
of code—we'll clean it up later.

Refactoring/Refactoring/ChangePasswordViewController.swift

```
@IBAction private func changePassword() {
    // 1. Validate inputs
    if oldPasswordTextField.text?.isEmpty ?? true {
        oldPasswordTextField.becomeFirstResponder()
        return
    }

    if newPasswordTextField.text?.isEmpty ?? true {
        let alertController = UIAlertController(
                title: nil,
                message: "Please enter a new password.",
                preferredStyle: .alert)
        let okButton = UIAlertAction(
                title: "OK",
                style: .default) { [weak self] _ in
            self?.newPasswordTextField.becomeFirstResponder()
        }
        alertController.addAction(okButton)
        alertController.preferredAction = okButton
        self.present(alertController, animated: true)
        return
    }

    if newPasswordTextField.text?.count ?? 0 < 6 {
        let alertController = UIAlertController(title: nil,
                message: "The new password should have at least 6 characters.",
                preferredStyle: .alert)
        let okButton = UIAlertAction(
                title: "OK",
                style: .default) { [weak self] _ in
```

```
        self?.newPasswordTextField.text = ""
        self?.confirmPasswordTextField.text = ""
        self?.newPasswordTextField.becomeFirstResponder()
    }
    alertController.addAction(okButton)
    alertController.preferredAction = okButton
    self.present(alertController, animated: true)
    return
}

if newPasswordTextField.text != confirmPasswordTextField.text {
    let alertController = UIAlertController(title: nil,
            message: "The new password and the confirmation password "
                    + "don't match. Please try again.",
            preferredStyle: .alert)
    let okButton = UIAlertAction(
            title: "OK",
            style: .default) { [weak self] _ in
        self?.newPasswordTextField.text = ""
        self?.confirmPasswordTextField.text = ""
        self?.newPasswordTextField.becomeFirstResponder()
    }
    alertController.addAction(okButton)
    alertController.preferredAction = okButton
    self.present(alertController, animated: true)
    return
}

// 2. Set up waiting appearance
oldPasswordTextField.resignFirstResponder()
newPasswordTextField.resignFirstResponder()
confirmPasswordTextField.resignFirstResponder()
cancelBarButton.isEnabled = false
view.backgroundColor = .clear
view.addSubview(blurView)
view.addSubview(activityIndicator)
NSLayoutConstraint.activate([
    blurView.heightAnchor.constraint(equalTo: view.heightAnchor),
    blurView.widthAnchor.constraint(equalTo: view.widthAnchor),
    activityIndicator.centerXAnchor.constraint(
            equalTo: view.centerXAnchor),
    activityIndicator.centerYAnchor.constraint(
            equalTo: view.centerYAnchor),
])
activityIndicator.startAnimating()

// 3. Attempt to change password
passwordChanger.change(
    securityToken: securityToken,
    oldPassword: oldPasswordTextField.text ?? "",
    newPassword: newPasswordTextField.text ?? "",
    onSuccess: { [weak self] in
```

```
            self?.activityIndicator.stopAnimating()
            self?.activityIndicator.removeFromSuperview()
            let alertController = UIAlertController(
                    title: nil,
                    message: "Your password has been successfully changed.",
                    preferredStyle: .alert)
            let okButton = UIAlertAction(
                    title: "OK",
                    style: .default) { [weak self] _ in
                self?.dismiss(animated: true)
            }
            alertController.addAction(okButton)
            alertController.preferredAction = okButton
            self?.present(alertController, animated: true)
        },
        onFailure: { [weak self] message in
            self?.activityIndicator.stopAnimating()
            self?.activityIndicator.removeFromSuperview()
            let alertController = UIAlertController(
                    title: nil,
                    message: message,
                    preferredStyle: .alert)
            let okButton = UIAlertAction(
                    title: "OK",
                    style: .default) { [weak self] _ in
                self?.oldPasswordTextField.text = ""
                self?.newPasswordTextField.text = ""
                self?.confirmPasswordTextField.text = ""
                self?.oldPasswordTextField.becomeFirstResponder()
                self?.view.backgroundColor = .white
                self?.blurView.removeFromSuperview()
                self?.cancelBarButton.isEnabled = true
            }
            alertController.addAction(okButton)
            alertController.preferredAction = okButton
            self?.present(alertController, animated: true)
        })
}
```

Once the action is in place, connect the Submit button to it. This action enforces the following rules:

- If the old password is empty, put the user input back in the old password field.

- If the new password is empty, show an alert. Tapping OK puts the user input back in the new password field.

- The new password must be at least six characters long. If not, show an alert explaining the requirement. Tapping OK clears the new password and confirm password fields, and puts the user input back in the new password field.

• The confirmation password must match the new password. If not, show an alert explaining the problem. Tapping OK clears the new password and confirm password fields, and puts the user input back in the new password field.

If the inputs satisfy these rules, then we do the following:

• Hide the keyboard.
• Disable the Cancel bar button.
• Show a blurring overlay with a spinning activity indicator.
• Call the password changer, passing the security token, the old password, and the new password.

The call to change the password may succeed or fail. If the call succeeds, stop the spinner and hide it. Show a success alert. Tapping OK dismisses the view.

If the call fails, stop the spinner and hide it. Show a failure alert displaying the failure message passed to the closure. Tapping OK resets the screen by doing the following:

• Clearing all text fields
• Putting the user input back in the old password field
• Removing the blur overlay
• Re-enabling the Cancel bar button

Try running the app, and see what happens if the inputs don't satisfy the rules. Then try with valid inputs. Remember, our fake password changer will alternate between failure and success.

To support the return key in the keyboard, we need a delegate for the text fields. First add UITextFieldDelegate conformance to the view controller definition:

Refactoring/Refactoring/ChangePasswordViewController.swift
```
class ChangePasswordViewController: UIViewController, UITextFieldDelegate {
```

In the storyboard, select each text field in turn and connect its delegate to the view controller as we did in Make a Place to Play, on page 169. Then add a method to ChangePasswordViewController to process the return key. It advances the keyboard focus from one text field to the next until it calls the same action as the Submit button:

Refactoring/Refactoring/ChangePasswordViewController.swift
```swift
func textFieldShouldReturn(_ textField: UITextField) -> Bool {
    if textField === oldPasswordTextField {
        newPasswordTextField.becomeFirstResponder()
    } else if textField === newPasswordTextField {
        confirmPasswordTextField.becomeFirstResponder()
    } else if textField === confirmPasswordTextField {
        changePassword()
    }
    return true
}
```

Run the app and try using the return key in each text field. Notice how the return key is disabled until some text is entered. See how tapping it advances the input focus.

Finally, run the app and enter passwords that meet the requirements. Apply Examine Console Output, on page 23 to see the console output for a change password request:

```
Initiate Change Password:
securityToken =
```

The security token is empty. This property needs to be set from the outside. Add the following method to ViewController (not to ChangePasswordViewController). It prepares for the segue to ChangePasswordViewController:

Refactoring/Refactoring/ViewController.swift
```swift
override func prepare(for segue: UIStoryboardSegue, sender: Any?) {
    super.prepare(for: segue, sender: sender)
    if segue.identifier == "changePassword" {
        let changePasswordVC = segue.destination
                as? ChangePasswordViewController
        changePasswordVC?.securityToken = "TOKEN"
    }
}
```

In the storyboard, select the first segue from the View Controller Scene to the Change Password Scene. In the Attributes Inspector, set its identifier to "changePassword." Now run the app again, submitting a valid password request. This time, the console output will show the following:

```
Initiate Change Password:
securityToken = TOKEN
```

Now we have functioning code. But before we start any refactoring, let's bring this code under test.

Replace the Difficult Dependency with a Mock Object

This chapter focuses on refactoring ChangePasswordViewController, so we want to bring it under test. But the class has an embedded dependency on Password-Changer. Even though PasswordChanger is a simulation, we need to break this dependency. We shouldn't have unit tests call an actual web service, not even one set up for testing. It's unreliable, too slow, and would pollute the service.

Instead, let's apply Extract a Protocol to Support Test Doubles, on page 131. In PasswordChanger.swift, define an empty protocol named PasswordChanging:

Refactoring/Refactoring/PasswordChanger.swift
```
protocol PasswordChanging {}
```

Then in ChangePasswordViewController, change the passwordChanger property to have an explicit type of PasswordChanging:

Refactoring/Refactoring/ChangePasswordViewController.swift
```
private var passwordChanger: PasswordChanging = PasswordChanger()
```

Xcode will show an error:

```
Value of type 'PasswordChanger' does not conform to specified type
    'PasswordChanging'
```

Since PasswordChanger is a type we own, we can make it conform to the protocol directly:

Refactoring/Refactoring/PasswordChanger.swift
```
final class PasswordChanger: PasswordChanging {
```

This in turn leads to the error:

```
Value of type 'PasswordChanging' has no member 'change'
```

Fix this by copying the method signature into the protocol:

Refactoring/Refactoring/PasswordChanger.swift
```
protocol PasswordChanging {
    func change(securityToken: String,
                oldPassword: String,
                newPassword: String,
                onSuccess: @escaping () -> Void,
                onFailure: @escaping (String) -> Void)
}
```

We've changed the property type to use the protocol. But its value is still fixed to a PasswordChanger instance. Let's make it possible for tests to substitute a different implementation of the protocol. Apply Use Properties, on page 87 by making the property lazy, and no longer private.

Refactoring/Refactoring/ChangePasswordViewController.swift
```
lazy var passwordChanger: PasswordChanging = PasswordChanger()
```

Now we're set up to create a mock object version of the PasswordChanging protocol. First, create a file named TestHelpers.swift in the RefactoringTests group with these mock object helpers:

Refactoring/RefactoringTests/TestHelpers.swift
```
import XCTest

func verifyMethodCalledOnce(
        methodName: String,
        callCount: Int,
        describeArguments: @autoclosure () -> String,
        file: StaticString = #file,
        line: UInt = #line) -> Bool {
    if callCount == 0 {
        XCTFail("Wanted but not invoked: \(methodName)",
                file: file, line: line)
        return false
    }
    if callCount > 1 {
        XCTFail("Wanted 1 time but was called \(callCount) times. " +
                "\(methodName) with \(describeArguments())",
                file: file, line: line)
        return false
    }
    return true
}

func verifyMethodNeverCalled(
        methodName: String,
        callCount: Int,
        describeArguments: @autoclosure () -> String,
        file: StaticString = #file,
        line: UInt = #line) {
    let times = callCount == 1 ? "time" : "times"
    if callCount > 0 {
        XCTFail("Never wanted but was called \(callCount) \(times). " +
                "\(methodName) with \(describeArguments())",
                file: file, line: line)
    }
}
```

(The first helper returns a Bool because we'll use it to decide whether to make more assertions. The second helper has no return type because we won't do any more checks.)

Using these helpers, let's create a new file, MockPasswordChanger.swift:

Refactoring/RefactoringTests/MockPasswordChanger.swift
```
@testable import Refactoring
```

```swift
import XCTest

final class MockPasswordChanger: PasswordChanging {
    private var changeCallCount = 0
    private var changeArgsSecurityToken: [String] = []
    private var changeArgsOldPassword: [String] = []
    private var changeArgsNewPassword: [String] = []
    private var changeArgsOnSuccess: [() -> Void] = []
    private var changeArgsOnFailure: [(String) -> Void] = []

    func change(
            securityToken: String,
            oldPassword: String,
            newPassword: String,
            onSuccess: @escaping () -> Void,
            onFailure: @escaping (String) -> Void) {
        changeCallCount += 1
        changeArgsSecurityToken.append(securityToken)
        changeArgsOldPassword.append(oldPassword)
        changeArgsNewPassword.append(newPassword)
        changeArgsOnSuccess.append(onSuccess)
        changeArgsOnFailure.append(onFailure)
    }

    func verifyChange(
            securityToken: String,
            oldPassword: String,
            newPassword: String,
            file: StaticString = #file,
            line: UInt = #line) {
        guard changeWasCalledOnce(file: file, line: line) else { return }
        XCTAssertEqual(changeArgsSecurityToken.last, securityToken,
                "security token", file: file, line: line)
        XCTAssertEqual(changeArgsOldPassword.last, oldPassword,
                "old password", file: file, line: line)
        XCTAssertEqual(changeArgsNewPassword.last, newPassword,
                "new password", file: file, line: line)
    }

    func verifyChangeNeverCalled(
            file: StaticString = #file, line: UInt = #line) {
        changeWasNeverCalled(file: file, line: line)
    }

    private func changeWasCalledOnce(
            file: StaticString = #file, line: UInt = #line) -> Bool {
        verifyMethodCalledOnce(
                methodName: changeMethodName,
                callCount: changeCallCount,
                describeArguments: changeMethodArguments,
                file: file, line: line)
    }
```

```
    private func changeWasNeverCalled(
            file: StaticString = #file, line: UInt = #line) {
        verifyMethodNeverCalled(
                methodName: changeMethodName,
                callCount: changeCallCount,
                describeArguments: changeMethodArguments,
                file: file, line: line)
    }
    private var changeMethodName: String {
        "change(securityToken:oldPassword:newPassword:onSuccess:onFailure:)"
    }
    private var changeMethodArguments: String {
        "oldPasswords: \(changeArgsOldPassword), " +
                "newPasswords: \(changeArgsNewPassword)"
    }
}
}
```

In addition to recording calls to the change() method, this mock object provides the following:

- verifyChange(securityToken:oldPassword:newPassword:) to verify one call with the given arguments
- verifyChangeNeverCalled() to verify no calls

We changed the production code to use a protocol instead of a direct reference. We made the property lazy so that tests can substitute a different value after loading the view controller from the storyboard. And we created a mock object to intercept calls to the protocol and let us test the arguments. Now onward to the tests.

Write the First Tests of the Change Password View Controller

Let's begin writing tests for ChangePasswordViewController. If RefactoringTests.swift is still lingering around from creating the project, delete the file. Add a new test suite named ChangePasswordViewControllerTests. Do the normal Test Zero steps to confirm that it's in the right place.

Then let's start easy by testing the outlets. Since we know we're going to be writing many tests, let's put the system under test into the test fixture from the start. Here's the content of the file so far:

Refactoring/RefactoringTests/ChangePasswordViewControllerTests.swift

```swift
@testable import Refactoring
import XCTest

final class ChangePasswordViewControllerTests: XCTestCase {
    private var sut: ChangePasswordViewController!

    override func setUp() {
        super.setUp()
        let storyboard = UIStoryboard(name: "Main", bundle: nil)
        sut = storyboard.instantiateViewController(
                identifier: String(
                        describing: ChangePasswordViewController.self))
        sut.loadViewIfNeeded()
    }

    override func tearDown() {
        sut = nil
        super.tearDown()
    }

    func test_outlets_shouldBeConnected() {
        XCTAssertNotNil(sut.cancelBarButton, "cancelButton")
        XCTAssertNotNil(sut.oldPasswordTextField, "oldPasswordTextField")
        XCTAssertNotNil(sut.newPasswordTextField, "newPasswordTextField")
        XCTAssertNotNil(sut.confirmPasswordTextField,
                "confirmPasswordTextField")
        XCTAssertNotNil(sut.submitButton, "submitButton")
    }
}
```

To get this to pass, we edit the view controller in Main.storyboard, copying the Class name into the Storyboard ID.

Next, let's test the attributes of each UI component from top to bottom. It would be nice to test the title shown in the navigation bar, but there's no way for tests to reach it. To provide that access, let's add an outlet to ChangePasswordViewController:

Refactoring/Refactoring/ChangePasswordViewController.swift

```swift
@IBOutlet private(set) var navigationBar: UINavigationBar!
```

In test_outlets_shouldBeConnected(), add an assertion for the new outlet:

Refactoring/RefactoringTests/ChangePasswordViewControllerTests.swift

```swift
XCTAssertNotNil(sut.navigationBar, "navigationBar")
```

This test will fail. Get it to pass by connecting the navigation bar to the outlet. Then we can write the test we wanted in the first place, checking the title:

Refactoring/RefactoringTests/ChangePasswordViewControllerTests.swift
```
func test_navigationBar_shouldHaveTitle() {
    XCTAssertEqual(sut.navigationBar.topItem?.title, "Change Password")
}
```

Moving down, how can we check the "System Item" setting of the Bar Button Item? UIKit doesn't expose it as a property, but we can still peek at it since it's Objective-C underneath. (Peering into Apple's implementation details is inadvisable in production code. But in test code, it's a necessary evil when Apple chooses not to expose something that would be useful for tests.)

Add a function to TestHelpers.swift, which uses value(forKey:) to ask a UIBarButtonItem for a hidden numeric property named systemItem. It converts that number into the UIBarButtonItem.SystemItem enumeration.

Refactoring/RefactoringTests/TestHelpers.swift
```
func systemItem(for barButtonItem: UIBarButtonItem) ->
        UIBarButtonItem.SystemItem {
    let systemItemNumber = barButtonItem.value(forKey: "systemItem") as! Int
    return UIBarButtonItem.SystemItem(rawValue: systemItemNumber)!
}
```

We'll use this helper to test the Cancel button is the right kind of system item.

Refactoring/RefactoringTests/ChangePasswordViewControllerTests.swift
```
func test_cancelBarButton_shouldBeSystemItemCancel() {
    XCTAssertEqual(systemItem(for: sut.cancelBarButton), .cancel)
}
```

The tests should pass. But remember the warning from Test Attributes and Wrangle UIKit Descriptions, on page 173 about older enumerations defined in Objective-C: they don't report mismatches well in Swift tests. To test this, edit the Bar Button Item in the storyboard. Temporarily change its system item to Done instead of Cancel, and run the tests again. You'll see an unhelpful test failure message:

```
XCTAssertEqual failed: ("UIBarButtonSystemItem") is not equal to
    ("UIBarButtonSystemItem")
```

To make the error reporting useful, let's have the system item conform to the CustomStringConvertible protocol. Add the following to TestHelpers.swift:

Refactoring/RefactoringTests/TestHelpers.swift
```
extension UIBarButtonItem.SystemItem: CustomStringConvertible {
    public var description: String {
        switch self {
        case .done: return "done"
        case .cancel: return "cancel"
        case .edit: return "edit"
        case .save: return "save"
```

```
        case .add: return "add"
        case .flexibleSpace: return "flexibleSpace"
        case .fixedSpace: return "fixedSpace"
        case .compose: return "compose"
        case .reply: return "reply"
        case .action: return "action"
        case .organize: return "organize"
        case .bookmarks: return "bookmarks"
        case .search: return "search"
        case .refresh: return "refresh"
        case .stop: return "stop"
        case .camera: return "camera"
        case .trash: return "trash"
        case .play: return "play"
        case .pause: return "pause"
        case .rewind: return "rewind"
        case .fastForward: return "fastForward"
        case .undo: return "undo"
        case .redo: return "redo"
        case .pageCurl: return "pageCurl"
        case .close: return "close"
        @unknown default: fatalError("Unknown UIBarButtonItem.SystemItem")
        }
    }
}
```

Run tests again. This time, you should see the following test failure:

```
XCTAssertEqual failed: ("done") is not equal to ("cancel")
```

That's more like it. Change the system item back to Cancel. Run tests again to make sure we're back to a clean state.

Tests for the text field placeholders and the Submit button title are straight-forward:

Refactoring/RefactoringTests/ChangePasswordViewControllerTests.swift
```
func test_oldPasswordTextField_shouldHavePlaceholder() {
    XCTAssertEqual(sut.oldPasswordTextField.placeholder, "Current Password")
}

func test_newPasswordTextField_shouldHavePlaceholder() {
    XCTAssertEqual(sut.newPasswordTextField.placeholder, "New Password")
}

func test_confirmPasswordTextField_shouldHavePlaceholder() {
    XCTAssertEqual(sut.confirmPasswordTextField.placeholder,
            "Confirm New Password")
}

func test_submitButton_shouldHaveTitle() {
    XCTAssertEqual(sut.submitButton.titleLabel?.text, "Submit")
}
```

The Current Password text field is set up to receive password input and to enable the Return key. Let's write a test that confirms those attributes:

Refactoring/RefactoringTests/ChangePasswordViewControllerTests.swift
```
func test_oldPasswordTextField_shouldHavePasswordAttributes() {
    let textField = sut.oldPasswordTextField!
    XCTAssertEqual(textField.textContentType, .password, "textContentType")
    XCTAssertTrue(textField.isSecureTextEntry, "isSecureTextEntry")
    XCTAssertTrue(textField.enablesReturnKeyAutomatically,
            "enablesReturnKeyAutomatically")
}
```

Make similar tests for newPasswordTextField and confirmPasswordTextField but change their textContentType assertions to check for .newPassword.

Now we have tests for the basic configuration of the UI elements on the Change Password view controller. Next, let's begin adding tests of behavior, starting with button taps.

Test the Cancel Button

Tapping the Cancel button should get the active text field to resign input focus so that the keyboard goes away. We know from Test Input Focus, on page 180 that we need to put the view controller's view into a UIWindow. We also know that we need to take extra steps to clean up this UIWindow by executing the run loop. And all this starts by tapping Cancel, which is a UIBarButtonItem. Add the following helpers to TestHelpers.swift, along with import UIKit:

Refactoring/RefactoringTests/TestHelpers.swift
```
func tap(_ button: UIBarButtonItem) {
    _ = button.target?.perform(button.action, with: nil)
}

func putInViewHierarchy(_ vc: UIViewController) {
    let window = UIWindow()
    window.addSubview(vc.view)
}

func executeRunLoop() {
    RunLoop.current.run(until: Date())
}
```

To make it easier to activate a particular text field as the first responder, let's add a helper method to ChangePasswordViewControllerTests:

Refactoring/RefactoringTests/ChangePasswordViewControllerTests.swift
```
private func putFocusOn(textField: UITextField) {
    putInViewHierarchy(sut)
    textField.becomeFirstResponder()
}
```

Since this adds the system under test's view to a UIWindow, execute the run loop in tearDown() to delete the window:

Refactoring/RefactoringTests/ChangePasswordViewControllerTests.swift
```
override func tearDown() {
    executeRunLoop() // Clean out UIWindow
    sut = nil
    super.tearDown()
}
```

Now we can use these pieces to put input focus on one text field, then tap the Cancel button. The test confirms that the text field is no longer the first responder.

Refactoring/RefactoringTests/ChangePasswordViewControllerTests.swift
```
func test_tappingCancel_withFocusOnOldPassword_shouldResignThatFocus() {
    putFocusOn(textField: sut.oldPasswordTextField)
    XCTAssertTrue(sut.oldPasswordTextField.isFirstResponder, "precondition")

    tap(sut.cancelBarButton)

    XCTAssertFalse(sut.oldPasswordTextField.isFirstResponder)
}
```

Repeat this test for newPasswordTextField and confirmPasswordTextField.

The other thing the Cancel button does is dismiss the modal presentation of the Change Password view controller. To check this, we will use another verifier from ViewControllerPresentationSpy, the DismissalVerifier. First, follow the steps from Add the Helper Framework to the Project, on page 108 to add ViewControllerPresentationSpy to the test target. Add import ViewControllerPresentationSpy to the top of ChangePasswordViewControllerTests.swift. Then we can write the following test:

Refactoring/RefactoringTests/ChangePasswordViewControllerTests.swift
```
func test_tappingCancel_shouldDismissModal() {
    let dismissalVerifier = DismissalVerifier()

    tap(sut.cancelBarButton)

    dismissalVerifier.verify(animated: true, dismissedViewController: sut)
}
```

This verify() call checks the following:

- That dismiss(animated:completion:) was called once
- That the dismissal was animated
- That the dismissed view controller was the system under test

That takes care of the Cancel button. Let's move on to the Submit button.

Test the Submit Button

The behavior of the Submit button is defined in the changePassword() method. This is a big one. The method has 116 lines with three sections. The first section checks the inputs. The second sets up the appearance of the view while we wait for the password call to finish. The third section passes the inputs to the password changer and handles success or failure. Let's test this, step by step.

Since our tests will be tapping the Submit button, let's add a helper to TestHelpers.swift to make these tests more expressive:

```
Refactoring/RefactoringTests/TestHelpers.swift
func tap(_ button: UIButton) {
    button.sendActions(for: .touchUpInside)
}
```

The Submit button interacts with the password changer. We created a Mock-PasswordChanger in Replace the Difficult Dependency with a Mock Object, on page 220, which we'll need now. There are also several different alerts, so let's also set up an AlertVerifier. Put both into the test fixture, injecting the mock into the system under test as the password changer:

```
Refactoring/RefactoringTests/ChangePasswordViewControllerTests.swift
    private var sut: ChangePasswordViewController!
➤   private var passwordChanger: MockPasswordChanger!
➤   private var alertVerifier: AlertVerifier!

    override func setUp() {
        super.setUp()
        let storyboard = UIStoryboard(name: "Main", bundle: nil)
        sut = storyboard.instantiateViewController(
                identifier: String(
                    describing: ChangePasswordViewController.self))
➤       passwordChanger = MockPasswordChanger()
➤       sut.passwordChanger = passwordChanger
➤       alertVerifier = AlertVerifier()
        sut.loadViewIfNeeded()
    }

    override func tearDown() {
        executeRunLoop() // Clean out UIWindow
        sut = nil
➤       passwordChanger = nil
➤       alertVerifier = nil
        super.tearDown()
    }
```

Make sure your tests still pass with these changes.

Validate the Inputs

Most of our tests will need valid entries in the text fields. To test an invalid entry, we can set up valid entries, then change one of them. Let's make a helper to set up valid entries. The old password has to be non-empty. The new password has to have at least six characters. And the confirmation password has to match the new password.

Refactoring/RefactoringTests/ChangePasswordViewControllerTests.swift
```
private func setUpValidPasswordEntries() {
    sut.oldPasswordTextField.text = "NONEMPTY"
    sut.newPasswordTextField.text = "123456"
    sut.confirmPasswordTextField.text = sut.newPasswordTextField.text
}
```

If the old password input is empty and the user taps Submit, we don't submit anything to the password changer. And we move input focus to the old password.

We can express this with two tests:

Refactoring/RefactoringTests/ChangePasswordViewControllerTests.swift
```
func test_tappingSubmit_withOldPasswordEmpty_shouldNotChangePassword() {
    setUpValidPasswordEntries()
    sut.oldPasswordTextField.text = ""

    tap(sut.submitButton)

    passwordChanger.verifyChangeNeverCalled()
}

func test_tappingSubmit_withOldPasswordEmpty_shouldPutFocusOnOldPassword() {
    setUpValidPasswordEntries()
    sut.oldPasswordTextField.text = ""
    putInViewHierarchy(sut)

    tap(sut.submitButton)

    XCTAssertTrue(sut.oldPasswordTextField.isFirstResponder)
}
```

If the new password is empty, we don't submit the change request. And we show an alert with a message. The alerts throughout this view controller are the same, except for the message and the behavior of the OK button. Let's write a helper to verify the basics of these alerts:

Refactoring/RefactoringTests/ChangePasswordViewControllerTests.swift
```
private func verifyAlertPresented(
        message: String, file: StaticString = #file, line: UInt = #line) {
    alertVerifier.verify(
            title: nil,
            message: message,
```

```
            animated: true,
            actions: [
                .default("OK"),
            ],
            presentingViewController: sut,
            file: file,
            line: line
    )
    XCTAssertEqual(alertVerifier.preferredAction?.title, "OK",
            "preferred action", file: file, line: line)
}
```

Now we can write our first two tests of what should happen when the new password field is empty:

Refactoring/RefactoringTests/ChangePasswordViewControllerTests.swift
```
func test_tappingSubmit_withNewPasswordEmpty_shouldNotChangePassword() {
    setUpValidPasswordEntries()
    sut.newPasswordTextField.text = ""

    tap(sut.submitButton)

    passwordChanger.verifyChangeNeverCalled()
}

func test_tappingSubmit_withNewPasswordEmpty_shouldShowPasswordBlankAlert() {
    setUpValidPasswordEntries()
    sut.newPasswordTextField.text = ""

    tap(sut.submitButton)

    verifyAlertPresented(message: "Please enter a new password.")
}
```

Then we can test that tapping OK in the alert puts the input focus on the new password field:

Refactoring/RefactoringTests/ChangePasswordViewControllerTests.swift
```
func test_tappingOKPasswordBlankAlert_shouldPutFocusOnNewPassword() throws {
    setUpValidPasswordEntries()
    sut.newPasswordTextField.text = ""
    tap(sut.submitButton)
    putInViewHierarchy(sut)

    try alertVerifier.executeAction(forButton: "OK")

    XCTAssertTrue(sut.newPasswordTextField.isFirstResponder)
}
```

What if the new password is too short? Then we don't submit it to the password changer, and we show a different alert. But if the rules about what's considered too short change, we don't want to make repeated changes across the tests. So let's make a shared helper to set up the input we need for the "too short" case:

Refactoring/RefactoringTests/ChangePasswordViewControllerTests.swift
```
private func setUpEntriesNewPasswordTooShort() {
    sut.oldPasswordTextField.text = "NONEMPTY"
    sut.newPasswordTextField.text = "12345"
    sut.confirmPasswordTextField.text = sut.newPasswordTextField.text
}
```

Now we can use this helper to write our first tests of this case:

Refactoring/RefactoringTests/ChangePasswordViewControllerTests.swift
```
func test_tappingSubmit_withNewPasswordTooShort_shouldNotChangePassword() {
    setUpEntriesNewPasswordTooShort()

    tap(sut.submitButton)

    passwordChanger.verifyChangeNeverCalled()
}

func test_tappingSubmit_withNewPasswordTooShort_shouldShowTooShortAlert() {
    setUpEntriesNewPasswordTooShort()

    tap(sut.submitButton)

    verifyAlertPresented(
            message: "The new password should have at least 6 characters.")
}
```

A few things happen with this alert's OK action. It should clear the text fields for the new password and the confirmation password. But it should leave the old password field alone. And it should put input focus on the new password. Here are our tests for this action:

Refactoring/RefactoringTests/ChangePasswordViewControllerTests.swift
```
func test_tappingOKInTooShortAlert_shouldClearNewAndConfirmation() throws {
    setUpEntriesNewPasswordTooShort()
    tap(sut.submitButton)

    try alertVerifier.executeAction(forButton: "OK")

    XCTAssertEqual(sut.newPasswordTextField.text?.isEmpty, true, "new")
    XCTAssertEqual(sut.confirmPasswordTextField.text?.isEmpty, true,
            "confirmation")
}

func test_tappingOKInTooShortAlert_shouldNotClearOldPasswordField() throws {
    setUpEntriesNewPasswordTooShort()
    tap(sut.submitButton)

    try alertVerifier.executeAction(forButton: "OK")

    XCTAssertEqual(sut.oldPasswordTextField.text?.isEmpty, false)
}
```

```
func test_tappingOKInTooShortAlert_shouldPutFocusOnNewPassword() throws {
    setUpEntriesNewPasswordTooShort()
    tap(sut.submitButton)
    putInViewHierarchy(sut)

    try alertVerifier.executeAction(forButton: "OK")

    XCTAssertTrue(sut.newPasswordTextField.isFirstResponder)
}
```

(That first test adds descriptive messages to the assertions because the test has more than one assertion.)

Finally, what if the confirmation password doesn't match the new password? Same as the others, we don't change the password, but instead show an alert. Let's write a helper to express this input case:

Refactoring/RefactoringTests/ChangePasswordViewControllerTests.swift
```
private func setUpMismatchedConfirmationEntry() {
    sut.oldPasswordTextField.text = "NONEMPTY"
    sut.newPasswordTextField.text = "123456"
    sut.confirmPasswordTextField.text = "abcdef"
}
```

Here are the first two tests for a mismatch:

Refactoring/RefactoringTests/ChangePasswordViewControllerTests.swift
```
func test_tappingSubmit_withConfirmationMismatch_shouldNotChangePassword() {
    setUpMismatchedConfirmationEntry()

    tap(sut.submitButton)

    passwordChanger.verifyChangeNeverCalled()
}

func test_tappingSubmit_withConfirmationMismatch_shouldShowMismatchAlert() {
    setUpMismatchedConfirmationEntry()

    tap(sut.submitButton)

    verifyAlertPresented(
            message: "The new password and the confirmation password " +
                    "don't match. Please try again.")
}
```

Just like the "password too short" case, the alert's OK action should clear the new and confirmation fields, leaving the old password field alone. And the input focus should go back on the new password field. So copy and paste the tappingOKInTooShortAlert tests, changing their names and using setUpMismatched-ConfirmationEntry() instead.

Set the Appearance of the Waiting State

If the input fields are okay, the next step is to set the appearance while we wait for the password change request to finish. The first thing that happens is we dismiss the keyboard. Add a test that puts input focus on the first text field and confirms that it loses this focus:

```
Refactoring/RefactoringTests/ChangePasswordViewControllerTests.swift
func test_tappingSubmit_withValidFieldsFocusedOnOldPassword_resignsFocus() {
    setUpValidPasswordEntries()
    putFocusOn(textField: sut.oldPasswordTextField)
    XCTAssertTrue(sut.oldPasswordTextField.isFirstResponder, "precondition")

    tap(sut.submitButton)

    XCTAssertFalse(sut.oldPasswordTextField.isFirstResponder)
}
```

Repeat this same test for the new password field and for the confirmation field.

We want to prevent user interaction while the change password call is happening. This includes disabling the Cancel button. Here's a test for that.

```
Refactoring/RefactoringTests/ChangePasswordViewControllerTests.swift
func test_tappingSubmit_withValidFields_shouldDisableCancelBarButton() {
    setUpValidPasswordEntries()
    XCTAssertTrue(sut.cancelBarButton.isEnabled, "precondition")

    tap(sut.submitButton)

    XCTAssertFalse(sut.cancelBarButton.isEnabled)
}
```

We blur the entire screen, then put a spinning activity indicator on top. We'll test this in two ways. First, we'll test if blurView and activityIndicator have a superview. To make these properties accessible from the tests, edit ChangePasswordViewController, removing the private modifiers. Then add the following tests:

```
Refactoring/RefactoringTests/ChangePasswordViewControllerTests.swift
func test_tappingSubmit_withValidFields_shouldShowBlurView() {
    setUpValidPasswordEntries()
    XCTAssertNil(sut.blurView.superview, "precondition")

    tap(sut.submitButton)

    XCTAssertNotNil(sut.blurView.superview)
}
func test_tappingSubmit_withValidFields_shouldShowActivityIndicator() {
    setUpValidPasswordEntries()
    XCTAssertNil(sut.activityIndicator.superview, "precondition")
```

```
    tap(sut.submitButton)

    XCTAssertNotNil(sut.activityIndicator.superview)
}

func test_tappingSubmit_withValidFields_shouldStartActivityAnimation() {
    setUpValidPasswordEntries()
    XCTAssertFalse(sut.activityIndicator.isAnimating, "precondition")

    tap(sut.submitButton)

    XCTAssertTrue(sut.activityIndicator.isAnimating)
}
```

The blur visual effect looks best if the background color is clear. Let's add a test for that:

Refactoring/RefactoringTests/ChangePasswordViewControllerTests.swift
```
func test_tappingSubmit_withValidFields_shouldClearBackgroundColorForBlur() {
    setUpValidPasswordEntries()
    XCTAssertNotEqual(sut.view.backgroundColor, .clear, "precondition")

    tap(sut.submitButton)

    XCTAssertEqual(sut.view.backgroundColor, .clear)
}
```

These tests confirm some basic state about the views, but not how they look. To capture the layout, let's add a snapshot test. A snapshot is slower than a regular unit test, so let's apply Slow Snapshots: Keep Them in Their Own Corner, on page 203 and create a separate test suite. Give it the name ChangePasswordViewControllerSnapshotTests.

Then follow Add FBSnapshotTestCase to a Test Target, on page 196 to add the library and Set the Location for Reference Images, on page 198 to set the environment variable. Change the superclass of the snapshot suite from XCTestCase to FBSnapshotTestCase.

Copy the Test Fixture from ChangePasswordViewControllerTests, including setUp() and tearDown(). In setUp(), add the record mode for the snapshot:

Refactoring/RefactoringTests/ChangePasswordViewControllerSnapshotTests.swift
```
super.setUp()
recordMode = false
let storyboard = UIStoryboard(name: "Main", bundle: nil)
```

Also copy the setUpValidPasswordEntries() helper from the unit tests to the snapshot tests. Then add the following test:

Refactoring/RefactoringTests/ChangePasswordViewControllerSnapshotTests.swift
```
func test_blur() {
    setUpValidPasswordEntries()

    tap(sut.submitButton)

    FBSnapshotVerifyViewController(sut)
}
```

Set your destination to the iOS simulator you want to use for snapshots. Temporarily change recordMode to true, and run tests. Find the recorded image. On the first try, it doesn't look correct. The navigation bar is missing. To fix that, follow What If the Snapshot Doesn't Look Right?, on page 201 by creating the following helper:

Refactoring/RefactoringTests/ChangePasswordViewControllerSnapshotTests.swift
```
private func verifySnapshot(file: StaticString = #file, line: UInt = #line) {
    let window = UIWindow(frame: UIScreen.main.bounds)
    window.addSubview(sut.view)
    FBSnapshotVerifyViewController(sut, file: file, line: line)
}
```

Change the last line in the test to verifySnapshot(). Run the tests again and check the recorded image. This time the positioning is correct. The blur effect isn't the same as in real life, but it shows an approximation, which is good enough. Change recordMode back to false and rerun the tests to see them pass.

Now we have unit tests that check the state of the blur view and the activity indicator, and snapshot tests that check their appearance.

Call the Password Changer

Our last tests of the Submit button check the interactions with the password changer. These tests will all deal with the mock object. The first test sets up some valid inputs, along with a security token. We want to make sure the code sends these to the password changer. But instead of using setUpValidPasswordEntries() where the input values are somewhat hidden, let's set them right from the test. That way, it's obvious where the values in the mock object's verifyChange() call come from.

Refactoring/RefactoringTests/ChangePasswordViewControllerTests.swift
```
func test_tappingSubmit_withValidFields_shouldRequestChangePassword() {
    sut.securityToken = "TOKEN"
    sut.oldPasswordTextField.text = "OLD456"
    sut.newPasswordTextField.text = "NEW456"
    sut.confirmPasswordTextField.text = sut.newPasswordTextField.text

    tap(sut.submitButton)
```

```
    passwordChanger.verifyChange(
            securityToken: "TOKEN",
            oldPassword: "OLD456",
            newPassword: "NEW456"
    )
}
```

The rest of the password changer tests are for the closures, which handle success or failure. To make it easy to invoke these closures, let's add some more methods to MockPasswordChanger:

Refactoring/RefactoringTests/MockPasswordChanger.swift
```
func changeCallSuccess(file: StaticString = #file, line: UInt = #line) {
    guard changeWasCalledOnce(file: file, line: line) else { return }
    changeArgsOnSuccess.last!()
}

func changeCallFailure(message: String,
                       file: StaticString = #file, line: UInt = #line) {
    guard changeWasCalledOnce(file: file, line: line) else { return }
    changeArgsOnFailure.last!(message)
}
```

Let's test the success closure. First, it should stop the spinning animation on the activity indicator and remove it from the view:

Refactoring/RefactoringTests/ChangePasswordViewControllerTests.swift
```
func test_changePasswordSuccess_shouldStopActivityIndicatorAnimation() {
    setUpValidPasswordEntries()
    tap(sut.submitButton)
    XCTAssertTrue(sut.activityIndicator.isAnimating, "precondition")

    passwordChanger.changeCallSuccess()

    XCTAssertFalse(sut.activityIndicator.isAnimating)
}

func test_changePasswordSuccess_shouldHideActivityIndicator() {
    setUpValidPasswordEntries()
    tap(sut.submitButton)
    XCTAssertNotNil(sut.activityIndicator.superview, "precondition")

    passwordChanger.changeCallSuccess()

    XCTAssertNil(sut.activityIndicator.superview)
}
```

This should also be true for the failure closure. Duplicate these tests, but change their names and have them call the failure closure:

Refactoring/RefactoringTests/ChangePasswordViewControllerTests.swift
```
passwordChanger.changeCallFailure(message: "DUMMY")
```

The success closure should show a success alert notifying the user. Tapping OK in the alert should dismiss the modal. Here are the tests for this:

Refactoring/RefactoringTests/ChangePasswordViewControllerTests.swift
```
func test_changePasswordSuccess_shouldShowSuccessAlert() {
    setUpValidPasswordEntries()
    tap(sut.submitButton)

    passwordChanger.changeCallSuccess()

    verifyAlertPresented(
        message: "Your password has been successfully changed.")
}
func test_tappingOKInSuccessAlert_shouldDismissModal() throws {
    setUpValidPasswordEntries()
    tap(sut.submitButton)
    passwordChanger.changeCallSuccess()
    let dismissalVerifier = DismissalVerifier()

    try alertVerifier.executeAction(forButton: "OK")

    dismissalVerifier.verify(animated: true, dismissedViewController: sut)
}
```

If the call to the password changer fails, it will call the failure closure. Let's call the closure with a pretend error message, confirming that this shows an alert with that message:

Refactoring/RefactoringTests/ChangePasswordViewControllerTests.swift
```
func test_changePasswordFailure_shouldShowFailureAlertWithGivenMessage() {
    setUpValidPasswordEntries()
    tap(sut.submitButton)

    passwordChanger.changeCallFailure(message: "MESSAGE")

    verifyAlertPresented(message: "MESSAGE")
}
```

We have several tests of the OK action in the failure alert. Let's make it easier to get to this alert by creating a helper method:

Refactoring/RefactoringTests/ChangePasswordViewControllerTests.swift
```
private func showPasswordChangeFailureAlert() {
    setUpValidPasswordEntries()
    tap(sut.submitButton)
    passwordChanger.changeCallFailure(message: "DUMMY")
}
```

The upcoming tests of the OK action for failure show the following:

- It clears the text fields to start all over.

- It puts input focus on the first text field.

- It sets the background color to back to white. (We used a clear background color underneath the blur effect.)

- It removes the blur from the view.

- It enables the Cancel button.

- It doesn't dismiss the modal.

Refactoring/RefactoringTests/ChangePasswordViewControllerTests.swift
```swift
func test_tappingOKInFailureAlert_shouldClearAllFieldsToStartOver() throws {
    showPasswordChangeFailureAlert()

    try alertVerifier.executeAction(forButton: "OK")

    XCTAssertEqual(sut.oldPasswordTextField.text?.isEmpty, true, "old")
    XCTAssertEqual(sut.newPasswordTextField.text?.isEmpty, true, "new")
    XCTAssertEqual(sut.confirmPasswordTextField.text?.isEmpty, true,
            "confirmation")
}

func test_tappingOKInFailureAlert_shouldPutFocusOnOldPassword() throws {
    showPasswordChangeFailureAlert()
    putInViewHierarchy(sut)

    try alertVerifier.executeAction(forButton: "OK")

    XCTAssertTrue(sut.oldPasswordTextField.isFirstResponder)
}

func test_tappingOKInFailureAlert_shouldSetBackgroundBackToWhite() throws {
    showPasswordChangeFailureAlert()
    XCTAssertNotEqual(sut.view.backgroundColor, .white, "precondition")

    try alertVerifier.executeAction(forButton: "OK")

    XCTAssertEqual(sut.view.backgroundColor, .white)
}

func test_tappingOKInFailureAlert_shouldHideBlur() throws {
    showPasswordChangeFailureAlert()
    XCTAssertNotNil(sut.blurView.superview, "precondition")

    try alertVerifier.executeAction(forButton: "OK")

    XCTAssertNil(sut.blurView.superview)
}

func test_tappingOKInFailureAlert_shouldEnableCancelBarButton() throws {
    showPasswordChangeFailureAlert()
    XCTAssertFalse(sut.cancelBarButton.isEnabled, "precondition")

    try alertVerifier.executeAction(forButton: "OK")

    XCTAssertTrue(sut.cancelBarButton.isEnabled)
}
```

```
func test_tappingOKInFailureAlert_shouldNotDismissModal() throws {
    showPasswordChangeFailureAlert()
    let dismissalVerifier = DismissalVerifier()

    try alertVerifier.executeAction(forButton: "OK")

    XCTAssertEqual(dismissalVerifier.dismissedCount, 0)
}
```

We're nearly done. We have one last method to test, a UITextField delegate method.

Test the Text Field Delegate Method

We've finished testing the long method for the Submit button action. Here's the last method we want to test. It determines what happens when you press the Return key from within each text field.

Refactoring/Refactoring/ChangePasswordViewController.swift
```
func textFieldShouldReturn(_ textField: UITextField) -> Bool {
    if textField === oldPasswordTextField {
        newPasswordTextField.becomeFirstResponder()
    } else if textField === newPasswordTextField {
        confirmPasswordTextField.becomeFirstResponder()
    } else if textField === confirmPasswordTextField {
        changePassword()
    }
    return true
}
```

We'll follow the approach laid out in Test Delegate Methods, on page 177. As a first test, let's make sure each text field has its delegate hooked up:

Refactoring/RefactoringTests/ChangePasswordViewControllerTests.swift
```
func test_textFieldDelegates_shouldBeConnected() {
    XCTAssertNotNil(sut.oldPasswordTextField.delegate,
            "oldPasswordTextField")
    XCTAssertNotNil(sut.newPasswordTextField.delegate,
            "updatedPasswordTextField")
    XCTAssertNotNil(sut.confirmPasswordTextField.delegate,
            "confirmPasswordTextField")
}
```

To call the method through the text field delegate, add a function to TestHelpers.swift:

Refactoring/RefactoringTests/TestHelpers.swift
```
@discardableResult func shouldReturn(in textField: UITextField) -> Bool? {
    textField.delegate?.textFieldShouldReturn?(textField)
}
```

Now we can test that hitting Return in the first two fields moves the input focus to the next field:

Refactoring/RefactoringTests/ChangePasswordViewControllerTests.swift

```swift
func test_hittingReturnFromOldPassword_shouldPutFocusOnNewPassword() {
    putInViewHierarchy(sut)

    shouldReturn(in: sut.oldPasswordTextField)

    XCTAssertTrue(sut.newPasswordTextField.isFirstResponder)
}
func test_hittingReturnFromNewPassword_shouldPutFocusOnConfirmPassword() {
    putInViewHierarchy(sut)

    shouldReturn(in: sut.newPasswordTextField)

    XCTAssertTrue(sut.confirmPasswordTextField.isFirstResponder)
}
```

Hitting Return from the Confirmation field should fire off the change password request:

Refactoring/RefactoringTests/ChangePasswordViewControllerTests.swift

```swift
func test_hittingReturnFromConfirmPassword_shouldRequestPasswordChange() {
    sut.securityToken = "TOKEN"
    sut.oldPasswordTextField.text = "OLD456"
    sut.newPasswordTextField.text = "NEW456"
    sut.confirmPasswordTextField.text = sut.newPasswordTextField.text

    shouldReturn(in: sut.confirmPasswordTextField)

    passwordChanger.verifyChange(
            securityToken: "TOKEN",
            oldPassword: "OLD456",
            newPassword: "NEW456")
}
```

This last test passes because of the call to the changePassword() method. But what if that call moves outside the if statement? Imagine what would happen if we put it right before the return statement. Our tests would still pass.

To make sure this doesn't happen, let's add two more tests. Hitting the Return key from the first text field shouldn't start the change password task, so let's test that:

Refactoring/RefactoringTests/ChangePasswordViewControllerTests.swift

```swift
func test_hittingReturnFromOldPassword_shouldNotRequestPasswordChange() {
    setUpValidPasswordEntries()

    shouldReturn(in: sut.oldPasswordTextField)

    passwordChanger.verifyChangeNeverCalled()
}
```

Then duplicate this test using the new password field.

Congratulations, we're finally done bringing the code under test! That was a long haul, so put this book down and take a break. When you come back, let's start refactoring the production code.

Refactor to Break Up a Long Function

You may have already noticed a few things about the production code, which you'd like to clean up. But instead of making a lot of changes all at once, let's apply the principles of refactoring. That's why we have all these unit tests.

We could start anywhere, but for this worked example, let's begin with a *code smell*. Martin Fowler describes what these are:

> A code smell is a surface indication that usually corresponds to a deeper problem in the system....A smell by definition is something that's quick to spot.[3]

The changePassword() method has the *Long Function smell*. As we noted earlier, this one method has 116 lines. This makes it more difficult to understand. There are three sections, each marked by a comment, so it also has the *comments smell*.

Inside the back cover of *Refactoring*, there's a catalog of smells. Each smell has a list of common refactorings we can apply. For Long Function, the most common refactoring is *Extract Function*.

Let's lean on automated refactoring when we can. Select the third section in changePassword(), which has the comment 3. Attempt to change password. In the Refactor menu, select *Extract to Method*.

 The context menu is a simpler way to access the Refactor menu. Either tap with two fingers or control-click. Then you can access the Refactor menu without moving the cursor up to the menu bar.

Xcode will extract the function and prompt you for its name. The comment describes what it does, so let's name it attemptToChangePassword().

Now we come to the most important part of the refactoring: running the tests. This follows my definition that "disciplined refactoring is changing code in small steps, with automated verification of each step." This is true for automated steps as well as manual steps.

---

3.   https://martinfowler.com/bliki/CodeSmell.html

Xcode places the new method above its origin, with a fileprivate modifier. I prefer the more restrictive private modifier. I also prefer to place helper methods below their point of call. This follows the newspaper metaphor from *Clean Code: A Handbook of Agile Software Craftsmanship [Mar08]*:

> We would like a source file to be like a newspaper article. …The topmost parts of the source file should provide the high-level concepts and algorithms. Detail should increase as we move downward, until at the end we find the lowest level functions and details in the source file.

So move the extracted method to the bottom of the ChangePasswordViewController class. Change its access control modifier from fileprivate to private.

Thanks to the name of the new method, the comment is now redundant. Delete the comment. Now run tests to confirm that moving the method and deleting the comment did no harm.

Follow these same steps to extract the section with the comment 2. Set up waiting appearance. Name the new method setUpWaitingAppearance(). Run tests. Then move the new method down, placing it above attemptToChangePassword(). Delete the superfluous comment. Test.

If you try this with the remaining first section, you'll find that Xcode has disabled "Extract to Method." That's because this section has early return statements. But that's okay because we can always follow the manual steps of the *Extract Function* refactoring.

The bulk of the refactoring book is a catalog of refactorings. Each refactoring entry has a Mechanics section, describing the steps to follow. For *Extract Function*, the first step is as follows:

• Create a new function and name it after the intent of the function.

To support the early return statements, let's return a Boolean flag indicating if the input is valid. Here's the skeleton of the new function:

Refactoring/Refactoring/ChangePasswordViewController.swift

```
private func validateInputs() -> Bool {
    return true
}
```

The next step is to do the following:

• Copy the extracted code from the source function into the new target function.

Paste the copied code above the return statement.

Xcode shows us four errors: "Non-void function should return a value" next to each return statement. Since these early returns handle failure, change each to return false.

There are further steps about handling local variables. We happen not to have any. This brings us to the next step:

- Compile after all variables are dealt with.

This build confirms that the new function compiles, even before anything calls it.

Now that we have a destination function, the next step is to do the following:

- Replace the extracted code in the source function with a call to the target function.

To express this as literally as possible, let's call the new function. If any inputs are invalid, do an early return:

Refactoring/Refactoring/ChangePasswordViewController.swift
```
guard validateInputs() else {
    return
}
```

Then we're ready for the big step to confirm it all:

- Test.

The final step in the Mechanics section is to "look for other code that's the same or similar to the code just extracted." That doesn't apply this time.

The new version of changePassword() now looks like this:

Refactoring/Refactoring/ChangePasswordViewController.swift
```
@IBAction private func changePassword() {
    guard validateInputs() else {
        return
    }
    setUpWaitingAppearance()
    attemptToChangePassword()
}
```

It clearly expresses what the action does in each section, while concealing the details.

Some programmers would do all this extracting in a single step, followed by one run of the tests. But following disciplined refactoring, this is what we did:

1. "Extract to Method" (automated), then test.
2. Move things around, then test.
3. "Extract to Method" again (automated), then test.
4. Move things around, then test.
5. *Extract Function* (manual):
   a. Define new target function, then build. (Nothing calls it yet, so building is a sufficient check.)

   b. Replace original code with call to target function, then test.

By moving in smaller steps, any failure in building or testing has a smaller scope. So fixing any problems is simpler and takes less time.

Extract a Method with Parameters

You may have noticed that ChangePasswordViewController has a lot of repeated code. In the newly extracted validateInputs() method, find the first alert code shown here:

```
Refactoring/Refactoring/ChangePasswordViewController.swift
if newPasswordTextField.text?.isEmpty ?? true {
    let alertController = UIAlertController(
            title: nil,
            message: "Please enter a new password.",
            preferredStyle: .alert)
    let okButton = UIAlertAction(
            title: "OK",
            style: .default) { [weak self] _ in
        self?.newPasswordTextField.becomeFirstResponder()
    }
    alertController.addAction(okButton)
    alertController.preferredAction = okButton
    self.present(alertController, animated: true)
    return false
}
```

There are many places that present an alert like this. It makes sense to think about extracting the common code into a new method. But if we apply the *Extract Function* refactoring without preparing the code, we'll end up with code we can't reuse.

Looking through the other places with alerts, we can see that they're the same except for these two things:

- The alert message
- The closure for the OK action

Here's a basic strategy for extracting reusable code, giving the extracted code input parameters:

1. *Extract Variable*
2. *Extract Function*
3. *Inline Variable*

In other words, let's first move aside the parts that change. We want to create a core section that we can reuse, then pull this core out into a function call. Then if we want to, we can move those changing parts back, putting them directly in the function arguments.

That's the large strategy. Let's dive into the nitty-gritty details.

Perform "Extract Variable" on the Alert Message

First, select the literal string "Please enter a new password." and look at the Refactor menu. As of this writing, Xcode doesn't enable "Extract to Variable" on this string literal, but maybe you'll be luckier with a newer release of Xcode. If so, use the automated refactoring and name the extracted variable message. Otherwise, let's follow the manual instructions.

The refactoring book lists the following steps for *Extract Variable*. First, it asks us to ensure that the expression we're extracting has no side effects. We're good there. On to the next step:

- Declare an immutable variable. Set it to a copy of the expression you want to name:

Refactoring/Refactoring/ChangePasswordViewController.swift
```
let message = "Please enter a new password."
```

Followed by:

- Replace the original expression with the new variable:

Refactoring/Refactoring/ChangePasswordViewController.swift
```
let alertController = UIAlertController(
    title: nil,
    message: message,
    preferredStyle: .alert)
```

And finally:

- Test.

Perform "Extract Variable" on the Alert Action Closure

Next, we want to extract the closure for the OK action. Select the trailing closure passed to the UIAlertController initializer. In the Refactor menu, select *Extract to Variable*. Name the new variable okAction. This creates a new variable:

Refactoring/Refactoring/ChangePasswordViewController.swift
```
let okAction: (UIAlertAction) -> Void = { [weak self] _ in
    self?.newPasswordTextField.becomeFirstResponder()
}
```

However, Xcode currently leaves the variable use dangling past the end of the initializer:

Refactoring/Refactoring/ChangePasswordViewController.swift
```
let okButton = UIAlertAction(
        title: "OK",
        style: .default) okAction
```

Fix this up by moving the closure variable inside the initializer parameters, using the argument label handler:

Refactoring/Refactoring/ChangePasswordViewController.swift
```
let okButton = UIAlertAction(
    title: "OK",
    style: .default,
    handler: okAction)
```

Run all tests to validate these changes.

Perform "Slide Statements" to Move the Closure Variable

Before we can do an *Extract Function* refactoring, we need to move things around. The extracted code should start with the creation of the UIAlertController and end with the call to present it. But now we have the okAction closure variable sitting in the middle.

We can't perform the extraction with that variable there, so let's move it further up. To do this, we'll use the *Slide Statements* refactoring.

The first step in the Mechanics section is to see if moving the statement will create any interference. It looks fine. So here are the remaining steps:

- Cut the fragment from the source and paste into the target position.
- Test.

This leaves us with the two newly extracted variables sitting together. They're above the code we want to extract, which is where we want them.

```
Refactoring/Refactoring/ChangePasswordViewController.swift
let message = "Please enter a new password."
let okAction: (UIAlertAction) -> Void = { [weak self] _ in
    self?.newPasswordTextField.becomeFirstResponder()
}
```

Perform "Extract Function" on the Alert Code

We've extracted variables for the parts that can vary when presenting an alert. We've moved those variables out of the way. Now we're ready to *Extract Function*. Let's use the automated version.

Start a multiline selection from the line defining the alertController variable. Finish the selection on the self.present() call. Then from the Refactor menu, select *Extract to Method*. Name the new function showAlert().

The resulting code has an error to fix and other ways we can refine it. Here's the error:

```
Passing non-escaping parameter 'okAction' to function expecting an @escaping
    closure
```

Xcode offers a suggestion, so select *Editor ▶ Fix All Issues* in the menu to define the okAction parameter as an escaping closure. Run the tests.

We'll use this new function throughout the code, so let's move it to the very bottom of the class. Do a *Slide Statements* refactoring and change the access control modifier from fileprivate to private. Run tests.

Now let's look at the signature of the new function. Xcode extracted it with no argument labels:

```
Refactoring/Refactoring/ChangePasswordViewController.swift
private func showAlert(_ message: String,
                      _ okAction: @escaping (UIAlertAction) -> Void) {
```

This leaves the call site looking rather bare.

```
Refactoring/Refactoring/ChangePasswordViewController.swift
showAlert(message, okAction)
```

To give the arguments names, we can apply the simplest mechanics of the *Change Function Declaration* refactoring, assisted by Xcode. First, we remove the underscores from the declaration:

```
Refactoring/Refactoring/ChangePasswordViewController.swift
private func showAlert(message: String,
                      okAction: @escaping (UIAlertAction) -> Void) {
```

Xcode shows a fixable error about "Missing argument labels," Apply the suggestion to have Xcode fix it up. The call site will look like this:

Refactoring/Refactoring/ChangePasswordViewController.swift
```
showAlert(message: message, okAction: okAction)
```

Here's what the extracted function looks like as a whole. Confirm what we've done by running all tests:

Refactoring/Refactoring/ChangePasswordViewController.swift
```
private func showAlert(message: String,
                       okAction: @escaping (UIAlertAction) -> Void) {
    let alertController = UIAlertController(
        title: nil,
        message: message,
        preferredStyle: .alert)
    let okButton = UIAlertAction(
        title: "OK",
        style: .default,
        handler: okAction)
    alertController.addAction(okButton)
    alertController.preferredAction = okButton
    self.present(alertController, animated: true)
}
```

Perform "Inline Variable" to Simplify the Call Site

Here's what the call site looks like now:

Refactoring/Refactoring/ChangePasswordViewController.swift
```
let message = "Please enter a new password."
let okAction: (UIAlertAction) -> Void = { [weak self] _ in
    self?.newPasswordTextField.becomeFirstResponder()
}
showAlert(message: message, okAction: okAction)
```

We extracted those variables so that we could do *Extract Function*. But now their job is complete. Let's move their values directly into the function call with the *Inline Variable* refactoring.

These are freshly extracted variables, so we know they're free of side effects and are immutable. So we can skip the first two steps of the Mechanics. The next step is to do the following:

• Find the first reference to the variable and replace it with the right-hand side of the assignment:

Refactoring/Refactoring/ChangePasswordViewController.swift
```
let message = "Please enter a new password."
let okAction: (UIAlertAction) -> Void = { [weak self] _ in
    self?.newPasswordTextField.becomeFirstResponder()
}
showAlert(message: "Please enter a new password.", okAction: okAction)
```

The next step is "Test."

There are no more references to replace. So the last two steps are these:

- Remove the declaration and assignment of the variable.
- Test.

In other words, we remove the entire let message statement and then test.

This completes the inlining of the string. Follow the same steps to inline the closure:

1. Copy the closure and paste it as the okAction argument of the showAlert() method. Test.

2. Delete the entire definition of the okAction variable. Test again.

The call site is now fairly simple:

Refactoring/Refactoring/ChangePasswordViewController.swift
```
showAlert(message: "Please enter a new password.",
          okAction: { [weak self] _ in
              self?.newPasswordTextField.becomeFirstResponder()
          })
```

You may like the explicit labeling of the closure as okAction. Or you may prefer to use Swift's trailing closure syntax. For our example, let's make it a trailing closure:

Refactoring/Refactoring/ChangePasswordViewController.swift
```
showAlert(message: "Please enter a new password.") { [weak self] _ in
    self?.newPasswordTextField.becomeFirstResponder()
}
```

Run the tests.

This completes our strategy for extracting a method with parameters. The new function looks good. The first call site looks good.

The next steps are to use the new method wherever we can. The name of this refactoring is *Replace Inline Code with Function Call*. The steps are simple: replace the code and then test.

I leave this as an exercise for you. Change each chunk of alert code to use the new method. Be sure to do this one alert at a time, not all at once.

If you encounter any test failures, here's a strategy for fixing them:

- If you can quickly figure out the problem, try to fix it. Run the tests.

- If the attempt at a fix didn't work, or you couldn't figure out a fix in a short time, undo. Go backward until the tests pass. Then take a breath, clear your mind, and start over.

The beauty of refactoring in small steps is that if a test fails, you don't have to hunt for the source. You know it's in the last change you made.

Using AppCode for Its Automated Refactoring

The alternative IDE AppCode[a] brings greater power to automated refactoring than Xcode. Working through the earlier example we see the following:

- AppCode's "Extract Variable" works on the string literal. It also works on closures. It even converts the former trailing closure to use the argument label.

- AppCode has "Move Statement Up" and "Move Statement Down" commands to help perform *Slide Statements*. These commands move entire statements.

- To select a portion to extract, place the cursor inside the code. Use the "Extend Selection" command to repeatedly increase the selected scope. If you go too far, use "Shrink Selection."

- "Extract to Method" works more often. It puts the extracted code below, following the Newspaper Metaphor. It sets the access modifier to private by default (you can change this). It names the arguments, gives them sensible names, and gives you a chance to change the argument names before doing the extraction.

No IDE is perfect, and Xcode is stronger in some areas. But AppCode is the tool to prefer for automated refactoring.

———————
a.   https://www.jetbrains.com/objc/

Clean Up a Few More Places

We've broken a big method into pieces. And we've extracted the most repeated section of code to show alerts. Let's finish with a little more cleanup.

Instead of doing a fine-grained walk-through, this time I will give rough descriptions. Remember to move in small steps, verifying each step as you go.

First, we have a UITextFieldDelegate method mixed in along with the rest of the code. Move it into its own extension:

Refactoring/Refactoring/ChangePasswordViewController.swift
```
extension ChangePasswordViewController: UITextFieldDelegate {
    func textFieldShouldReturn(_ textField: UITextField) -> Bool {
        if textField === oldPasswordTextField {
            newPasswordTextField.becomeFirstResponder()
        } else if textField === newPasswordTextField {
            confirmPasswordTextField.becomeFirstResponder()
        } else if textField === confirmPasswordTextField {
            changePassword()
        }
        return true
    }
}
```

Now that this is in an extension, remove the UITextFieldDelegate conformance from the ChangePasswordViewController declaration at the top of the file. Run tests to confirm.

There are two places that dismiss the keyboard with code like this:

Refactoring/Refactoring/ChangePasswordViewController.swift
```
oldPasswordTextField.resignFirstResponder()
newPasswordTextField.resignFirstResponder()
confirmPasswordTextField.resignFirstResponder()
```

We can do this more simply by using a UIView method that resigns the first responder of any subview. Change both to the following code. (Do one at a time, running tests after each change.)

Refactoring/Refactoring/ChangePasswordViewController.swift
```
view.endEditing(true)
```

Then in validateInputs(), the last two checks show alerts with the same closures for the OK action. Perform the *Extract Function* refactoring by creating a new method, resetNewPasswords():

Refactoring/Refactoring/ChangePasswordViewController.swift
```
private func resetNewPasswords() {
    newPasswordTextField.text = ""
    confirmPasswordTextField.text = ""
    newPasswordTextField.becomeFirstResponder()
}
```

Build with the new method. Then replace each call site, testing after each replacement.

Next, in attemptToChangePassword(), both the onSuccess and onFailure closures start with the same two lines:

Refactoring/Refactoring/ChangePasswordViewController.swift
```
self?.activityIndicator.stopAnimating()
self?.activityIndicator.removeFromSuperview()
```

Perform the *Extract Function* refactoring to pull these out to a new method named hideSpinner().

Finally in the onFailure closure, there's an alert that has another closure for the OK action. This inner closure is rather long and makes attemptToChangePassword() harder to read. This is a Long Function code smell. Perform the *Extract Function* refactoring to pull the contents of the inner closure into a new method named startOver().

This leaves the onFailure closure with code that gives a higher-level description of everything it does:

Refactoring/Refactoring/ChangePasswordViewController.swift
```
onFailure: { [weak self] message in
    self?.hideSpinner()
    self?.showAlert(message: message) { [weak self] _ in
        self?.startOver()
    }
})
```

If we were to express this code in English, it would read like this: If the attempt to change the password change fails, we get a message. First, we hide the waiting spinner. Then we show an alert with the given message. When the user dismisses the alert, start over.

The smaller details are hidden, making the larger intent clearer.

Key Takeaways

Stepping back from the exercise, here are the larger points you should remember:

- Refactoring means changing code in very small steps, with each step verified by tests.

- Quick feedback from automated tests makes this kind of refactoring possible.

- Use automated refactoring when possible. (AppCode makes this easier.)

- To perform manual refactoring, see *Refactoring: Improving the Design of Existing Code, 2nd Edition [Fow18]* for a catalog of refactorings. Follow the steps listed in the Mechanics sections.

- Whether the refactoring was automatic or manual, run the tests afterward.

- When moving code manually, don't perform the move in a single step. Put the new code in place and verify. Then remove the old code and verify.

- With each step verified by tests, if you get a failure, it happened because of something in the last change. Try to "fix it forward" once. If that doesn't work, go back to when the tests were passing and start over.

Here are the manual refactoring moves we introduced in this chapter:

- *Extract Function*
- *Extract Variable*
- *Inline Variable*
- *Replace Inline Code with Function Call*
- *Slide Statements*

(The chapters in Part III don't have Activities for your own code.)

What's Next?

Hopefully this chapter has given you a clearer picture of what it's like to make small changes in a safe manner. We can transform code by taking one small step after another.

Taking enough small steps can reveal larger possibilities for change that were harder to see before. For example, we can break a large class into multiple classes. In the next chapter, we'll refactor toward the model-view-view-model (MVVM) architecture.

CHAPTER 18

Refactoring: Moving to MVVM

In the previous chapter, we established the basic rhythm of refactoring: take a small step; run the tests. We used this to clean up a view controller, with high confidence that we didn't break anything. Now let's go further. That view controller followed a plain old model-view-controller (MVC) UI pattern. Another UI pattern popular among iOS developers is model-view-view-model or MVVM.

In this chapter, let's see how we can transform the view controller from MVC to MVVM. You'll learn how to do this using refactoring. With enough test coverage, you'll be able to adopt MVVM in your view controllers in a safe way.

What Is MVVM?

The basic idea of MVVM is to create a separate type that represents the current state of the view. We call this type a *view model*. Once we have a view model that captures the current state, it can also make decisions based on that state.

The view model then holds the business rules that affect the user interface. This makes it easier to reason about the business rules. The UIViewController becomes simpler because it doesn't have to handle the rules. Its job is to observe the view model and update the view to match.

The view model's representation should be independent of the view's technology. I find it helps to imagine that I have a different user interface, like a command-line tool one uses in Terminal. Then I ask myself, could I use this same view model for a Terminal-based UI?

Let's make this more concrete using our Change Password example. In the workflow, the Cancel button is usually enabled but is sometimes disabled. We can represent this in a view model with a Boolean variable:

```
var isCancelButtonEnabled: Bool
```

This variable doesn't know that the Cancel button is a UIBarButtonItem. That's not its job. But the ChangePasswordViewController does know how to communicate with the Cancel button. So in this chapter's example, we'll set up a simple way for the view controller to observe changes in the view model and respond to those changes. And we're going to refactor our way there, step by step.

For this worked example, we'll continue with the code we created and refactored in Chapter 17, Unleash the Power of Refactoring, on page 209. Let's duplicate the Refactoring source code into a new folder named MVVM. The project name will continue to be "Refactoring."

Replace String Literals to Use a View Model

The simplest place to begin a view model is to look for string literals. Search through ChangePasswordViewController, looking for double quotes. You will find:

- Various empty strings
- Alert messages
- The "OK" alert action label

The empty strings can remain. But let's pull the other string literals into a view model. These strings don't change, so we can start with a view model that doesn't change state at first. Let's begin by defining an empty view model. Add this file to the project:

MVVM/Refactoring/ChangePasswordViewModel.swift
```
struct ChangePasswordViewModel {
}
```

Then add it as a property in ChangePasswordViewController. In our case, we're using a storyboard supporting iOS versions before iOS 13, so it needs to be an implicitly unwrapped var property. (Otherwise, we could get rid of the ! and set it through an initializer.)

MVVM/Refactoring/ChangePasswordViewController.swift
```
var viewModel: ChangePasswordViewModel!
```

We use a new instance of ChangePasswordViewController in three places:

- Preparing for the segue in ViewController
- In the setUp() of ChangePasswordViewControllerTests
- In the setUp() of ChangePasswordViewControllerSnapshotTests

In each place, set the viewModel property to a new ChangePasswordViewModel. So in ViewController, we'll have:

MVVM/Refactoring/ViewController.swift
```
override func prepare(for segue: UIStoryboardSegue, sender: Any?) {
```

```
    super.prepare(for: segue, sender: sender)
    if segue.identifier == "changePassword" {
        let changePasswordVC = segue.destination
                as! ChangePasswordViewController
        changePasswordVC.securityToken = "TOKEN"
        changePasswordVC.viewModel = ChangePasswordViewModel()
    }
}
```

And each test suite will set the property on the system under test:

MVVM/RefactoringTests/ChangePasswordViewControllerTests.swift
```
sut = storyboard.instantiateViewController(
        identifier: String(describing: ChangePasswordViewController.self))
sut.viewModel = ChangePasswordViewModel()
```

We're not using viewModel yet, but everything should build. From the Xcode menu, select *Product ▶ Build For ▶ Testing* to build everything.

For our first string literal, let's move the "OK" from the alert action. Add the following to the view model:

MVVM/Refactoring/ChangePasswordViewModel.swift
```
let okButtonLabel: String
```

This now fails to build because the places that make ChangePasswordViewModel need to supply the string. Select *Editor ▶ Fix All Issues* in the Xcode menu to fill in the missing parameter, and set "OK" as the value:

MVVM/Refactoring/ViewController.swift
```
changePasswordVC.viewModel = ChangePasswordViewModel(okButtonLabel: "OK")
```

Repeat this with the setUp() code in the test suites. Then in ChangePasswordView-Controller, change showAlert(message:okAction:) to use the view model instead of the string literal:

MVVM/Refactoring/ChangePasswordViewController.swift
```
private func showAlert(message: String,
                       okAction: @escaping (UIAlertAction) -> Void) {
    let alertController = UIAlertController(
        title: nil,
        message: message,
        preferredStyle: .alert)
    let okButton = UIAlertAction(
        title: viewModel.okButtonLabel,
        style: .default,
        handler: okAction)
    alertController.addAction(okButton)
    alertController.preferredAction = okButton
    self.present(alertController, animated: true)
}
```

Run the tests, which should pass. But because they were passing before, the tests passing now could mean we didn't hook things up. Confirm that we're using the view model by temporarily changing the okButtonLabel value in the setUp() of ChangePasswordViewControllerTests. Running tests with a value other than "OK" will produce a lot of failures.

Repeat this process for the error alert messages. Add these strings to the view model one at a time, replacing the string literals:

- enterNewPasswordMessage
- newPasswordTooShortMessage
- confirmationPasswordDoesNotMatchMessage

One alert remains, for the success case. Start by setting up a successMessage property in the view model. But replacing the literal with viewModel.successMessage doesn't work, because Xcode complains:

```
Reference to property 'viewModel' in closure requires explicit 'self.' to
    make capture semantics explicit.
```

Applying the Fix-it suggestion to Insert 'self.' leads to a different error because we're inside a closure where self is weak. A common approach is to convert the weak self into a strong one with a guard statement:

```
guard let self = self else { return }
```

But let's use this as an opportunity to practice a refactoring technique. Instead of "fixing it forward," let's go back to a clean state where all tests pass, and try a different approach. Revert any changes to attemptToChangePassword(), but keep the unused successMessage property in the view model.

Instead of a guard to convert self from weak to strong, let's apply the *Extract Function* refactoring. A method is a function that happens to have implicit access to self, so this will simplify things. Xcode doesn't want to help us extract a closure into a method, so let's apply the mechanics of manual refactoring:

1. Create the skeleton of a new private function named handleSuccess().

2. Copy and paste the contents of the onSuccess closure into the new function.

3. Apply "Fix All Issues" so that the new code compiles.

4. Replace the body of the onSuccess closure with a call to the new function:

   ```
   self?.handleSuccess()
   ```

5. Run tests.

Now we can do the view model replacement we were attempting in the first place. In handleSuccess(), replace the string literal with a call to access successMessage from the view model. This time, the replacement goes smoothly. Run tests. Confirm the replacement by altering the successMessage in ChangePasswordViewControllerTests and checking for test failure.

Finally, we can remove each self-dot because we're no longer inside a closure. The method now looks as follows. As always, run tests to check the changes.

MVVM/Refactoring/ChangePasswordViewController.swift

```
private func handleSuccess() {
    hideSpinner()
    showAlert(message: viewModel.successMessage) { [weak self] _ in
        self?.dismiss(animated: true)
    }
}
```

(This also helps readability because we no longer have a closure inside a closure. In fact, let's repeat these same steps for the onFailure closure even though it doesn't need the view model. This reduces the complexity of the attemptToChangePassword() method.)

Overwrite Storyboard Labels

String literals in code aren't the only source of text in this view controller. We also have the labels we set in the storyboard. Let's supply that text in the view model as well.

Why Place Any Strings in the View Model?

Why bother overwriting labels, when Apple provides a way to localize storyboards? In fact, why not keep the earlier string literals in code, using NSLocalizedString() to convert them?

Well, it gives us a simple starting point to begin working on MVVM. If you have an existing localization workflow, you may not want to move strings into view models. And that's fine.

But moving strings does allow the UI components to be ignorant of the workflow. They'll just show whatever they're given. Separating concerns makes code easier to maintain. And if both storyboard and code-based strings live in a common place, it can simplify the localization workflow.

To help us set various labels, define an empty private function named setLabels() and call it from the end of viewDidLoad():

MVVM/Refactoring/ChangePasswordViewController.swift

```
override func viewDidLoad() {
    super.viewDidLoad()
    submitButton.layer.borderWidth = 1
    submitButton.layer.borderColor = UIColor(
            red: 55/255.0, green: 147/255.0, blue: 251/255.0, alpha: 1
    ).cgColor
    submitButton.layer.cornerRadius = 8
    blurView.translatesAutoresizingMaskIntoConstraints = false
    activityIndicator.translatesAutoresizingMaskIntoConstraints = false
    activityIndicator.color = .white
    setLabels()
}
```

One at a time, add the following properties to ChangePasswordViewModel:

- Set title to "Change Password"
- Set oldPasswordPlaceholder to "Current Password"
- Set newPasswordPlaceholder to "New Password"
- Set confirmPasswordPlaceholder to "Confirm New Password"
- Set submitButtonLabel to "Submit"

As each property is added, use it in setLabels() to set the appropriate label. Eventually, the method will grow to look like this:

MVVM/Refactoring/ChangePasswordViewController.swift

```
private func setLabels() {
    navigationBar.topItem?.title = viewModel.title
    oldPasswordTextField.placeholder = viewModel.oldPasswordPlaceholder
    newPasswordTextField.placeholder = viewModel.newPasswordPlaceholder
    confirmPasswordTextField.placeholder =
            viewModel.confirmPasswordPlaceholder
    submitButton.setTitle(viewModel.submitButtonLabel, for: .normal)
}
```

Run tests after each property is used by setLabels(). Remember to temporarily change the text of each property to make sure at least one test fails.

We now have a simple view model in place. It's simple because its contents never change. Let's take it further into a view model that changes, having it update the UI.

Respond to Changes in the View Model

So far, our view model is a set of strings that don't change. The view controller just looks up these strings as it needs them. But that only scratches the surface. MVVM becomes more powerful when the UI responds to changes in the view model.

When a view model property changes, we need a way for the view controller to use the new value. We can do this in various ways, from Apple's Key-Value Observing to third-party frameworks like Reactive Swift. For our example, we'll use a simple way built into the Swift language: the didSet observer.

We'll use this observation technique to move one view concept at a time, starting with whether the Cancel button is enabled.

Is the Cancel Button Enabled?

Add the following property to ChangePasswordViewModel. We'll use it to determine whether the Cancel bar button item is enabled.

MVVM/Refactoring/ChangePasswordViewModel.swift
```
var isCancelButtonEnabled = true
```

Note that this is a var property, not a let property like the others. This flag should be true initially. By giving it an initial value at its declaration, we don't need to add a custom initializer.

Now let's respond to changes in the view model. Our viewModel is already a var property because we're using old-fashioned storyboard injection. (If you defined it as a constant let property, change it now to a var.) Then add a didSet observer. Inside the observer, compare the old value of the property with the new value. If the property changed, use the new value to set cancelBarButton.isEnabled.

MVVM/Refactoring/ChangePasswordViewController.swift
```
var viewModel: ChangePasswordViewModel! {
    didSet {
        guard isViewLoaded else { return }
        if oldValue.isCancelButtonEnabled != viewModel.isCancelButtonEnabled {
            cancelBarButton.isEnabled = viewModel.isCancelButtonEnabled
        }
    }
}
```

Run tests to make sure nothing we haven't broken anything so far.

Why is that guard statement there? Try removing it and run tests again. Because we set viewModel before the view controller loads up the views, IBOutlets are still nil the first time through. The guard avoids this problem by not doing anything until the view controller's isViewLoaded property is true.

Now search for all references to cancelBarButton.isEnabled. Wherever it's set to true, set viewModel.isCancelButtonEnabled = true instead. Do the same for false. Run the tests.

This moves all direct manipulation of cancelBarButton.isEnabled into the view model's didSet observer. Everything else is indirect, by changing the view model property.

> ## Why Check If the Property Changed?
>
> Using if statements to check whether a property changed isn't always necessary. This is especially true for *idempotent operations*—that is, any operation you can apply multiple times without changing the result. Setting isEnabled on a UIControl is an example of such an operation. It doesn't matter if you set it to its own value.
>
> But remember that we're using a struct for the view model. As we add more mutable properties, when any of them change value, Swift will replace the entire struct. This fires off the didSet observer. Unless we're careful, it will update everything, whether we want it to or not.
>
> By comparing the old and new values of a property, we give the observer more granular control. Instead of updating everything, we can update only what changed. This granular control is important when gradually refactoring a view controller to use MVVM.

Which Text Field Has Input Focus?

Let's move another piece of state into the view model. This example is going to take us through interesting territory: *What should you do if you try a refactoring but some tests fail?*

We have several places that set a particular text field as the first responder for keyboard focus. There are also two places that dismiss the keyboard. We can model these with an enum showing which field has input focus, where the initial value is .noKeyboard.

MVVM/Refactoring/ChangePasswordViewModel.swift
```
var inputFocus: InputFocus = .noKeyboard

enum InputFocus {
    case noKeyboard
    case oldPassword
    case newPassword
    case confirmPassword
}
```

Then back in ChangePasswordViewController, add the following private method:

MVVM/Refactoring/ChangePasswordViewController.swift
```
private func updateInputFocus() {
    switch viewModel.inputFocus {
    case .noKeyboard:
        view.endEditing(true)
```

```
    case .oldPassword:
        oldPasswordTextField.becomeFirstResponder()
    case .newPassword:
        newPasswordTextField.becomeFirstResponder()
    case .confirmPassword:
        confirmPasswordTextField.becomeFirstResponder()
    }
}
```

Call this method from the didSet observer, wrapped in an if statement to see if the property value changed:

MVVM/Refactoring/ChangePasswordViewController.swift
```
if oldValue.inputFocus != viewModel.inputFocus {
    updateInputFocus()
}
```

Run tests. Now we want to take each case statement and replace other occurrences of that code with a view model change. So search for this statement outside of the didSet observer:

MVVM/Refactoring/ChangePasswordViewController.swift
```
view.endEditing(true)
```

The first occurrence is in cancel(). Replace it with code that sets the view model's inputFocus property to .noKeyboard:

MVVM/Refactoring/ChangePasswordViewController.swift
```
viewModel.inputFocus = .noKeyboard
```

Run tests. Unfortunately, this gives us a few errors related to tapping Cancel. Why? Each failing test starts by calling a helper method putFocusOn(textField:). And there we can see the test directly tells the given text field to becomeFirstResponder(), but the view model isn't updated.

We can make a new test helper that uses the view model to put focus on a specific text field. But the first thing we should do is get back to a state where our tests pass.

 Don't refactor while tests are failing. In disciplined refactoring, a move starts from "green" and ends in "green" without going through "red." That is, the tests should pass before the change, and continue to pass after the change.

Revert the last change, setting cancel() back to calling view.endEditing(true). Run tests to make sure they pass. Then let's start with our new strategy. Make a new test helper:

MVVM/RefactoringTests/ChangePasswordViewControllerTests.swift
```
private func putFocusOn(_ inputFocus: ChangePasswordViewModel.InputFocus) {
    putInViewHierarchy(sut)
    sut.viewModel.inputFocus = inputFocus
}
```

Now replace calls to putFocusOn(textField:) with calls to the new helper. For example, where you see:

MVVM/RefactoringTests/ChangePasswordViewControllerTests.swift
```
putFocusOn(textField: sut.oldPasswordTextField)
```

change it to:

MVVM/RefactoringTests/ChangePasswordViewControllerTests.swift
```
putFocusOn(.oldPassword)
```

Run tests after each replacement. When there are no more callers to the old helper, remove it.

Then let's go back to the line we wanted to change in the first place. In cancel(), change view.endEditing(true) back to viewModel.inputFocus = .noKeyboard. Run the tests. This time, it works fine. Repeat for other occurrences of view.endEditing(true). Then do the same for the other cases in the updateInputFocus() method.

Now the didSet observer is the only place that calls endEditing(_) or becomeFirstResponder(). We've moved more of our direct controlling of views into the view model observer. The rest of the code in the view controller is starting to express things at a higher level of abstraction. For example, here's the delegate method that handles the Return key for each text field:

MVVM/Refactoring/ChangePasswordViewController.swift
```
func textFieldShouldReturn(_ textField: UITextField) -> Bool {
    if textField === oldPasswordTextField {
        viewModel.inputFocus = .newPassword
    } else if textField === newPasswordTextField {
        viewModel.inputFocus = .confirmPassword
    } else if textField === confirmPasswordTextField {
        changePassword()
    }
    return true
}
```

With a little explanation, we can now read over this together with the product owner to make sure this is the behavior the product owner wants for the Return key.

Is the Blur View Showing?

The next thing we can move into the view model is whether the blur view is showing. We can represent this with a Boolean property. Name it isBlurViewShowing and initialize it to false:

MVVM/Refactoring/ChangePasswordViewModel.swift
```
var isBlurViewShowing = false
```

In the didSet observer, check whether this property changed. If it did, call a new method we'll write next:

MVVM/Refactoring/ChangePasswordViewController.swift
```
if oldValue.isBlurViewShowing != viewModel.isBlurViewShowing {
    updateBlurView()
}
```

Create a skeleton for this new method that does one thing if the new value is true, and something else if it's false:

MVVM/Refactoring/ChangePasswordViewController.swift
```
private func updateBlurView() {
    if viewModel.isBlurViewShowing {
    } else {
    }
}
```

Make sure there are no compiler errors so far. Then let's find where we show the blur view. It's the method setUpWaitingAppearance(). Copy the entire body of this method into the if clause of updateBlurView(). Remove anything that doesn't pertain to either blurView or view.backgroundColor. This leaves the following in the if clause:

MVVM/Refactoring/ChangePasswordViewController.swift
```
view.backgroundColor = .clear
view.addSubview(blurView)
NSLayoutConstraint.activate([
    blurView.heightAnchor.constraint(equalTo: view.heightAnchor),
    blurView.widthAnchor.constraint(equalTo: view.widthAnchor),
])
```

Back in setUpWaitingAppearance(), remove the lines that now live in updateBlurView(). Replace them with the following line:

MVVM/Refactoring/ChangePasswordViewController.swift
```
viewModel.isBlurViewShowing = true
```

Run tests to confirm this move was successful.

Next, find the two lines in startOver() that remove the blur view and set the background color back to white. Copy and paste them into the else clause:

MVVM/Refactoring/ChangePasswordViewController.swift
```
blurView.removeFromSuperview()
view.backgroundColor = .white
```

Change the original lines in startOver() to viewModel.isBlurViewShowing = false and run tests.

Moving this into the view model and its didSet observer takes the somewhat complicated show/hide commands that lived in two places and brings them together. Now we can see them in one place. The symmetry of the two halves makes visual inspection of the code easier.

MVVM/Refactoring/ChangePasswordViewController.swift
```
private func updateBlurView() {
    if viewModel.isBlurViewShowing {
        view.backgroundColor = .clear
        view.addSubview(blurView)
        NSLayoutConstraint.activate([
            blurView.heightAnchor.constraint(equalTo: view.heightAnchor),
            blurView.widthAnchor.constraint(equalTo: view.widthAnchor),
        ])
    } else {
        blurView.removeFromSuperview()
        view.backgroundColor = .white
    }
}
```

Is the Activity Indicator Showing?

Let's do much the same thing to move the spinning activity indicator into ChangePasswordViewModel. Add a Boolean property isActivityIndicatorShowing and initialize it to false:

MVVM/Refactoring/ChangePasswordViewModel.swift
```
var isActivityIndicatorShowing = false
```

In the didSet observer, call a new helper method if the property changed:

MVVM/Refactoring/ChangePasswordViewController.swift
```
if oldValue.isActivityIndicatorShowing !=
        viewModel.isActivityIndicatorShowing {
    updateActivityIndicator()
}
```

Define the new helper with a skeleton for whether the property is true or false:

MVVM/Refactoring/ChangePasswordViewController.swift
```
private func updateActivityIndicator() {
    if viewModel.isActivityIndicatorShowing {
    } else {
    }
}
```

Find the lines in setUpWaitingAppearance() that handle the activityIndicator. Copy those lines into the if clause of updateActivityIndicator():

MVVM/Refactoring/ChangePasswordViewController.swift
```
view.addSubview(activityIndicator)
NSLayoutConstraint.activate([
    activityIndicator.centerXAnchor.constraint(equalTo: view.centerXAnchor),
    activityIndicator.centerYAnchor.constraint(equalTo: view.centerYAnchor),
])
activityIndicator.startAnimating()
```

If there are no compiler errors, replace the original lines with viewModel.isActivityIndicatorShowing = true and run tests.

The helper hideSpinner() has the code to hide the activity indicator. Copy its body into the else clause of updateActivityIndicator():

MVVM/Refactoring/ChangePasswordViewController.swift
```
activityIndicator.stopAnimating()
activityIndicator.removeFromSuperview()
```

In handleSuccess(), replace the call to hideSpinner() with a view model change view-Model.isActivityIndicatorShowing = false. Run tests.

MVVM/Refactoring/ChangePasswordViewController.swift
```
private func handleSuccess() {
    viewModel.isActivityIndicatorShowing = false
    showAlert(message: viewModel.successMessage) { [weak self] _ in
        self?.dismiss(animated: true)
    }
}
```

Once again, we've pulled code for showing or hiding something that used to live in two places, bringing them close together. And the remaining view controller code is now more expressive. Look at the method that sets the appearance while the app sends the change password request. This is what it looked like before:

MVVM/Refactoring/ChangePasswordViewController.swift
```
private func setUpWaitingAppearance() {
    view.endEditing(true)
    cancelBarButton.isEnabled = false
    view.backgroundColor = .clear
    view.addSubview(blurView)
```

```
    view.addSubview(activityIndicator)
    NSLayoutConstraint.activate([
        blurView.heightAnchor.constraint(equalTo: view.heightAnchor),
        blurView.widthAnchor.constraint(equalTo: view.widthAnchor),
        activityIndicator.centerXAnchor.constraint(
                equalTo: view.centerXAnchor),
        activityIndicator.centerYAnchor.constraint(
                equalTo: view.centerYAnchor),
    ])
    activityIndicator.startAnimating()
}
```

Here it is now:

MVVM/Refactoring/ChangePasswordViewController.swift
```
private func setUpWaitingAppearance() {
    viewModel.inputFocus = .noKeyboard
    viewModel.isCancelButtonEnabled = false
    viewModel.isBlurViewShowing = true
    viewModel.isActivityIndicatorShowing = true
}
```

The former is a mishmash of details. The latter is code we could review with the product owner to make sure we did everything the product owner wanted.

Move Logic into the View Model

Most of the logic of this view controller is in the validateInputs() method. For example, to see if the new password is too short, we have the following if statement:

MVVM/Refactoring/ChangePasswordViewController.swift
```
if newPasswordTextField.text?.count ?? 0 < 6 {
```

Because UITextField's text property is optional (due to legacy Objective-C code), this statement is extra fiddly. If the view model could express the content of each text field, we could separate this logic from UIKit.

So far, the interaction between the view model and the views has been one-way. Any changes to the view model cause the didSet observer to execute. This is *one-way data binding*: the views are bound to the view model.

We can expand this to *two-way data binding*, where changes to the views update values in the view model. To do this in a thorough fashion, we could have each UITextField copy user input to the view model. We'd need this if user input enabled or disabled the Submit button on each keystroke. But that's not how this view controller behaves.

We're not checking text field content until the user taps the Submit button. So we can use a simpler approach of copying the fields to the view model on-demand. Let's start by adding a property for each text field, showing what the user entered. Set their initial values to empty strings:

MVVM/Refactoring/ChangePasswordViewModel.swift
```
var oldPassword = ""
var newPassword = ""
var confirmPassword = ""
```

Back in ChangePasswordViewController, add the following method to copy the text property from each UITextField to the view model:

MVVM/Refactoring/ChangePasswordViewController.swift
```
private func updateViewModelToTextFields() {
    viewModel.oldPassword = oldPasswordTextField.text ?? ""
    viewModel.newPassword = newPasswordTextField.text ?? ""
    viewModel.confirmPassword = confirmPasswordTextField.text ?? ""
}
```

Add a line to the top of changePassword() that calls this new method:

MVVM/Refactoring/ChangePasswordViewController.swift
```
@IBAction private func changePassword() {
    updateViewModelToTextFields()
    guard validateInputs() else {
        return
    }
    setUpWaitingAppearance()
    attemptToChangePassword()
}
```

By applying nil-coalescing, the view model can hold regular strings instead of optional strings. This will simplify things as we move the conditionals into the view model. Start from the first conditional in validateInputs().

MVVM/Refactoring/ChangePasswordViewController.swift
```
if oldPasswordTextField.text?.isEmpty ?? true {
```

Define a new computed variable in the view model. Copy everything before the nil-coalescing operator ?? into the body of the computed variable.

MVVM/Refactoring/ChangePasswordViewModel.swift
```
var isOldPasswordEmpty: Bool { oldPassword.isEmpty }
```

Make sure there are no compiler errors. Then change the conditional in validateInputs() to use this computed property instead:

MVVM/Refactoring/ChangePasswordViewController.swift
```
if viewModel.isOldPasswordEmpty {
```

Run tests to make sure everything is still fine. Then repeat these steps to define the following computed properties in ChangePasswordViewModel, changing the conditionals to call them:

- isNewPasswordEmpty
- isNewPasswordTooShort
- isConfirmPasswordMismatched

The resulting validateInputs() method is cleaner, expressing things at a slightly higher level of abstraction:

```
MVVM/Refactoring/ChangePasswordViewController.swift
private func validateInputs() -> Bool {
    if viewModel.isOldPasswordEmpty {
        viewModel.inputFocus = .oldPassword
        return false
    }

    if viewModel.isNewPasswordEmpty {
        showAlert(message: viewModel.enterNewPasswordMessage) {
            [weak self] _ in
            self?.viewModel.inputFocus = .newPassword
        }
        return false
    }

    if viewModel.isNewPasswordTooShort {
        showAlert(message: viewModel.newPasswordTooShortMessage) {
            [weak self] _ in
            self?.resetNewPasswords()
        }
        return false
    }

    if viewModel.isConfirmPasswordMismatched {
        showAlert(
            message: viewModel.confirmationPasswordDoesNotMatchMessage) {
            [weak self] _ in
            self?.resetNewPasswords()
        }
        return false
    }

    return true
}
```

You should notice a few things:

- The conditionals are now expressed as ideas, without testing whether any UIKit properties are nil.

- The alert messages are now expressed as ideas, not as string literals.

- Changing input focus is now expressed as ideas, not as UIKit commands.

Business rules like "What's the minimum number of characters we require in a new password?" now live in the view model. Pulling such rules out of the view controller makes it easier to see them in one place. They're no longer scattered around code that's manipulating views.

There's also some nil-coalescing in attemptToChangePassword(). Since it's called after changePassword() updates the view model, we can replace them with references to the view model:

MVVM/Refactoring/ChangePasswordViewController.swift
```
private func attemptToChangePassword() {
    passwordChanger.change(
            securityToken: securityToken,
            oldPassword: viewModel.oldPassword,
            newPassword: viewModel.newPassword,
            onSuccess: { [weak self] in
                self?.handleSuccess()
            },
            onFailure: { [weak self] message in
                self?.handleFailure(message)
            })
}
```

If you start with MVVM, it's easier to write tests directly against the view model. But if you have a solid suite of tests on a view controller, you can adopt MVVM later. And you can do so in safe and gradual steps using disciplined refactoring.

Key Takeaways

Starting with a well-tested view controller in MVC, we were able to evolve it toward MVVM using refactoring. The following was our overall refactoring strategy:

- Set up infrastructure for the new thing.
- Lay down the new code without changing the old code.
- Change the old code so it uses the new code.

This was a smooth process most of the way. But sometimes a refactoring doesn't work out and you end up with failing tests. Rather than "fixing forward," a pure refactoring approach sticks to the safety of keeping tests passing:

- Try a change that causes tests to fail.

- Revert the code back to where tests were passing.

- Refactor the thing that caused the test failures. (In our case, we needed to refactor the test code.)

- Try again with the original change you wanted.

We were able to gradually shift to MVVM with these steps:

- Move string literals into the view model.

- Choose a way to do data binding from the view model to the views. In our example, we did this using Swift's ability to define `didSet` observers.

- If your view controller loads IBOutlets from a storyboard or XIB, start the observer with a check that short-circuits if the outlets aren't ready:

```
guard isViewLoaded else { return }
```

- Find ways to model the user interface ideas separate from UIKit.

- Move view state changes into the `didSet` observer. Replace occurrences of the code with changes to the view model.

- Move conditionals that use view state into the view model. You'll need to choose a way to do data binding from the views back to the view model. Replace the original code with queries to the view model.

What's Next?

Now you can begin extracting view models from any view controller that has good unit tests. Doing so introduces some separation between the view controller code and the actual manipulation of UIKit views. The view model will contain some of your business logic. The view controller will manage the UI at a higher abstraction.

But MVVM is just one approach for improving traditional model-view-controller code. Another UI pattern that lets us move more business logic out of the view controller is model-view-presenter (MVP). In the next chapter, we'll continue refactoring our view controller, this time to MVP.

CHAPTER 19

Refactoring: Moving to MVP

We've now seen some refactoring in action. Relying on a good set of unit tests, we took a plain view controller and evolved it to use MVVM.

But MVC and MVVM aren't the only UI patterns we have. Another pattern is model-view-presenter, or MVP. This pattern is less well-known among iOS developers but brings a lot of power.

In this chapter, we'll continue refactoring our example, this time to MVP. You'll see even more code move out of the view controller. And we'll continue to do it all with refactoring.

What Is MVP?

In MVVM, we represent the state of the view in the view model. The view controller does two things with the view model:

- It asks the view model for what to show. This information might be constant, or it may change depending on business logic.

- It responds to changes in the view model state. We did this by adding a didSet observer to the view model property.

The information flow is one-way. The view controller is in charge and asks questions like, "Is the Cancel button enabled right now?" The view model knows nothing about the view controller.

But in MVP, the view controller puts the *presenter* in charge. It does this by routing user commands (like button taps) to the presenter. The presenter decides what to do and tells the view controller what to update.

So the view controller has a reference to the presenter, and the presenter has a reference back to the view controller. But we don't want a strong bidirectional dependency—otherwise we'll have a retain cycle causing memory leaks. Let's make the reference back to the view controller an unowned reference to break this retain cycle.

We also don't want the presenter to know everything about the view controller. In particular, the presenter should know nothing about UIKit views or controls. Instead, we'll create a protocol that represents an abstraction of UI commands. The view controller will conform to this protocol to provide the commands. And the presenter will issue these commands to the protocol, without knowing what implements them. We can diagram these relationships as follows:

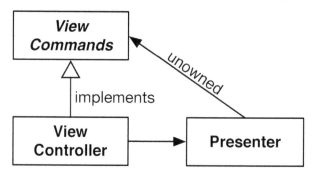

Set Up the MVP Types

Let's set up the new types we need for MVP and the relationships between them.

We'll continue where we left off with Chapter 18, Refactoring: Moving to MVVM, on page 255. There's no need to go through MVVM to get to MVP. But in our example, the responsibilities are clearer in the MVVM version, making it easier to work with. So duplicate the MVVM source code into a new folder named MVP. The project name will continue to be "Refactoring."

We'll start by setting up an empty View Commands protocol. Create a new file to hold a protocol named ChangePasswordViewCommands. Because the presenter's reference to it will be unowned, let's make it a class-only protocol to keep Swift happy:

MVP/Refactoring/ChangePasswordViewCommands.swift
```
protocol ChangePasswordViewCommands: AnyObject {
}
```

Add an extension to ChangePasswordViewController to conform to this protocol:

MVP/Refactoring/ChangePasswordViewController.swift
```
extension ChangePasswordViewController: ChangePasswordViewCommands {
}
```

Next, define ChangePasswordPresenter. It receives a ChangePasswordViewCommands implementor as its first initializer argument. (There will be more arguments later.) Hold on to it using an unowned property:

MVP/Refactoring/ChangePasswordPresenter.swift
```
class ChangePasswordPresenter {
    private unowned var view: ChangePasswordViewCommands!

    init(view: ChangePasswordViewCommands) {
        self.view = view
    }
}
```

Finally, add a property in ChangePasswordViewController to the presenter. We're going to pass self as the argument, so we'll delay construction of the property by making it a lazy property:

MVP/Refactoring/ChangePasswordViewController.swift
```
private lazy var presenter = ChangePasswordPresenter(view: self)
```

Now we have a View Commands protocol, and the view controller conforms to it. The view controller has a presenter. And the presenter points back to the view controller through the protocol. The pieces are empty, but we have what we need to begin refactoring to MVP.

Extract Methods into the View Commands Protocol

Here's the refactoring strategy we'll use to move responsibilities into MVP:

1. Use the *Extract Function* refactoring to take commands issued to views, and move them into the View Commands protocol.

2. Use the *Move Function* refactoring to move functions that call these View Commands. We'll move them from the view controller to the presenter.

Let's find something that issues commands to UIKit views. Since we used MVVM before, most of these will be in the didSet observer of viewModel. Looking at the bottom, we see it calls updateActivityIndicator(). Let's start there.

MVP/Refactoring/ChangePasswordViewController.swift
```
private func updateActivityIndicator() {
    if viewModel.isActivityIndicatorShowing {
        view.addSubview(activityIndicator)
        NSLayoutConstraint.activate([
            activityIndicator.centerXAnchor.constraint(
                    equalTo: view.centerXAnchor),
            activityIndicator.centerYAnchor.constraint(
                    equalTo: view.centerYAnchor),
        ])
        activityIndicator.startAnimating()
```

```
    } else {
        activityIndicator.stopAnimating()
        activityIndicator.removeFromSuperview()
    }
}
```

The else clause hides the activity indicator. Select those lines, then in the Refactor menu, select *Extract to Method*. Name the new method hideActivityIndi-cator(). Run tests.

We want this method to live in the extension at the bottom, which conforms the view controller to ChangePasswordViewCommands. To do this, we'll use the *Slide Statements* refactoring from *Refactoring: Improving the Design of Existing Code, 2nd Edition [Fow18]*. Basically, that means cutting and pasting to move it, then running tests.

Then remove the fileprivate access control. Copy this method signature into the protocol definition. Now the protocol declares one view command. Run tests.

MVP/Refactoring/ChangePasswordViewCommands.swift
```
protocol ChangePasswordViewCommands: AnyObject {
    func hideActivityIndicator()
}
```

Repeat these steps on the if clause of updateActivityIndicator(), extracting a method named showActivityIndicator(). Move it into the extension and copy its signature into ChangePasswordViewCommands.

Move Functionality out of the View Model

Here's what's left of updateActivityIndicator().

MVP/Refactoring/ChangePasswordViewController.swift
```
private func updateActivityIndicator() {
    if viewModel.isActivityIndicatorShowing {
        showActivityIndicator()
    } else {
        hideActivityIndicator()
    }
}
```

We want to change the places that set viewModel.isActivityIndicatorShowing to directly show or hide the activity indicator instead. When refactoring, we're looking for ways to move in small steps. The didSet observer calls this method whenever the property changes, so let's continue to set the property for now. Comment out the call to hideActivityIndicator(), so that the else clause is empty. Then at every call site that sets isActivityIndicatorShowing to false, add a call to hideActivityIndicator():

MVP/Refactoring/ChangePasswordViewController.swift
```
viewModel.isActivityIndicatorShowing = false
hideActivityIndicator()
```

Run tests. Then repeat the process to move the call to showActivityIndicator() out of the if clause. Run tests again.

Now delete the line in the didSet observer that calls updateActivityIndicator() and run tests. This leaves an empty if statement. Delete it and run tests. With nothing left that calls updateActivityIndicator(), delete the method and run tests.

The places that change the value of isActivityIndicatorShowing still cause the didSet observer to fire. But this no longer has any effect. One at a time, delete a line that changes the value of this view model property, and run tests. Repeat until there are no references to this property left in the view controller.

Now nothing even uses the view model property isActivityIndicatorShowing. Remove it from ChangePasswordViewModel, and run tests.

Can We Move to the Presenter? Not Until We Extract More

The View Commands protocol now defines two methods, showActivityIndicator() and hideActivityIndicator(). Let's see if we can move anything to the presenter. To move a method to the presenter, we need that method to call only the View Commands protocol and deal only with properties that exist in the presenter.

We call showActivityIndicator() from setUpWaitingAppearance(), but there are still other lines in there that manipulate the view model. It can wait until later.

The methods that call hideActivityIndicator() are much shorter. handleSuccess() calls hideActivityIndicator(), then shows an alert. The alert's OK action closure dismisses the view controller.

MVP/Refactoring/ChangePasswordViewController.swift
```
private func handleSuccess() {
    hideActivityIndicator()
    showAlert(message: viewModel.successMessage) { [weak self] _ in
        self?.dismiss(animated: true)
    }
}
```

Remember, our goal is to move methods to the presenter. To do that for this method, we need to define View Commands to show the alert and dismiss the modal. Let's start from the inside out and extract the dismiss(animated:) call.

Select the line. Control-click to bring up Xcode's context menu and select *Refactor ▶ Extract to Method*. Let's name the new method dismissModal() to describe what it does. The automated extraction leaves a couple of errors with

Fix-it suggestions. Select *Editor ▶ Fix All Issues* in the main menu to apply the first fixes. This creates a new error saying:

```
Value of optional type 'ChangePasswordViewController?' must be unwrapped to
    refer to member 'dismissModal' of wrapped base type
    'ChangePasswordViewController'
```

We can't "Fix All Issues" because it offers two suggestions. Click on the error and accept the fix to "Chain the optional." With no errors remaining, run tests.

Xcode's automated "Extract to Method" is helpful. But doing *Extract Function* manually has an important final step: "Look for other code that's the same or similar to the code just extracted." A search reveals another call to dismiss(animated:), from the cancel() action. Let's apply the *Replace Inline Code with Function Call* refactoring by changing it to call dismissModal() and then running tests.

> After doing an automated "Extract to Method" refactoring, look for other places that can call the new method.

Do a manual *Slide Statements* (cut and paste, then test) to move the new method dismissModal() down to the extension that provides the View Commands protocol methods. Remove the fileprivate modifier, then copy its method signature into the protocol definition in ChangePasswordViewCommands.swift. Run the tests again.

Since we already extracted a method to show alerts in Chapter 17, Unleash the Power of Refactoring, on page 209, it's tempting to move it into the protocol. But its okAction closure takes a UIAlertAction argument, which we ignore. We want to avoid UIKit types in the View Commands protocol so that it stays at an abstraction higher than UIKit. It would be nice to provide a closure without the argument, since we ignore the argument anyway.

So define a new method that takes an action with no argument. It will wrap the closure into the type UIKit needs, then call the method we already had before.

MVP/Refactoring/ChangePasswordViewController.swift
```swift
func showAlert(message: String,
              action: @escaping () -> Void) {
    let wrappedAction: (UIAlertAction) -> Void = { _ in action() }
    showAlert(message: message, okAction: { wrappedAction($0) })
}
```

One at a time, find the other calls to showAlert(message:okAction:). The preamble to each closure uses an underscore to show that it ignores the argument.

MVP/Refactoring/ChangePasswordViewController.swift

```
[weak self] _ in
```

Delete the underscore so the alert action closure starts as follows:

```
[weak self] in
```

This changes it to call the new method showAlert(message:action:) where the closure has no argument. Run tests.

Do *Slide Statements* on both showAlert() methods to pull them down into the extension. On the original one, which has the UIAlertAction closure argument, keep it private. Copy the signature of the new method showAlert(message:action:) with no closure argument into the ChangePasswordViewCommands protocol. Run tests.

 Avoid using UIKit types in the View Commands protocol so that the presenter can stay ignorant of UIKit.

Now everything inside of handleSuccess() calls things that are available to the presenter. So it's ready to move from the view controller to the presenter.

Move a Function into the Presenter

Let's now see how we can use *Move Function* to move handleSuccess() from the view controller to the presenter. We'll walk through the steps from the Mechanics section of this refactoring.

• Examine all the program elements used by the chosen function in its current context. Consider whether they should move too.

Everything in handleSuccess() is a call to one of the View Commands with one exception. The alert message comes from viewModel.successMessage. So we'll need to pass viewModel to the presenter.

The view model has begun to shrink, and may shrink down to only string literals, which we can store in a let property. But for now, since the view controller holds it as a mutable var, let's have the presenter also hold it as a var. Add viewModel as an initializer argument, which sets the property:

MVP/Refactoring/ChangePasswordPresenter.swift

```
class ChangePasswordPresenter {
    private unowned var view: ChangePasswordViewCommands!
    private var viewModel: ChangePasswordViewModel
```

```
    init(view: ChangePasswordViewCommands,
         viewModel: ChangePasswordViewModel) {
        self.view = view
        self.viewModel = viewModel
    }
```

This creates a "Missing argument" build error where the presenter is created. Fix it up by adding the new argument:

MVP/Refactoring/ChangePasswordViewController.swift
```
private lazy var presenter = ChangePasswordPresenter(view: self,
                                        viewModel: viewModel)
```

Run tests to make sure nothing is broken. Now that the presenter has a way to access the strings in the view model, let's continue doing *Move Function*.

• Check if the chosen function is a polymorphic method.

The method only exists at the ChangePasswordViewController level, so it's not poly-morphic.

• Copy the function to the target context. Adjust it to fit in its new home.

Here, we copy handleSuccess() and paste it into ChangePasswordPresenter as a method. This causes a couple of "Use of unresolved identifier" errors where it's trying to call the ChangePasswordViewCommands protocol. The presenter already has this in its view property, so add view. in front of each call. Also remove the private modifier:

MVP/Refactoring/ChangePasswordPresenter.swift
```
func handleSuccess() {
    view.hideActivityIndicator()
    view.showAlert(message: viewModel.successMessage) { [weak self] in
        self?.view.dismissModal()
    }
}
```

• Perform static analysis.

To do static analysis in Xcode, select *Product* ▶ *Analyze* from the menu.

• Figure out how to reference the target function from the source context.

ChangePasswordViewController has a property holding the ChangePasswordPresenter. And we've already made the target function non-private. So we're good.

• Turn the source function into a delegating function.

This changes the original handleSuccess() in ChangePasswordViewController so that it does nothing but call the new function:

MVP/Refactoring/ChangePasswordViewController.swift
```
private func handleSuccess() {
    presenter.handleSuccess()
}
```

• Test.

Everything should continue to pass.

• Consider *Inline Function* on the source function.

This step is directing us to perform another refactoring, which has its own steps. We'll follow them below:

1. Check that this isn't a polymorphic method. (We already know it's not.)
2. Find all the callers of the function.
3. Replace each call with the function's body.
4. Test after each replacement.

There is one caller, from attemptToChangePassword() inside the onSuccess closure argument. Change it to call the presenter, then test:

MVP/Refactoring/ChangePasswordViewController.swift
```
self?.presenter.handleSuccess()
```

With no more callers, we can take the final *Move Function* step:

• Remove the function definition.

So we delete the original handleSuccess() method.

The migration of this function from the view controller to the presenter is complete. Now you've experienced the process of moving one function, which calls back to the view controller through the protocol.

Remove the didSet Observer

Having moved handleSuccess() from the view controller to the presenter, it would be nice to do the same for handleFailure(). But its alert action calls startOver(), which touches several view model properties. So let's shift the effects of those properties into View Commands.

Let's follow the same refactoring steps we used in Move Functionality out of the View Model, on page 276, applying them to updateBlurView():

1. Extract the else clause into a function named hideBlurView(). Slide it down into the extension, then declare it in the ChangePasswordViewCommands protocol.

2. Extract the if clause into a function named showBlurView(). Slide it into the extension and declare it in the protocol.

3. Comment out the call to hideBlurView(). Add the call after every place that sets isBlurViewShowing to false. Run the tests.

4. Comment out the call to showBlurView(). Add the call after every place that sets isBlurViewShowing to true. Test.

5. Delete the didSet line that calls updateBlurView(), then test. Delete the now-empty conditional, then test. Delete updateBlurView() entirely, then test again.

6. Find a line that sets the viewModel.isBlurViewShowing. Delete it and run tests. Repeat until they're gone.

7. Delete the isBlurViewShowing property from ChangePasswordViewModel itself. Test.

The code that handles changes to isCancelButtonEnabled lives directly inside the didSet observer. Let's extract it. To separate it from the view model, first do the *Extract Variable* refactoring on viewModel.isCancelButtonEnabled. Xcode's automated refactoring isn't helping us, so do it by hand:

MVP/Refactoring/ChangePasswordViewController.swift
```
if oldValue.isCancelButtonEnabled != viewModel.isCancelButtonEnabled {
➤    let enabled = viewModel.isCancelButtonEnabled
➤    cancelBarButton.isEnabled = enabled
}
```

Test. Now we can use Xcode's "Extract to Method" to extract that last line to a method named setCancelButtonEnabled(_:). Test again.

From this point, we'll follow the same steps as before, except that there's one function to move into View Commands. Comment out the call to setCancelButtonEnabled(), and add calls with true or false arguments after each line that sets isCancelButtonEnabled. Then start deleting until the view model no longer has that property.

This leaves one last property observed by didSet, the inputFocus property. It calls updateInputFocus():

MVP/Refactoring/ChangePasswordViewController.swift
```
private func updateInputFocus() {
    switch viewModel.inputFocus {
    case .noKeyboard:
        view.endEditing(true)
    case .oldPassword:
        oldPasswordTextField.becomeFirstResponder()
    case .newPassword:
        newPasswordTextField.becomeFirstResponder()
    case .confirmPassword:
        confirmPasswordTextField.becomeFirstResponder()
    }
}
```

This is nicely contained, except for the reference to the view model. Let's fix this by passing viewModel.inputFocus in as a parameter. We can get there in a few steps. We need to apply the *Change Function Declaration* refactoring. This refactoring has two sets of mechanics. The simple mechanics are to make the change and fix up the callers. If you can adjust everything in less than a minute, this is appropriate. Otherwise, use the following migration mechanics to avoid breaking the build.

- If necessary, refactor the body of the function to make it easy to do the following extraction step.

To move the reference to viewModel.inputFocus outside the main body of this function, do a manual *Extract Variable* refactoring and run tests:

MVP/Refactoring/ChangePasswordViewController.swift
```
let inputFocus = viewModel.inputFocus
switch inputFocus {
```

- Use *Extract Function* on the function body to create the new function.

Select the entire switch statement and select "Extract to Method" from Xcode's Refactoring menu. Thanks to Swift's function overloading, we can give the new method the same name. Run tests.

- Apply *Inline Function* to the old function.

We'll do this in two inline steps. First, do *Inline Variable* on the variable we extracted right before extracting the new method:

MVP/Refactoring/ChangePasswordViewController.swift
```
private func updateInputFocus() {
    updateInputFocus(viewModel.inputFocus)
}
```

Then do *Inline Function* so that the didSet observer calls the method with the added parameter. Now follow the usual steps of doing *Slide Statements* to move the updateInputFocus(_:) method into the extension. Then copy its signature into the View Commands protocol:

MVP/Refactoring/ChangePasswordViewCommands.swift
```
func updateInputFocus(_ inputFocus: ChangePasswordViewModel.InputFocus)
```

Next, comment out the call to updateInputFocus(_:). At every call site that sets viewModel.inputFocus, add a call to the new method. For example, here's what we do with the cancel() method:

MVP/Refactoring/ChangePasswordViewController.swift
```
@IBAction private func cancel() {
    viewModel.inputFocus = .noKeyboard
    updateInputFocus(.noKeyboard)
    dismissModal()
}
```

Run tests...and we get several failures! But the name of each failing test says something about testing with the focus on a specific field. These tests each call the test helper putFocusOn(_:) in their Arrange sections. Fix up this helper by adding a call to updateInputFocus(_:):

MVP/RefactoringTests/ChangePasswordViewControllerTests.swift
```
private func putFocusOn(_ inputFocus: ChangePasswordViewModel.InputFocus) {
    putInViewHierarchy(sut)
    sut.viewModel.inputFocus = inputFocus
    sut.updateInputFocus(inputFocus)
}
```

This time, all tests should pass. (If you have any failures, you probably overlooked some viewModel.inputFocus changes.) Delete the preceding line that sets sut.viewModel.inputFocus, then test again.

Now the didSet has an empty if statement. Delete it and test. Then delete each line that sets viewModel.inputFocus. Run tests afterward.

Delete the inputFocus property from ChangePasswordViewModel.

Finally, what's left in the didSet does nothing useful. Delete it, leaving the view model as a plain property with no observer:

MVP/Refactoring/ChangePasswordViewController.swift
```
var viewModel: ChangePasswordViewModel!
```

All tests should continue to pass. We've succeeded in shifting away from an observed view model to a set of commands. We can now continue moving functions into the MVP style.

Use Refactoring Principles to Reparent a Swift Type

We still declare the InputFocus enumeration inside ChangePasswordViewModel as a nested type. But there's nothing left in the view model that references it, so it no longer makes sense for it to live there. It would be nice to move it to ChangePasswordCommands.swift, next to the protocol that uses it.

Three files use this enumeration. In this small example, we could just move it and fix all the references. But what if there were many more references?

Let's put on our refactoring thinking caps. What we want are mechanics that allow us to move in small steps. This would let us make gradual progress without breaking the build. That way, having a refactoring in progress would not impact us or anyone else.

In Swift, we can use a typealias as temporary scaffolding. That is, we can set up the scaffolding, gradually shift references, then remove the scaffolding. Here are the mechanics to move a type from one parent to another:

- Copy the entire type definition from its current location. Paste it into the desired location.

- Build.

- Change the original type definition into a typealias pointing to the new type. If the new type has no parent, reference it by the module name (the implicit parent).

- Test.

- Replace references to the original type with the new type. Build after each change.

- Remove the typealias definition.

- Test.

Let's do this for InputFocus. First, copy it from ChangePasswordViewModel and paste it inside ChangePasswordCommands.swift, below the protocol definition. Make sure that builds.

Then change the old definition into the following typealias. We can't say InputFocus = InputFocus so prefix it with the module name:

MVP/Refactoring/ChangePasswordViewModel.swift
```
typealias InputFocus = Refactoring.InputFocus
```

Everything should continue to pass. Now one by one, find the references to the old type name ChangePasswordViewModel.InputFocus. Change them to InputFocus, building after each change.

Finally, remove the typealias and run tests.

This completes the reparenting of the type. And it's an example of applying the principles of *Refactoring: Improving the Design of Existing Code, 2nd Edition* *[Fow18]* in new ways. The important goal is to find a gradual transformation that avoids breaking the build or the tests.

Move Several Functions to the Presenter

The effects that the view model used to control now live in View Commands. Let's keep working on moving other functions into the presenter.

It helps to move lower-level functions first, so let's start from the methods at the bottom and move up. Here's what startOver() looks like now:

MVP/Refactoring/ChangePasswordViewController.swift
```
private func startOver() {
    oldPasswordTextField.text = ""
    newPasswordTextField.text = ""
    confirmPasswordTextField.text = ""
    updateInputFocus(.oldPassword)
    hideBlurView()
    setCancelButtonEnabled(true)
}
```

The last three lines are all View Commands. But the first three lines can't move to the presenter. Extract them into a method named clearAllPasswordFields(). Move it into the extension, and copy its signature into the protocol. You know to run the tests often during this process, right?

Now we can do *Move Function* on startOver(). Follow the steps shown in Move a Function into the Presenter, on page 279. The end result should be that the alert action of handleFailure(_:) calls the following presenter method:

MVP/Refactoring/ChangePasswordPresenter.swift
```
func startOver() {
    view.clearAllPasswordFields()
    view.updateInputFocus(.oldPassword)
    view.hideBlurView()
    view.setCancelButtonEnabled(true)
}
```

Moving higher, handleFailure(_:) is the next function to move. Follow the same steps. Here's how it looks living in the presenter:

MVP/Refactoring/ChangePasswordPresenter.swift
```
func handleFailure(_ message: String) {
    view.hideActivityIndicator()
    view.showAlert(message: message) { [weak self] in
        self?.startOver()
    }
}
```

Now that the line that calls startOver() is also in the presenter, we can mark startOver() as private. All tests should continue to pass.

The attemptToChangePassword() method is up next. But it has references to the view controller properties passwordChanger and securityToken. So we'll need to pass these to the presenter's initializer:

```
MVP/Refactoring/ChangePasswordPresenter.swift
init(view: ChangePasswordViewCommands,
     viewModel: ChangePasswordViewModel,
     securityToken: String,
     passwordChanger: PasswordChanging) {
    self.view = view
    self.viewModel = viewModel
    self.securityToken = securityToken
    self.passwordChanger = passwordChanger
}
```

Fix anything the compiler complains about. Namely, add new properties in the presenter (declaring them private). And pass the extra arguments at the call site.

Now we can move attemptToChangePassword(). It's the one that calls handleSuccess() and handleFailure(_:), so those two methods can become private after the function moves.

Then move setUpWaitingAppearance() to the presenter.

Next up, resetNewPasswords():

```
MVP/Refactoring/ChangePasswordViewController.swift
private func resetNewPasswords() {
    newPasswordTextField.text = ""
    confirmPasswordTextField.text = ""
    updateInputFocus(.newPassword)
}
```

Its first two lines clear the new and confirm password fields. Extract those lines into a new method named clearNewPasswordFields(). Move it into the extension, and add it to the ChangePasswordViewCommands protocol.

Now move resetNewPasswords() into the presenter. Follow the steps to turn the original method in the view controller into a delegating function. There are two call sites in validateInputs(). Change one at a time, running tests. Then delete the original method.

We've now moved several things into the presenter. Take a moment to celebrate before we face the last obstacle.

Extract Password Validation into Its Own Type

Moving up the view controller helper methods, the next ones are updateViewMod-elToTextFields() and validateInputs(). They involve the view model's validation of the inputs to the password fields. Let's find a way to move that validation out of the view model.

The view model has methods that check the password inputs against business rules. Rather than moving these into the presenter, it would make sense to extract them into their own type. Let's apply the *Extract Class* refactoring, which has the following mechanics:

- Decide how to split the responsibilities of the class.

What we'd like to end up with is a value type that takes the three password inputs and answers questions about their validity. I'm picturing a struct with three properties, and a handful of methods.

- Create a new child class to express the split-off responsibilities.

Make a new file that defines the following empty type:

MVP/Refactoring/PasswordInputs.swift
```
struct PasswordInputs {
}
```

- Create an instance of the child class when constructing the parent and add a link from parent to child.

Because the validation currently takes place in ChangePasswordViewModel, we'll add the instance there. Declare it as a mutable var property for now. We can try to make it immutable later, but the property itself may move around or even vanish. Let's cross the immutability bridge when we get there.

MVP/Refactoring/ChangePasswordViewModel.swift
```
var passwordInputs = PasswordInputs()
```

- Use *Move Field* on each field you wish to move. Test after each move.

Here it refers to another refactoring that's new to us. *Move Field* starts with adding getter and setter methods so that one can flexibly change them into forwarding functions. Swift lets us avoid these mechanics by using computed properties. We can have getters and setters, but the call sites continue to reference the property. (Swift gives us the best of both worlds.)

Let's move oldPassword from ChangePasswordViewModel to PasswordInputs. First, define it in the target. Give it the same default value that it has in the origin:

MVP/Refactoring/PasswordInputs.swift
```
var oldPassword = ""
```

Then change the original property to use a custom getter and setter that point to the new property:

MVP/Refactoring/ChangePasswordViewModel.swift
```
var oldPassword: String {
    get { passwordInputs.oldPassword }
    set { passwordInputs.oldPassword = newValue }
}
```

All tests should continue to pass. Now change all references to the original property to use the new property instead. The following computed property body is a good place to start. Change its implementation from referencing oldPassword to passwordInputs.oldPassword:

MVP/Refactoring/ChangePasswordViewModel.swift
```
var isOldPasswordEmpty: Bool { passwordInputs.oldPassword.isEmpty }
```

Run tests. Change the other references in the presenter and the view controller, running tests after each change. Then once everything has been updated to use the new property, delete the original oldPassword property from ChangePasswordViewModel, then test again.

This completes the *Move Field* refactoring for one field. Repeat this process for the newPassword and confirmPassword properties.

Now we return to the mechanics of the *Extract Class* refactoring.

- Use *Move Function* to move methods to the new child. Start with lower-level methods (those being called rather than calling). Test after each move.

We know how to do this. Start by copying the first function, the isOldPasswordEmpty computed property, from ChangePasswordViewModel. Paste it into PasswordInputs, adjusting it to fit by deleting the reference to passwordInputs:

MVP/Refactoring/PasswordInputs.swift
```
var isOldPasswordEmpty: Bool { oldPassword.isEmpty }
```

Then change the old ChangePasswordViewModel function so it delegates to the new one (and test):

MVP/Refactoring/ChangePasswordViewModel.swift
```
var isOldPasswordEmpty: Bool { passwordInputs.isOldPasswordEmpty }
```

Change the call site in validateInputs() to call the new method (and test):

MVP/Refactoring/ChangePasswordViewController.swift
```swift
if viewModel.passwordInputs.isOldPasswordEmpty {
```

Finally, delete the old function (and test).

Repeat this process to move isNewPasswordEmpty, isNewPasswordTooShort, and isConfirmPasswordMismatched into PasswordInputs.

- Review the interfaces of both classes, remove unneeded methods, change names to better fit the new circumstances.

Now we must remember our original goal, which was to move validation of the view model. The validation functions now live in the PasswordInputs, but validateInputs() references it through viewModel.passwordInputs. What if, instead, we pass the PasswordInputs in as an argument to validateInputs()?

We can do this with a *Change Function Declaration* refactoring. First, add it as an argument:

MVP/Refactoring/ChangePasswordViewController.swift
```swift
private func validateInputs(passwordInputs: PasswordInputs) -> Bool {
```

Fix up the call site to pass this argument:

MVP/Refactoring/ChangePasswordViewController.swift
```swift
guard validateInputs(passwordInputs: viewModel.passwordInputs) else {
```

Now in validateInputs(_:), change each reference to viewModel.passwordInputs to use the passwordInputs argument instead. Test. The only viewModel references left in the method should be to access strings.

Next, we can do *Move Function* to move validateInputs(_:) from the view controller to the presenter. Start with copy and paste, fixing it up by adding view references and removing presenter references:

MVP/Refactoring/ChangePasswordPresenter.swift
```swift
func validateInputs(passwordInputs: PasswordInputs) -> Bool {
    if passwordInputs.isOldPasswordEmpty {
        view.updateInputFocus(.oldPassword)
        return false
    }

    if passwordInputs.isNewPasswordEmpty {
        view.showAlert(message: viewModel.enterNewPasswordMessage) {
            [weak self] in
            self?.view.updateInputFocus(.newPassword)
        }
        return false
    }

    if passwordInputs.isNewPasswordTooShort {
```

```
        view.showAlert(message: viewModel.newPasswordTooShortMessage) {
            [weak self] in
            self?.resetNewPasswords()
        }
        return false
    }

    if passwordInputs.isConfirmPasswordMismatched {
        view.showAlert(
                message: viewModel.confirmationPasswordDoesNotMatchMessage) {
            [weak self] in
            self?.resetNewPasswords()
        }
        return false
    }

    return true
}
```

Change the original function so it calls the new one in the presenter. Don't forget to conclude this refactoring by inlining the original function into the call site in the changePassword() method. This is a big one, and worth celebrating.

The last remaining use of viewModel.passwordInputs is in updateViewModelToTextFields(). Let's first do *Inline Function* to move its contents into changePassword(). (Replace the call with the body, run tests, then delete the original method and then test again.)

Instead of using viewModel.passwordInputs, we want changePassword() to create its own instance of PasswordInputs. Let's add this below the references to viewModel.passwordInputs we just inlined:

MVP/Refactoring/ChangePasswordViewController.swift
```
viewModel.passwordInputs.oldPassword = oldPasswordTextField.text ?? ""
viewModel.passwordInputs.newPassword = newPasswordTextField.text ?? ""
viewModel.passwordInputs.confirmPassword =
        confirmPasswordTextField.text ?? ""
let passwordInputs = PasswordInputs(
        oldPassword: oldPasswordTextField.text ?? "",
        newPassword: newPasswordTextField.text ?? "",
        confirmPassword: confirmPasswordTextField.text ?? "")
```

Change the following line to pass passwordInputs instead of viewModel.passwordInputs:

MVP/Refactoring/ChangePasswordViewController.swift
```
guard presenter.validateInputs(passwordInputs: passwordInputs) else {
```

Run the tests to see that they still pass. But now try deleting the preceding three lines that reference viewModel.passwordInputs, and run tests again. Two tests fail! What went wrong? It turns out that in the presenter, attemptToChangePassword() still references viewModel.passwordInputs. It's a good thing we have unit tests to catch such mistakes right away.

Let's fix this up. Do *Change Function Declaration* to pass the PasswordInputs instance into attemptToChangePassword(). Add the argument to the caller. Build to check this change, without running the tests yet.

MVP/Refactoring/ChangePasswordViewController.swift
```
presenter.attemptToChangePassword(passwordInputs: viewModel.passwordInputs)
```

Now fix up attemptToChangePassword() to use the argument instead of viewModel.passwordInputs. This should pass all tests.

MVP/Refactoring/ChangePasswordPresenter.swift
```
private func attemptToChangePassword(passwordInputs: PasswordInputs) {
    passwordChanger.change(
            securityToken: securityToken,
            oldPassword: passwordInputs.oldPassword,
            newPassword: passwordInputs.newPassword,
            onSuccess: { [weak self] in
                self?.handleSuccess()
            },
            onFailure: { [weak self] message in
                self?.handleFailure(message)
            })
}
```

Now we can go back to changePassword() in ChangePasswordViewController. Delete the three lines above the creation of PasswordInputs that reference viewModel.passwordInputs. Run tests to confirm that everything still works.

There's nothing remaining that references the passwordInputs property in ChangePasswordViewModel. Delete it and test.

There should be nothing left that sets the PasswordInputs properties from the outside. Give them explicit types of String with no default values. Then change the properties from var to let. Run tests.

MVP/Refactoring/PasswordInputs.swift
```
let oldPassword: String
let newPassword: String
let confirmPassword: String
```

Password validation now lives in this new type, reducing our reliance on the view model. This was the last thing keeping us from moving things into the presenter. We're in the final stretch.

Finish Up the Refactoring to MVP

We've moved all sorts of helper methods from the view controller to the presenter. All that remains are the two IBAction methods, cancel() and changePassword().

Let's start with cancel(). Though it has only two lines, we want those two lines to live in the presenter. That way, nothing in the view controller calls the View Commands—only the presenter does.

Select those two lines and use Xcode's "Extract to Method" command. We want to name this new method cancel() as well when it lives in the presenter. But we can't do that while it coexists with the IBAction. So let's use a temporary name that stands out, like zz_cancel(). Run tests.

Then do *Move Function* to move it into the presenter. Using our usual technique, copy it to the presenter but give it the desired name cancel(). Make zz_cancel() delegate to the new method and then test. Then *Inline Function* so that that IBAction calls presenter.cancel().

Now on changePassword(). Select everything below the creation of PasswordInputs. Xcode doesn't want to let us do an automated extraction, so do a manual *Extract Method* of those lines. Call the new method zz_changePassword(). Give it a PasswordInputs parameter so it builds and tests pass.

MVP/Refactoring/ChangePasswordViewController.swift
```
func zz_changePassword(passwordInputs: PasswordInputs) {
    guard presenter.validateInputs(passwordInputs: passwordInputs) else {
        return
    }
    presenter.setUpWaitingAppearance()
    presenter.attemptToChangePassword(passwordInputs: passwordInputs)
}
```

Here we are at the last step. Do a *Move Function* but name it changePassword(_:) in the presenter. Inline it so that the IBAction calls it directly.

Everything is now in the presenter. Let's do some final cleanup. First, the only methods we need to expose are the initializer, cancel(), and changePassword(_:). Make everything else private and run tests.

ChangePasswordViewModel now contains nothing but immutable strings, so there's no benefit in keeping it a var property in the presenter. Change it to let.

Finally, ChangePasswordViewModel is no longer a view model. It's a set of labels to show to the user. Use Xcode's "Rename" refactoring command to rename it to ChangePasswordLabels. And rename viewModel properties to labels. (I'll leave this step to you to avoid complicating the downloadable sample code with this change.)

Now that we shifted to an MVP design, what does it look like? Everything in the view controller deals with the actual views. The job of the IBAction methods is to pull information out of the inputs and send it to the presenter, nothing more.

MVP/Refactoring/ChangePasswordViewController.swift
```
@IBAction private func cancel() {
    presenter.cancel()
}

@IBAction private func changePassword() {
    let passwordInputs = PasswordInputs(
            oldPassword: oldPasswordTextField.text ?? "",
            newPassword: newPasswordTextField.text ?? "",
            confirmPassword: confirmPasswordTextField.text ?? "")
    presenter.changePassword(passwordInputs)
}
```

The presenter (with all its helper methods) does the work. All updates to the user interface are calls to the View Commands.

The View Commands themselves are an abstraction of the user interface specific to this view.

MVP/Refactoring/ChangePasswordViewCommands.swift
```
protocol ChangePasswordViewCommands: AnyObject {
    func setCancelButtonEnabled(_ enabled: Bool)
    func updateInputFocus(_ inputFocus: InputFocus)
    func showBlurView()
    func hideBlurView()
    func showActivityIndicator()
    func hideActivityIndicator()
    func dismissModal()
    func clearNewPasswordFields()
    func clearAllPasswordFields()
    func showAlert(message: String, action: @escaping () -> Void)
}
```

The view controller implements these commands, turning them into updates to the views. You now have a complete example of how the MVP pattern works.

(MVP is command-centric and so may be a better fit for imperative, command-based UI. Meanwhile, MVVM is state-centric and so is likely better for declarative UI.)

If you start a view controller following MVP, it would be simpler to write tests for the presenter first. Tests for the view controller could then inject a spy to make sure it's calling the presenter correctly. This leads to simpler tests because there are fewer combinations to test.

But in our example, we started with a comprehensive test suite against the view controller. This let us change our minds about the UI pattern to use, shifting from MVVM to MVP. And we accomplished this shift in small, well-tested steps. This shows the power of disciplined refactoring.

Key Takeaways

Starting with a well-tested view controller, we were able to change it to the MVP pattern. First, we set up the relationships:

- Create an initially empty protocol to house the View Commands.
- Conform the view controller to the protocol.
- Create a presenter with an unowned reference to the protocol.
- Create a lazy view controller property to the presenter, passing itself as the implementor of the protocol.

Then we followed this approach:

- Extract functions to manipulate the views. Make these functions available through the View Commands protocol. These commands call the views but should avoid using UIKit types in their function signatures.

- Move functions that call View Commands into the presenter. Pass anything else these functions need to the presenter but nothing that uses UIKit.

- View controller actions should extract information from inputs, then call a presenter method, nothing more.

We did all this with disciplined refactoring, relying on a thorough set of unit tests. The tests check the end result we want, but are ignorant of the UI pattern we use. This allowed us to change from MVC to MVVM to MVP, with only minor changes in test code. In other words, the tests check the behavior, not the implementation.

Here are the manual refactoring moves we discussed in this chapter:

- *Change Function Declaration*
- *Extract Class*
- *Inline Function*
- *Move Field*
- *Move Function*

What's Next?

Now you've seen how the small steps of refactoring can add up to big changes. We put these steps to work to do basic cleanup in Chapter 17, Unleash the Power of Refactoring, on page 209. We used them to adopt MVVM in Chapter 18, Refactoring: Moving to MVVM, on page 255. And in this chapter, we applied these small steps to adopt the model-view-presenter pattern.

And you now have a feel for how disciplined refactoring works. A large refactoring such as "use MVVM" or "use MVP" is composed of smaller refactoring moves. Each refactoring move has a prescribed set of steps designed to keep the code working at all times. "I can't commit my changes, I'm in the middle of refactoring" is something we should never have to say.

Disciplined refactoring is moving in small steps, verifying each step as you go. Unit tests are the secret sauce that make such refactoring possible.

But let's not stop there! You're ready to go all the way into test-driven development (TDD), which we'll look at in the final chapter.

CHAPTER 20

Test-Driven Development Beckons to You

Adding tests after the production code is written is hard work. What could we do to make this process easier? This question leads us to test-driven development, or TDD. Writing a unit test before changing production code may sound backward. But it's easier, and the resulting code tends to be better (both the production code and the test code).

In Part I of this book, we laid the foundations of unit testing using XCTest. In Part II, we explored various tricks for testing the specifics of iOS apps. And so far in Part III, we've seen how unit tests can empower us to change the design of our code using refactoring. So you have most of the ingredients you need to do test-driven development. Why not go all the way?

In this chapter, we'll look at the three steps of TDD. You'll learn how to let the tests determine how much code to write. And you'll see what it looks like to allow a solution to gradually evolve.

What Is TDD?

Test-driven development adds functionality by following three repeating steps:

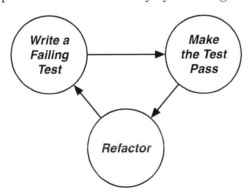

These steps are easy to remember as "red, green, refactor." The colors tell us whether we want a failing test (red) or a passing test (green). Let's examine each step and the transitions between them.

Write a Failing Test

The first step is to write a failing test. Note that this is one test, not a suite of tests. That doesn't mean you can't sketch out a plan for several test cases. But you turn only one at a time into code.

You have some experience with writing tests by doing the worked exercises from Part II of this book. For example, you know how to ensure that a button outlet is connected and how to write a test that taps that button. So you're already ahead of the game.

But what's tricky at first is writing test code before writing production code. What does that mean? We'll explore this in the coming worked example.

Make the Test Pass

Once we have a failing test, we can do whatever it takes to get it to pass, or turn green. All the other tests should continue to pass as well.

What's interesting is that the production code change can be a quick and dirty hack. It can be dirty, because we'll take time to clean it up in the third step. The code can be long-winded or use hard-coded values or have code smells. It doesn't matter as long as it causes the test to go from red to green.

Refactor

Now that the test passes, we can clean up code. If you've done the earlier exercises in Part III, then you have some experience with refactoring.

This step includes cleaning up test code as well as production code. At no point should this step cause tests to fail. Refactoring needs to start in green and end in green without going through red.

Separating the second and third steps is a discipline of concentrating on different goals. It's much like writing a book. As I write this, I'm trying to express my ideas in words, even if the first draft is clumsy. But then I switch hats, from author to editor. In the editing phase, I examine my words critically. I look for anything that feels awkward. I see if the new words fit into the larger picture.

Switching hats between creating and critiquing leads to better results. The second and third steps of TDD lead us in this direction, except we're writing code instead of prose.

Let's work through an example so you see what these three steps look like.

Make a New Place to Play with TDD

Let's create a new project. Unlike the projects for the other chapters, we don't need a full iOS app for what we're about to do. We can make a framework instead to keep things simple.

Make a new Xcode project, selecting iOS Framework. Use the product name TDD. As always, make sure you've selected the "Include Unit Tests" check box.

Delete the initial test file TDDTests.swift. Now we have a blank framework, with no tests. We don't need to set up any production code yet, because this time we're going to start from the test code.

Define the Requirements of the Time-of-Day Greeter

For our example, let's make code to greet someone by name, according to the time of day. These are the greetings we'll use:

5:00 a.m.–11:59 a.m. Good morning.

12:00 p.m.–4:59 p.m. Good afternoon.

5:00 p.m.–4:59 a.m. Good evening.

For example, if we've provided the name "Jon" and the time is 3:56 p.m., the greeting should be, "Good afternoon, Jon."

If no name is provided, the greeting should omit the name and simply say, "Good afternoon."

Those are the requirements. Take a moment to think about what test cases we need to capture these requirements. In particular, think about the boundary conditions. At 11:59 a.m., it should say, "Good morning." At noon, it should say, "Good afternoon." So those are two test cases right there. You may want to sketch out the test cases on a piece of paper.

Now let's begin turning this into code in a test-driven way.

Design the First Failing Test with Bare Production Code

When you're new to test-driven development, writing the first test can feel counterintuitive. How are you supposed to test something that doesn't exist?

The answer is to create just enough production code to get the test to compile. By writing the test first, we focus on designing the interface from the point of view of the caller. The test code is the first call site.

The requirements don't describe the interface. That's up to us to figure out and depends on the context. With little context to guide us, let's make some educated guesses. Let's assume the name of the person won't change often. But the time of day keeps changing.

Remember from Chapter 6, Manage Difficult Dependencies, on page 73 that the current time is a difficult dependency. We don't want the code to call Date() directly because it would make it hard to write tests. Instead, let's tell it the time using some form of dependency injection. That way, tests can pass in any time they need.

So let's aim for a type that takes a name in its initializer. If there is no name, let's pass in any empty string. To get the time-of-day greeting, we'll call a method that takes a Date argument.

Now we need to think of some names. Let's call the new type Greeter. To write test code first, create a new test file named GreeterTests.swift. Start the test suite with Test Zero, deleting the test when it gives you the expected failure message.

Next, let's decide what the first test will be. A good way to find a starting point is to ask yourself, what's the simplest functionality we can deliver? In our case, it would be to have no name, which we decided to represent with an empty string. And "Good morning" seems like a good greeting to start with.

According to our requirements, "Good morning" should cover any time between 5:00 a.m. and 11:59 a.m. The boundary condition at noon is interesting, and a test for that would drive more behavior. So let's plan on noon as our second test. For our first test, let's use 11:59 a.m.

Let's express this in the test name. To do this we'll create a new test named test_greet_with1159am_shouldSayGoodMorning().

Remember what we've decided:

- We'll name the new type Greeter.
- It'll have an initializer that takes a name.
- We're starting by passing an empty string as the name.

That's enough information to start entering some test code to express this:

TDD/TDDTests/GreeterTests.swift
```
Greeter(name: "")
```

Of course, this doesn't compile yet. But we've done a fair bit of design work to get here. This is the first call site, so we can pay attention to how it feels. Ask yourself questions like, "Do I like the type name? Do I like the initializer parameters? Am I passing the right type, or is there something more expressive that would eliminate impossible state?"

To get this to build, create a new file in production code named Greeter.swift. We'll make a new struct inside called Greeter. Define an initializer that takes a name of type String:

TDD/TDD/Greeter.swift
```
struct Greeter {
    init(name: String) {
    }
}
```

> AppCode provides a way to generate production code from a call site. All you do is place the cursor inside the code that doesn't compile. A light bulb icon appears. Clicking the light bulb shows various options. Select "Create type 'Greeter' in a new file," and it's done. No typing involved.
>
> Using an IDE that generates code helps me stay focused on what I was doing in the first place: writing the test.

This is enough to satisfy the compiler. And it shows one of the rhythms of TDD, especially for the first test. We write just enough test code to call production code into existence. And we write only enough production code to satisfy the test code. Initially, a new type has no properties, and a new method has no behavior. But we can create an instance, and we can call the method.

Back in the test, assign the newly created Greeter to a variable. This will be the system under test, so name it sut:

TDD/TDDTests/GreeterTests.swift
```
let sut = Greeter(name: "")
```

Next, we'd like to call a new method, passing in a time argument. The time will be a Date with 11:59 a.m. as the time of day, so let's create this input using DateComponents:

TDD/TDDTests/GreeterTests.swift
```
let components = DateComponents(
        calendar: Calendar.current, hour: 11, minute: 59)
let time = components.date!
```

Now we can pass this time to our new method, which doesn't exist yet:

TDD/TDDTests/GreeterTests.swift
```
let result: String = sut.greet(time: time)
```

If you're used to omitting explicit types in Swift, it may look odd to specify the String type for result. But this completely defines the interface we're designing. We can always remove the explicit type later. (This also gives AppCode the information it needs to generate the correct function stub.)

Let's define just enough production code by declaring a new method so that this builds. It has to return a String, so what string should we use for a bare implementation? An empty string sometimes works, but it may also happen to be valid output. We want to provide invalid output if possible. So for strings, we can return a nonsense value like "BOGUS".

TDD/TDD/Greeter.swift
```
func greet(time: Date) -> String {
    return "BOGUS"
}
```

 When creating the skeleton of a method to make your test compile, try to return output you know is invalid. This will help make the test fail. Remember, the first step of TDD is to get a test to fail in the way you want it to.

Now we're ready for the assertion in our first test. At one minute before noon, the greeter should say, "Good morning."

TDD/TDDTests/GreeterTests.swift
```
XCTAssertEqual(result, "Good morning.")
```

Run the test. We expect it to fail. And it does, with the message:

```
XCTAssertEqual failed: ("BOGUS") is not equal to ("Good morning.")
```

The test fails in the way we want it to, with a clear message. We've succeeded at the first step of TDD! This is worth celebrating, because the very first test took a lot of work:

- We put some thought into designing the interface.
- We came up with the name for a new type.
- We decided what the first test should do.
- We designed the initializer.

- We created a bare type with the initializer.
- We designed the call to the method.
- We created a bare method that returns a nonsense value.
- We expressed the desired return value in an assertion.
- We watched the test fail. This not only satisfies the first step of TDD, it also gives us a way to check that the failure message is expressive.

Make the First Test Pass with "Good Morning"

We now have a failing test. The second step of TDD is to get this test to pass. At this point, people new to TDD often start adding code to examine the time argument of greet(time:). When you haven't yet built up muscle memory of the TDD steps, it's easy to fall back on old habits.

No, our job for the second step is to get the test to pass, and that's all. The passing code can look silly and unsophisticated. The important thing is to avoid adding code that goes beyond the current set of tests. By keeping the production code from running beyond what the tests ask for, we are allowing the tests to be in control.

The test wants the function to return "Good morning" Here's the quickest way to do that:

TDD/TDD/Greeter.swift
```
func greet(time: Date) -> String {
    return "Good morning."
}
```

This may bother you because you know the code is incomplete. Where's "Good afternoon" or "Good evening"? Those will come as we add tests that expect those results.

 The nagging feeling that the production code is incomplete is a signal that you have more tests to write.

"Incomplete" is not the same as "incorrect." Our greeter now works correctly —as long as you give it no name and call it during the morning hours.

Refactor the First Test to Make It More Expressive

The third step of TDD is to refactor. Now that we have a passing test, we can look for opportunities to do cleanup. We want to take time to look critically at both the production code and the test code.

The production code has hardly anything in it so far. There's usually no clean-up to do here after the first test passes.

But in the test code, we should ask: Does the test express what is important while hiding what is unimportant? Here's what the first test looks like now:

TDD/TDDTests/GreeterTests.swift
```swift
func test_greet_with1159am_shouldSayGoodMorning() {
    let sut = Greeter(name: "")
    let components = DateComponents(
            calendar: Calendar.current, hour: 11, minute: 59)
    let time = components.date!

    let result: String = sut.greet(time: time)

    XCTAssertEqual(result, "Good morning.")
}
```

Creating the Greeter with no name looks fine. But the code to make the time 11:59 a.m. has noisy details. The system under test doesn't care about Date-Components. Let's create a test helper to create a Date with a given hour and minute:

- Apply *Extract Variable* refactorings to pull 11 into a variable named hour and 59 into a variable named minute.

- Apply the *Extract Function* refactoring to extract the creation of DateCompo-nents, and the call to create a Date from it, into a method named date(hour:minute:).

- Apply the *Inline Variable* refactoring to inline the hour and the minute.

- Apply *Inline Variable* again on the time variable so that the call to greet(time:) directly expresses the time.

TDD/TDDTests/GreeterTests.swift
```swift
func test_greet_with1159am_shouldSayGoodMorning() {
    let sut = Greeter(name: "")

    let result: String = sut.greet(time: date(hour: 11, minute: 59))

    XCTAssertEqual(result, "Good morning.")
}

private func date(hour: Int, minute: Int) -> Date {
    let components = DateComponents(
            calendar: Calendar.current, hour: hour, minute: minute)
    return components.date!
}
```

The test now does a better job at hiding irrelevant details.

There's one more thing we can refactor, and that's to remove the explicit String type of the result. It helped us make the interface explicit while we were still defining it. But it was a stepping-stone we can now remove.

TDD/TDDTests/GreeterTests.swift
```
let result = sut.greet(time: date(hour: 11, minute: 59))
```

This concludes our first journey through the three steps. We have an expressive test that passes, with minimal production code to satisfy it.

Repeat the TDD Steps for the Second Test

Let's add a second test for noon, the border where the greeting changes to "Good afternoon." For step 1 (red), we want a failing test. Duplicate the first test, changing its input, output, and test name:

TDD/TDDTests/GreeterTests.swift
```
func test_greet_with1200pm_shouldSayGoodAfternoon() {
    let sut = Greeter(name: "")

    let result = sut.greet(time: date(hour: 12, minute: 00))

    XCTAssertEqual(result, "Good afternoon.")
}
```

Run tests. This new test fails as expected, with this message:

```
XCTAssertEqual failed: ("Good morning.") is not equal to ("Good afternoon.")
```

On to step 2 (green), getting this test to pass. What's the simplest thing we can do? We can add a conditional that checks if the hour is 12. To determine the hour of the given time, we can use DateComponents again, but this time in production code:

TDD/TDD/Greeter.swift
```
func greet(time: Date) -> String {
➤    let components = Calendar.current.dateComponents([.hour], from: time)
➤    if components.hour! == 12 {
➤        return "Good afternoon."
➤    }
    return "Good morning."
}
```

The tests pass. Again, we know this code is incomplete. "Good afternoon" will be the greeting for more than when the hour is 12. This tells us that we'll need another "Good afternoon" test at the far end of the boundary condition.

And this code is inelegant. But remember, we'll have an opportunity to clean it up soon in step 3. The important thing for step 2 is that all tests pass.

Now on to step 3 (refactor). Let's start by cleaning up production code. The first nagging thing is where we're force-unwrapping the hour from the date components. While it should be safe because we asked for .hour components, let's avoid force-unwrapping in production code. Change this to nil-coalesce, returning 0 if the hour is missing for any reason:

TDD/TDD/Greeter.swift
```
if components.hour ?? 0 == 12 {
```

Run tests to confirm this refactoring.

The next thing we can clean up is to extract the bit that determines the hour. To separate this from the comparison against 12, let's apply the *Extract Variable* refactoring. Select components.hour ?? 0 and extract it using Xcode's automated refactoring if it lets you. Run tests.

Then use the *Extract Function* refactoring to create and call the following method:

TDD/TDD/Greeter.swift
```
private func hour(for time: Date) -> Int {
    let components = Calendar.current.dateComponents([.hour], from: time)
    return components.hour ?? 0
}
```

This makes the code for greet(time:) easier to read. As always, run tests to confirm these changes:

TDD/TDD/Greeter.swift
```
func greet(time: Date) -> String {
    if hour(for: time) == 12 {
        return "Good afternoon."
    }
    return "Good morning."
}
```

Let's turn our attention to cleaning up the test code. There's duplication around creating the Greeter, passing it an empty name. But we know that later we'll have tests where we do pass in a name.

The choice we face is whether to create a new instance in each test or to create separate test suites with different setUp() methods. This varies by context and can be a matter of preference. For the sake of example, let's plan to use separate test suites—so let's extract the repeated code into a test fixture:

TDD/TDDTests/GreeterTests.swift

```swift
private var sut: Greeter!

override func setUp() {
    super.setUp()
    sut = Greeter(name: "")
}

override func tearDown() {
    sut = nil
    super.tearDown()
}
```

With this fixture in place, delete let sut = Greeter(name: "") from both tests. To make the meaning of this common SUT more obvious, rename the class from GreeterTests to GreeterWithoutNameTests. (Don't use Xcode's "Rename" refactoring for this because we want to keep the same file name. Just change the class name by hand.) Run tests to confirm these changes.

This completes our three steps for the new test case of 12:00 p.m.

Add Tests to Expand "Good Afternoon"

The greeting for "Good afternoon" should start at 12:00 p.m., and continue through 4:59 p.m. The production code is incomplete because it checks for hour 12 and nothing else. Let's stretch it to the next boundary by adding a new failing test:

TDD/TDDTests/GreeterTests.swift

```swift
func test_greet_with459pm_shouldSayGoodAfternoon() {
    let result = sut.greet(time: date(hour: 16, minute: 59))

    XCTAssertEqual(result, "Good afternoon.")
}
```

This fails, fulfilling the red step. The quickest way to get this test to pass is to extend the conditional to check for hour 16 (that is, four in the afternoon).

TDD/TDD/Greeter.swift

```swift
if hour(for: time) == 12 || hour(for: time) == 16 {
```

This passes, fulfilling the green step. Now let's clean it up for the refactor step. First, repeatedly extracting the same hour is wasteful. Let's apply the *Extract Variable* refactoring to pull out the call to hour(for: time) to a variable. We can't call it hour because that name would clash with our helper method. So let's name it theHour:

TDD/TDD/Greeter.swift

```swift
let theHour = hour(for: time)
if theHour == 12 || theHour == 16 {
```

We want the conditional to check for a range of hours, not just the boundary endpoints. So we've discovered a missing test. Let's go back to step 1 and add a test with a time somewhere in the middle of the range.

Duplicate the previous test, changing the input time to 2:00 p.m.—that is, hour 14. Run the test to watch it fail. Now let's go from red to green in the quickest way, by adding one more check to our conditional:

TDD/TDD/Greeter.swift
```
if theHour == 12 || theHour == 14 || theHour == 16 {
```

This passes. Now that we're in green, we can clean up this code by checking for a range of hours:

TDD/TDD/Greeter.swift
```
if 12 <= theHour && theHour <= 16 {
```

Remember to run tests to confirm this refactoring.

Implement "Good Evening"

Let's continue on to the "Good evening" greeting. The requirements say this greeting should apply for any time from 5:00 p.m. to 4:59 a.m.

But in 24-hour notation, this starts at hour 17 and continues through the end of hour 4. It'll be easier if we split this into two ranges: one from 5:00 p.m. through 11:59 p.m., and one from 12:00 a.m. through 4:59 a.m.

Continue in the same manner we used for the "Good afternoon" tests by testing for the beginning of a range, the end of a range, and a time in between. So use TDD the first range using the following times:

- date(hour: 17, minute: 00)
- date(hour: 23, minute: 59)
- date(hour: 20, minute: 00)

These inputs should all return the greeting "Good evening." Then do the same with the second range from midnight on:

- date(hour: 0, minute: 00)
- date(hour: 4, minute: 59)
- date(hour: 2, minute: 00)

Your resulting code, grown gradually to satisfy each test in turn, may look like this:

TDD/TDD/Greeter.swift
```
func greet(time: Date) -> String {
    let theHour = hour(for: time)
```

```
    if 12 <= theHour && theHour <= 16 {
        return "Good afternoon."
    }
    if 0 <= theHour && theHour <= 4 ||
               17 <= theHour && theHour <= 23 {
        return "Good evening."
    }
    return "Good morning."
}
```

At this point, we know the final "Good morning" result will apply to any time that wasn't scooped up by the "Good afternoon" or "Good evening" ranges. But sometimes it helps to deviate from TDD and add tests we think will already pass. We already have a "Good morning." test for 11:59 a.m. Let's add two more:

- date(hour: 5, minute: 00)
- date(hour: 8, minute: 00)

The purpose of these tests isn't to drive the creation of any more code. But they can help our anxious brains relax by filling in gaps.

 If adding a passing test helps you sleep better at night, add it.

The greeting now works for all times of day. But now, let's take a step back and look at the method we created.

Step Back to Refactor the Method as a Whole

Each conditional in greet(time:) is doing an important job. But looking at them all together makes me feel uncomfortable. Code should not only work, it should be easy to change. What happens if the customer asks us to change the starting time of "Good evening" from 5:00 p.m. to 6:00 p.m.? We'd have to change two lines: not only the starting time of "Good evening," but the ending time of "Good afternoon."

Even though we followed the three steps to apply TDD to what we have, repeating similar steps can sometimes lead to a narrow focus. So let's take a step back and expand our focus. What can we do to make this method easier to maintain?

Now we encounter another principle of refactoring. Sometimes things look similar, but not quite the same. See how we repeat comparisons using different ranges? The more similar we can make these repeated comparisons, the more opportunities we'll have for further refactoring.

Separate a Complex Conditional

Let's start by splitting the complex conditional for "Good evening" into two. We can turn it into one conditional for midnight on, and another for 5:00 p.m. on. Let's do this in steps. First, duplicate the entire conditional.

TDD/TDD/Greeter.swift

```swift
func greet(time: Date) -> String {
    let theHour = hour(for: time)
    if 12 <= theHour && theHour <= 16 {
        return "Good afternoon."
    }
    if 0 <= theHour && theHour <= 4 ||
            17 <= theHour && theHour <= 23 {
        return "Good evening."
    }
    if 0 <= theHour && theHour <= 4 ||
            17 <= theHour && theHour <= 23 {
        return "Good evening."
    }
    return "Good morning."
}
```

Run tests, which should still pass. (Remember, try to avoid any test failures during refactoring.)

Next, take the first of the repeated conditionals. Delete the second half, leaving the first half. Run tests. On the second "Good evening" conditional, delete the first half, leaving the second half. Run tests.

TDD/TDD/Greeter.swift

```swift
if 0 <= theHour && theHour <= 4 {
    return "Good evening."
}
if 17 <= theHour && theHour <= 23 {
    return "Good evening."
}
```

Reorder the Comparisons and Fill a Gap

Now we can sort the comparisons by hour. Do a *Slide Statements* refactoring to move the 0-to-4 hour comparison so it comes first.

This leaves a strange gap in the hours, where "Good morning" is handled at the end by falling through other conditionals. To make things more uniform, add a conditional so that the "Good morning" range is spelled out in the code. Run tests. We should never reach the final return statement, but Swift demands it. Change it to return an empty string and run tests again.

```
TDD/TDD/Greeter.swift
func greet(time: Date) -> String {
    let theHour = hour(for: time)
    if 0 <= theHour && theHour <= 4 {
        return "Good evening."
    }
➤    if 5 <= theHour && theHour <= 11 {
➤        return "Good morning."
➤    }
    if 12 <= theHour && theHour <= 16 {
        return "Good afternoon."
    }
    if 17 <= theHour && theHour <= 23 {
        return "Good evening."
    }
➤    return ""
}
```

This is looking more uniform.

Repeat Values by Changing Comparisons

Changing a boundary of a greeting still requires us to edit two lines. Let's make the relationships between the ranges clearer. Change the ending boundary check from <= 4 to < 5. Run tests. Repeat this change for each conditional, testing after each change.

```
TDD/TDD/Greeter.swift
func greet(time: Date) -> String {
    let theHour = hour(for: time)
➤    if 0 <= theHour && theHour < 5 {
        return "Good evening."
    }
➤    if 5 <= theHour && theHour < 12 {
        return "Good morning."
    }
➤    if 12 <= theHour && theHour < 17 {
        return "Good afternoon."
    }
➤    if 17 <= theHour && theHour < 24 {
        return "Good evening."
    }
    return ""
}
```

The integers at the end of one conditional and the beginning of the next now repeat. This makes their meaning clearer and would provide a visual clue if we were to change any of them.

Introduce a Lookup Table

Let's go further. Add a new property to the Greeter type.

TDD/TDD/Greeter.swift
```
private let greetingTimes: [(from: Int, greeting: String)] = [
    (0, "Good evening."),
    (5, "Good morning."),
    (12, "Good afternoon."),
    (17, "Good evening."),
]
```

This defines an array of tuples with a starting hour and greeting, which we'll use as a lookup table. Make sure this compiles. Then, let's start replacing the string literals in greet with array references. So where we have the first "Good evening." replace that with greetingTimes[0].greeting. Run tests. Continue to replace each string literal, until we get the following:

TDD/TDD/Greeter.swift
```
func greet(time: Date) -> String {
    let theHour = hour(for: time)
    if 0 <= theHour && theHour < 5 {
        return greetingTimes[0].greeting
    }
    if 5 <= theHour && theHour < 12 {
        return greetingTimes[1].greeting
    }
    if 12 <= theHour && theHour < 17 {
        return greetingTimes[2].greeting
    }
    if 17 <= theHour && theHour < 24 {
        return greetingTimes[3].greeting
    }
    return ""
}
```

Now we can begin replacing the integer literals. Replace 0 with greeting-Times[0].from and run tests. Repeat for the remaining integers until you come to 24. To make this uniform, let's add a sentinel value to the end of the greetingTimes array:

TDD/TDD/Greeter.swift
```
(24, "SENTINEL"),
```

Now we can replace 24 with a reference to this last entry. The resulting code looks like this:

TDD/TDD/Greeter.swift
```swift
func greet(time: Date) -> String {
    let theHour = hour(for: time)
    if greetingTimes[0].from <= theHour && theHour < greetingTimes[1].from {
        return greetingTimes[0].greeting
    }
    if greetingTimes[1].from <= theHour && theHour < greetingTimes[2].from {
        return greetingTimes[1].greeting
    }
    if greetingTimes[2].from <= theHour && theHour < greetingTimes[3].from {
        return greetingTimes[2].greeting
    }
    if greetingTimes[3].from <= theHour && theHour < greetingTimes[4].from {
        return greetingTimes[3].greeting
    }
    return ""
}
```

By making the code more similar, this now looks like an unrolled loop. Let's replace it with an actual loop. We'll enumerate over each entry in greetingTimes:

TDD/TDD/Greeter.swift
```swift
func greet(time: Date) -> String {
    let theHour = hour(for: time)
    for (index, greetingTime) in greetingTimes.enumerated() {
        if greetingTime.from <= theHour &&
                theHour < greetingTimes[index + 1].from {
            return greetingTime.greeting
        }
    }
    return ""
}
```

Instead of a bunch of literals in code, we now do a lookup in a data structure. This lookup makes the code tighter and easier to change. We could even substitute the data to localize the greeting to different customs.

Note that we got here not by following a grand plan but by looking for opportunities to make the code more similar.

Making code more similar reveals opportunities for refactoring that were initially hard to see.

Add the Name to the Greeting

So far, we've handled the greeting for every time of day, as long as the name is empty. Now let's add a test that specifies a name. We decided to use separate test suites for the test cases with and without names. First, let's do a little preparatory refactoring. We want to reuse the helper function date(hour:minute:), so it needs to move outside of GreeterWithoutNameTests. Move it to file scope (that is, outside of the test class), and run tests to confirm this refactoring.

Red: Test with One Name

Inside GreeterTests.swift, add a new test suite named GreeterWithNameTests. Give it the following test using the name Alberto:

TDD/TDDTests/GreeterTests.swift
```
final class GreeterWithNameTests: XCTestCase {

    func test_greetMorning_withAlberto_shouldSayGoodMorningAlberto() {
        let sut = Greeter(name: "Alberto")

        let result = sut.greet(time: date(hour: 5, minute: 0))

        XCTAssertEqual(result, "Good morning, Alberto.")
    }
}
```

Run tests to watch this fail.

Green: Hard-Code the Name

How shall we get this test to pass? The initializer takes a name argument but ignores it. Let's first save the name in a property:

TDD/TDD/Greeter.swift
```
private let name: String

init(name: String) {
    self.name = name
}
```

We can now use this property in greet(time:). The quickest way to go from red to green is to return a hard-coded greeting if the name is not empty:

TDD/TDD/Greeter.swift
```
func greet(time: Date) -> String {
    if !name.isEmpty {
        return "Good morning, Alberto."
    }
    let theHour = hour(for: time)
```

Run tests to watch this pass.

Refactor: Reuse Existing Greetings

Now let's refactor. We have duplication between "Good morning" in this string literal and "Good morning" in the greetingTimes property.

The problem is, the string in the property ends with a period, which keeps us from using it in this new conditional. Let's refactor to move the period out.

Edit the greetingTimes array, removing the period from each greeting. Inside the for-in loop, append a period to the returned string:

TDD/TDD/Greeter.swift
```
return greetingTime.greeting + "."
```

Run tests to confirm that we successfully moved the period. With the period on the outside of the greeting, we can move Alberto's greeting so it uses the greetingTimes look-up:

TDD/TDD/Greeter.swift
```
func greet(time: Date) -> String {
    let theHour = hour(for: time)
    for (index, greetingTime) in greetingTimes.enumerated() {
        if greetingTime.from <= theHour &&
                theHour < greetingTimes[index + 1].from {
            if !name.isEmpty {
                return "\(greetingTime.greeting), Alberto."
            }
            return greetingTime.greeting + "."
        }
    }
    return ""
}
```

This shifts the Alberto case away from a hard-coded "Good morning" to use the proper greeting for the time of day.

Red: Test with Different Name Input

The greeting works—as long as your name is Alberto. Let's add another test with a different name. This will lead us to make the code more general.

TDD/TDDTests/GreeterTests.swift
```
func test_greetAfternoon_withBeryl_shouldSayGoodAfternoonBeryl() {
    let sut = Greeter(name: "Beryl")

    let result = sut.greet(time: date(hour: 15, minute: 0))

    XCTAssertEqual(result, "Good afternoon, Beryl.")
}
```

Watch this test fail.

Green: Use the Given Name

To get this test to pass, replace Alberto with the name property:

TDD/TDD/Greeter.swift
```
return "\(greetingTime.greeting), \(name)."
```

Refactor: Separate Name from Time

Now we have a solution that satisfies all the requirements. It correctly returns a greeting for any time of day, with or without a name. But once again, let's expand our focus past individual lines to look at things as a whole.

As it stands, greet(time:) mixes two responsibilities. First, it determines the appropriate greeting for the time of day. Then, it decides how to use this greeting depending on the given name. If either of these were to change, we'd have to separate the code in our minds to find the right part to change.

So instead of separating the code in our minds, let's actually separate them into two functions. It makes sense for the time-of-day greeting to become its own thing. Let's do this with these steps:

- Duplicate greet(time:), giving it a slightly different name.

- Simplify the return statement so it returns only greetingTime.greeting. No name, no punctuation.

- Declare this new method private.

TDD/TDD/Greeter.swift
```
private func greeting(for time: Date) -> String {
    let theHour = hour(for: time)
    for (index, greetingTime) in greetingTimes.enumerated() {
        if greetingTime.from <= theHour &&
                    theHour < greetingTimes[index + 1].from {
            return greetingTime.greeting
        }
    }
    return ""
}
```

Call this new method from greet(time:), assigning the results to a variable named hello. Strip out the call to determine theHour along with the contents of the for loop, leaving the name conditional. Replace occurrences of greetingTime.greeting with hello:

```
TDD/TDD/Greeter.swift
func greet(time: Date) -> String {
    let hello = greeting(for: time)
    if !name.isEmpty {
        return "\(hello), \(name)."
    }
    return hello + "."
}
```

Run tests to confirm these changes.

This is better. But the conditional checks the negative condition first, which is awkward. Let's flip the conditional and add an else:

```
TDD/TDD/Greeter.swift
func greet(time: Date) -> String {
    let hello = greeting(for: time)
➤   if name.isEmpty {
➤       return hello + "."
➤   } else {
➤       return "\(hello), \(name)."
➤   }
}
```

Run tests. Finally, let's unify the appearance of the two return statements by using string interpolation to append the period:

```
TDD/TDD/Greeter.swift
func greet(time: Date) -> String {
    let hello = greeting(for: time)
    if name.isEmpty {
➤       return "\(hello)."
    } else {
        return "\(hello), \(name)."
    }
}
```

Run all tests, which should pass. Now we have one method that handles the time of day and another that handles the name. Making changes to either responsibility will be easier because they're handled by separate pieces of code.

Key Takeaways

Test-driven development combines unit testing and refactoring into a discipline for creating new functionality:

- TDD emphasizes moving in small steps.

- The main steps are red, green, refactor: Create a single failing test. Get it to pass. Clean up code.

- Creating a failing test includes creating bare-bones production code that does nothing useful.

- Try to move from red to green quickly. The code can be ugly, because you'll clean it up in the refactor step.

- Refactoring includes cleaning up test code as well as production code. Try to change one or the other. Keep the tests passing while refactoring. Keep cleaning until you're satisfied.

- Create test helpers so your tests express what is important while hiding what is unimportant.

- It's okay for the production code to use hard-coded values. Such code isn't wrong; it's just incomplete. The feeling that it's wrong is telling you to write more tests.

- It's okay to add non-TDD-passing tests if they help demonstrate requirements. There's nothing wrong with extra reassurance that you didn't miss a particular edge case. (But remember to force an unwanted change in production code to make sure the test fails as desired.)

- After you've fleshed out a piece of functionality, take a step back. Expand your focus to look at the whole method or the whole type. Ask yourself how easy it will be to maintain when changes are requested. Refactor to make it easier to change.

- Making code more similar reveals further opportunities for refactoring.

This particular example demonstrates one more thing about TDD. The test input supplies both hour and minute to create instances of Date, so that we can see how the tests map to the requirements. But curiously, the production code only needs to pay attention to the hour. We didn't need to examine the minutes at all. This is an example of how code written with TDD can be simpler than code written without it.

What's Next?

We've reached the end of this book. You've grown in your unit testing. You've improved your refactoring skills. The next logical step is to begin mastering test-driven development.

Here are some next steps for you to take. First, try to use TDD the next time you need a piece of functionality that doesn't use UIKit. This is what we did for our time-of-day greeter.

Then combine TDD with the iOS testing tips and techniques in Part II. You might start with the following exercise: Use TDD to make an iOS app that shows two buttons. Tapping either button will push another view controller, showing a label. The text of the label depends on which button you tapped.

After this, use TDD to make the next new view controller in your actual code. A test-driven approach will lead you to identify any difficult dependencies right away. Sketch out a rough design on a whiteboard, but allow the actual design to emerge.

It shouldn't take long before you begin to experience the benefits of TDD. There is, of course, the big benefit of unit testing—safety. But TDD adds to this by making testability a requirement. You'll still puzzle over "How can I test this," but you'll ask that question first instead of at the end when it's too late. Testability leads to better designs where the components are more modular. This—and continuously asking, "How can I clean this up?"—will lead to code that's easier to change. The end result is that making changes will become faster.

Don't become discouraged if you find TDD hard at first. You are learning how to code backward. You have taken the first steps in a journey of discovery that never stops. Get help along the way to accelerate your progress, and have fun!

Bibliography

[Fea04]   Michael Feathers. *Working Effectively with Legacy Code.* Prentice Hall, Englewood Cliffs, NJ, 2004.

[Fow18]   Martin Fowler. *Refactoring: Improving the Design of Existing Code, 2nd Edition.* Addison-Wesley, Boston, MA, 2018.

[GHJV95]   Erich Gamma, Richard Helm, Ralph Johnson, and John Vlissides. *Design Patterns: Elements of Reusable Object-Oriented Software.* Addison-Wesley, Boston, MA, 1995.

[Lee12]   Graham Lee. *Test-Driven iOS Development.* Addison-Wesley, Boston, MA, 2012.

[Mar02]   Robert C. Martin. *Agile Software Development, Principles, Patterns, and Practices.* Prentice Hall, Englewood Cliffs, NJ, 2002.

[Mar08]   Robert C. Martin. *Clean Code: A Handbook of Agile Software Craftsmanship.* Prentice Hall, Englewood Cliffs, NJ, 2008.

[Mes07]   Gerard Meszaros. *xUnit Test Patterns.* Addison-Wesley, Boston, MA, 2007.

[Osh13]   Roy Osherove. *The Art of Unit Testing: with examples in C#, Second Edition.* Manning Publications Co., Greenwich, CT, 2013.

[vS19]   Steven van Deursen and Mark Seemann. *Dependency Injection Principles, Practices, and Patterns.* Manning Publications Co., Greenwich, CT, 2019.

Index

Thank you!

How did you enjoy this book? Please let us know. Take a moment and email us at support@pragprog.com with your feedback. Tell us your story and you could win free ebooks. Please use the subject line "Book Feedback."

Ready for your next great Pragmatic Bookshelf book? Come on over to https://pragprog.com and use the coupon code BUYANOTHER2020 to save 30% on your next ebook.

Void where prohibited, restricted, or otherwise unwelcome. Do not use ebooks near water. If rash persists, see a doctor. Doesn't apply to *The Pragmatic Programmer* ebook because it's older than the Pragmatic Bookshelf itself. Side effects may include increased knowledge and skill, increased marketability, and deep satisfaction. Increase dosage regularly.

And thank you for your continued support,

Andy Hunt, Publisher

Become an Effective Software Engineering Manager

Software startups make global headlines every day. As technology companies succeed and grow, so do their engineering departments. In your career, you'll may suddenly get the opportunity to lead teams: to become a manager. But this is often uncharted territory. How do you decide whether this career move is right for you? And if you do, what do you need to learn to succeed? Where do you start? How do you know that you're doing it right? What does "it" even mean? And isn't management a dirty word? This book will share the secrets you need to know to manage engineers successfully.

James Stanier
(396 pages) ISBN: 9781680507249. $45.95
https://pragprog.com/book/jsengman

Build Websites with Hugo

Rediscover how fun web development can be with Hugo, the static site generator and web framework that lets you build content sites quickly, using the skills you already have. Design layouts with HTML and share common components across pages. Create Markdown templates that let you create new content quickly. Consume and generate JSON, enhance layouts with logic, and generate a site that works on any platform with no runtime dependencies or database. Hugo gives you everything you need to build your next content site and have fun doing it.

Brian P. Hogan
(154 pages) ISBN: 9781680507263. $26.95
https://pragprog.com/book/bhhugo

Practical Microservices

MVC and CRUD make software easier to write, but harder to change. Microservice-based architectures can help even the smallest of projects remain agile in the long term, but most tutorials meander in theory or completely miss the point of what it means to be microservice based. Roll up your sleeves with real projects and learn the most important concepts of evented architectures. You'll have your own deployable, testable project and a direction for where to go next.

Ethan Garofolo
(290 pages) ISBN: 9781680506457. $45.95
https://pragprog.com/book/egmicro

Real-Time Phoenix

Give users the real-time experience they expect, by using Elixir and Phoenix Channels to build applications that instantly react to changes and reflect the application's true state. Learn how Elixir and Phoenix make it easy and enjoyable to create real-time applications that scale to a large number of users. Apply system design and development best practices to create applications that are easy to maintain. Gain confidence by learning how to break your applications before your users do. Deploy applications with minimized resource use and maximized performance.

Stephen Bussey
(326 pages) ISBN: 9781680507195. $45.95
https://pragprog.com/book/sbsockets

Programming Machine Learning

You've decided to tackle machine learning — because you're job hunting, embarking on a new project, or just think self-driving cars are cool. But where to start? It's easy to be intimidated, even as a software developer. The good news is that it doesn't have to be that hard. Master machine learning by writing code one line at a time, from simple learning programs all the way to a true deep learning system. Tackle the hard topics by breaking them down so they're easier to understand, and build your confidence by getting your hands dirty.

Paolo Perrotta
(340 pages) ISBN: 9781680506600. $47.95
https://pragprog.com/book/pplearn

Competing with Unicorns

Today's tech unicorns develop software differently. They've developed a way of working that lets them scale like an enterprise while working like a startup. These techniques can be learned. This book takes you behind the scenes and shows you how companies like Google, Facebook, and Spotify do it. Leverage their insights, so your teams can work better together, ship higher-quality product faster, innovate more quickly, and compete with the unicorns.

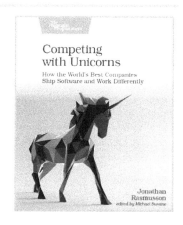

Jonathan Rasmusson
(138 pages) ISBN: 9781680507232. $26.95
https://pragprog.com/book/jragile

Programming Flutter

Develop your next app with Flutter and deliver native look, feel, and performance on both iOS and Android from a single code base. Bring along your favorite libraries and existing code from Java, Kotlin, Objective-C, and Swift, so you don't have to start over from scratch. Write your next app in one language, and build it for both Android and iOS. Deliver the native look, feel, and performance you and your users expect from an app written with each platform's own tools and languages. Deliver apps fast, doing half the work you were doing before and exploiting powerful new features to speed up development. Write once, run anywhere.

Carmine Zaccagnino
(368 pages) ISBN: 9781680506952. $47.95
https://pragprog.com/book/czflutr

Agile Web Development with Rails 6

Learn Rails the way the Rails core team recommends it, along with the tens of thousands of developers who have used this broad, far-reaching tutorial and reference. If you're new to Rails, you'll get step-by-step guidance. If you're an experienced developer, get the comprehensive, insider information you need for the latest version of Ruby on Rails. The new edition of this award-winning classic is completely updated for Rails 6 and Ruby 2.6, with information on processing email with Action Mailbox and managing rich text with Action Text.

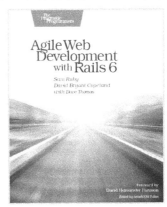

Sam Ruby and David Bryant Copeland
(494 pages) ISBN: 9781680506709. $57.95
https://pragprog.com/book/rails6

Modern Systems Programming with Scala Native

Access the power of bare-metal systems programming with Scala Native, an ahead-of-time Scala compiler. Without the baggage of legacy frameworks and virtual machines, Scala Native lets you re-imagine how your programs interact with your operating system. Compile Scala code down to native machine instructions; seamlessly invoke operating system APIs for low-level networking and IO; control pointers, arrays, and other memory management techniques for extreme performance; and enjoy instant start-up times. Skip the JVM and improve your code performance by getting close to the metal.

Richard Whaling
(260 pages) ISBN: 9781680506228. $45.95
https://pragprog.com/book/rwscala

Fixing Your Scrum

Broken Scrum practices limit your organization's ability to take full advantage of the agility Scrum should bring: The development team isn't cross-functional or self-organizing, the product owner doesn't get value for their investment, and stakeholders and customers are left wondering when something—anything—will get delivered. Learn how experienced Scrum masters balance the demands of these three levels of servant leadership, while removing organizational impediments and helping Scrum teams deliver real-world value. Discover how to visualize your work, resolve impediments, and empower your teams to self-organize and deliver using advanced coaching and facilitation techniques that honor and support the Scrum values and agile principles.

Ryan Ripley and Todd Miller
(240 pages) ISBN: 9781680506976. $45.95
https://pragprog.com/book/rrscrum

Software Estimation Without Guessing

Developers hate estimation, and most managers fear disappointment with the results, but there is hope for both. You'll have to give up some widely held misconceptions: let go of the notion that "an estimate is an estimate," and estimate for your particular need. Realize that estimates have a limited shelf-life, and re-estimate frequently as needed. When reality differs from your estimate, don't lament; mine that disappointment for the gold that can be the longer-term jackpot. We'll show you how.

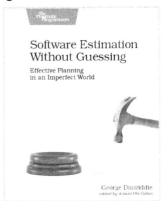

George Dinwiddie
(246 pages) ISBN: 9781680506983. $29.95
https://pragprog.com/book/gdestimate

Designing Elixir Systems with OTP

You know how to code in Elixir; now learn to think in it. Learn to design libraries with intelligent layers that shape the right data structures, flow from one function into the next, and present the right APIs. Embrace the same OTP that's kept our telephone systems reliable and fast for over 30 years. Move beyond understanding the OTP functions to knowing what's happening under the hood, and why that matters. Using that knowledge, instinctively know how to design systems that deliver fast and resilient services to your users, all with an Elixir focus.

James Edward Gray, II and Bruce A. Tate
(246 pages) ISBN: 9781680506617. $41.95
https://pragprog.com/book/jgotp

The Pragmatic Bookshelf

The Pragmatic Bookshelf features books written by professional developers for professional developers. The titles continue the well-known Pragmatic Programmer style and continue to garner awards and rave reviews. As development gets more and more difficult, the Pragmatic Programmers will be there with more titles and products to help you stay on top of your game.

Visit Us Online

This Book's Home Page
https://pragprog.com/book/jrlegios
Source code from this book, errata, and other resources. Come give us feedback, too!

Keep Up to Date
https://pragprog.com
Join our announcement mailing list (low volume) or follow us on twitter @pragprog for new titles, sales, coupons, hot tips, and more.

New and Noteworthy
https://pragprog.com/news
Check out the latest pragmatic developments, new titles and other offerings.

Save on the ebook

Save on the ebook versions of this title. Owning the paper version of this book entitles you to purchase the electronic versions at a terrific discount.

PDFs are great for carrying around on your laptop—they are hyperlinked, have color, and are fully searchable. Most titles are also available for the iPhone and iPod touch, Amazon Kindle, and other popular e-book readers.

Buy now at *https://pragprog.com/coupon*

Contact Us

Online Orders:	*https://pragprog.com/catalog*
Customer Service:	*support@pragprog.com*
International Rights:	*translations@pragprog.com*
Academic Use:	*academic@pragprog.com*
Write for Us:	*http://write-for-us.pragprog.com*
Or Call:	+1 800-699-7764

Milton Keynes UK
Ingram Content Group UK Ltd.
UKHW050610310524
443454UK00001B/6